THE GUARDIAN ANGEL

THE GUARDIAN ANGEL

MICHEL HOLLARD: THE RESISTANCE LEADER WHO STOPPED HITLER'S PLANS TO DESTROY LONDON

FLORIAN HOLLARD

Pen & Sword
MILITARY
AN IMPRINT OF PEN & SWORD BOOKS LTD.
YORKSHIRE – PHILADELPHIA

First published in France in 2005 by Cherche Midi as *Michel Hollard, Le Français Qui a Sauvé Londres*

First published in Great Britain in 2025 by
Pen & Sword Military
An imprint of
Pen & Sword Books Ltd
Yorkshire - Philadelphia

ISBN 978 152678 005 8

A CIP catalogue record for this book is available from the British Library.

Typeset in INDIA by IMPEC eSolutions
Printed and bound in England by CPI (UK) Ltd.

The Publisher's authorised representative in the EU for product safety is Authorised Rep Compliance Ltd., Ground Floor, 71 Lower Baggot Street, Dublin D02 P593, Ireland. www.arccompliance.com

For a complete list of Pen & Sword titles please contact

PEN & SWORD BOOKS LIMITED
47 Church Street, Barnsley, South Yorkshire, S70 2AS, England
E-mail: enquiries@pen-and-sword.co.uk
Website: www.pen-and-sword.co.uk

or

PEN AND SWORD BOOKS
1950 Lawrence Rd, Havertown, PA 19083, USA
E-mail: uspen-and-sword@casematepublishers.com
Website: www.penandswordbooks.com

FSC
www.fsc.org
MIX
Paper | Supporting responsible forestry
FSC® C013604

Contents

Preface by SIMONE VEIL

First Female President of the European Parliament
Former French Minister of State and Member of the Constitutional Council
Member of the Académie Française
President of the Foundation for the Memory of the Shoah

We are learning more and more about the Resistance movements, but the story of Michel Hollard remains largely unknown. As leader of Agir, a network independent from the FFI (French Forces of the Interior), he discovered the secret weapon that the Nazis had designed to destroy London. He was later deported and shared the same terrible experiences as so many prisoners in Neuengamme concentration camp.

The honours this man received after the war never besmirched the modesty and determination he was able to show, in such an exemplary manner, all throughout his life.

Engaged from the very beginning in the struggle for the freedom of his country, he ruled out even the simplest collusion with the enemy. In 1940, although managing a large firm making wood gas generators, whose technology replaced petrol which was in short supply in Western Europe, he refused to let the enemy benefit from his findings.

Subsequently, in all seasons, despite the infinite dangers he risked and the very real threat of arrest and sentencing, he crossed the Swiss border in both directions to bring strategic intelligence to the British and Swiss secret services in Bern: where troops were moving, where the main units were stationed and where the officers of the German Army were billeted. Around him, in all parts of the country, first in the Occupied Zone, then in the former Free Zone after the Allied landings in North Africa, patriotic men and women were unceasingly noting down information about an invader everybody considered as the enemy to be defeated, contrary to France's official position.

And yet, despite the discovery – vital for the course of the war – of the secret ramps the Germans set up to launch the infamous V-1 missiles at London from the coasts of Western Europe, Michel Hollard never wanted to believe he had done anything other than his duty. Despite his family's Christian obedience, which can be read in every line of this book, he refused to stop after his discovery which forever established his importance in the eyes of the English.

His story intertwines with those of other men, Swiss and English, all those to whom he brought vital information for the conduct of the war, and also a host of other more or less anonymous French people. These include railway workers, hotel owners, farmers – a 'morally committed' France that he inspired by his charisma to struggle against the occupier, that oft-forgotten face of France which, despite the dangers and the difficulties, did not yield totally under the German yoke.

After his betrayal and subsequent arrest at the Café des Chasseurs near the Gare du Nord, he was tortured by the Gestapo, but he showed selflessness despite the torture and did not denounce any of his own agents. He was then deported to Neuengamme concentration camp in 1944, where he suffered the hell of privations, abuse and forced labour. Yet he never gave up. Rather, he continued to gather men around his faith and optimism, giving them the courage to await the Liberation.

Beyond Michel Hollard's impressive series of heroic acts, told fervently by his son, I have retained the profound modesty of this man who said the following words to his former companions in the Resistance a few years after the war: 'You were all filled with patriotic zeal. All I did was awaken your indignation against the tyranny you were putting up with in silence.'

There are men whose lives are exemplary, not only for their heroism but equally for their humanity; a quality which in troubled times was lacking in so many others. Reading his story, it is easy to understand why Michel Hollard has left such a strong impression of respect and admiration. This man, driven by such rare faith, energy and sensitivity, deserves an eternal place of honour in the annals of history.

Foreword

When France capitulated on 21 June 1940, my father Michel Hollard, a reserve officer, was outraged. The sight of occupying troops marching past in the streets of Paris was unbearable for him. He decided to continue the struggle alongside the Allies, but family duty prevented him from following General de Gaulle to London.

As he was unable to get in touch with any of the groups of patriots who, according to public hearsay, were already operational in occupied France, he thought up an independent strategy and created his own underground network. After countless twists and turns, he found a way to gain access to heavily guarded military sites where the Germans were preparing to launch a top-secret weapon.

When Michel Hollard accomplished these feats, he was no longer hiding his underground activities from his wife, or even their three children. Such trust, perhaps close to foolhardiness, is quite surprising. But the head of the family's way of life was clearly so dangerous that, among those close to him, the law of silence had imposed itself upon everybody.

The incredible strategy he came across could have changed the course of history. With such a revolutionary arsenal, Hitler thought he held a trump card. He was counting on routing his enemies by first annihilating England's capital.

Chapter 1

Worrying Unrest

In the summer of 1943, an agent in Michel Hollard's network named Jean-Henri Daudemard, who worked as an engineer with SNCF (Société Nationale des Chemins de Fer Français), France's national railway company, drew Hollard's attention to the appearance of strange constructions the Germans were building in north-western France. Daudemard was lunching in one of Rouen's brasseries when a conversation at a neighbouring table caught his attention. The two speakers were public works contractors obliged by the occupying army to supply it with large quantities of building materials.

'Our clients,' said one of the men, 'want their strange buildings finished as soon as possible and to do this they have drafted in a huge number of labourers from both here and abroad. What's more, the technical demands specified by their engineers are very stringent…'

For some time now, Nazi propaganda had been stirring fears of a forthcoming deployment of mysterious machines of destruction the Reich claimed it possessed. Despite its scantiness, Michel Hollard thought the information was clear enough for him to believe the Germans were up to something on a large scale. He got ready at once to carry out his own investigation.

How was he going to find out where these mysterious construction sites were? He thought up a crafty ploy. Carrying an assortment of religious brochures and tracts exalting moral values, he took the train to Rouen. His luggage contained his little scout's compass, which was often very useful when exploring.

Pretending to be a representative from a charity, he went to the local labour office in the Norman administrative capital and knocked at the door of the social services. There, he spread out his collection of righteous literature, declaring he 'wanted to get in touch with the young people working on those large projects, since the uprooted workers were most certainly exposed to the most frightful temptations because of the easy money they were making'!

The civil servant seemed to be taken in by his explanation, or at least he acted like he was. Perhaps he guessed it was a stratagem and, cooperating without saying anything, he pretended to believe him. The main thing was that he agreed to give him a list of where these 'special constructions' were situated in the neighbourhood.

Back at Rouen station, Michel Hollard went to the public conveniences, came out wearing worker's overalls and put his suitcase containing his town clothes in the left luggage. After a thirty-minute trip he got off the train at Auffay, his haversack slung over his shoulder, and made enquiries among the locals. Either they didn't know or they didn't trust him; none of them said anything about the supposedly secret building work. He was convinced, however, that the official back in the labour office had not given him the information for nothing. As his perseverance sometimes amounted to stubbornness, he made a point of going around the neighbouring countryside methodically.

As Auffay was at the junction of a network of roads, he set off down one road for forty minutes, looking over the landscape carefully, without result. Coming back to where he'd started from, he did the same in another direction, but again in vain. The third road he tried led him to the hamlet of Bonnetot-le-Faubourg. After walking for almost 2.5 miles in that direction, he was about to turn back when he heard a distant rumbling noise. He carried on even more keenly, with the dull rustling sound accompanying his steps getting louder and louder.

He was soon able to make out a crowd of workers wielding spades and pickaxes within a vast enclosure. The rumbling sound of the concrete mixers echoed their blows, together with the din of an endless merry-go-round of backfiring motor vehicles. The rectangular-shaped construction site, measuring about 400 yards along its longest side, already had a maze of concrete paths, probably for serving a series of buildings under construction. German soldiers walked back and forth across the site and there were a lot of sentries on guard everywhere.

Trying to get into such a heavily protected area without a pass was wishful thinking. It was impossible to be the slightest bit curious and even just turning back would arouse suspicion, so he just had to carry straight on. Opportunity provided him with a wheelbarrow, abandoned by the side of the road. After hurriedly hiding his haversack in the nearby undergrowth, he grabbed the barrow and pushed it calmly onto the construction site. The guards saw him but did nothing.

Walking along a complicated network of concrete paths and cemented areas, he noted the beginnings of several forts and casemates of varying sizes. He went up to a group of labourers carrying breeze blocks and helped them without this seeming to surprise them. Speaking to one of them, he tried a question, asking him if he knew what it was they were building.

'According to the *vert-de-gris*,[1] they are building garages for lorries,' the man answered evasively, revealing his own disbelief. For everybody, the work in progress was more than just questionable, but nobody knew what it was for. Michel Hollard was quick to take in that the maze pathways all converged on an area set out with special care. A string was stretched out over 50 or so yards between two rows of perfectly parallel markers; it sloped gently upwards to the far end of the construction site.

'String stretched out in this manner could obviously only be used as a guide,' thought the exploring engineer. 'That particular implement is essential for doing well-calculated line-ups, or making rigorous settings.' Keeping an eye on a group of masons working nearby, the undercover visitor ventured closer to the layout, despite the presence of several German guards watching from a distance. Observing what they were doing and how they were all getting on, he took advantage of a moment of inattention to go and stand along the construction's alignment, facing where the string started. Following a sudden intuition, he took one of his most foolhardy initiatives: crouching down as if to tie-up his bootlaces, he remained in that position for a good ten seconds, time enough to take a compass reading of the layout's bearing.

Before beating a hasty retreat, the supposed workman went to the toilet area. There he ran into a foreman and asked him the same questions he'd asked others earlier.

'It's a mystery to me, too,' the man admitted. 'We're working blindly with no overall view of what it is. The German engineers are distrustful and curt; they only hand out information bit by bit. What's more, they keep making us go faster and faster all the time.'

'Do you know of any other sites like this one?'

'Don't you know that these things are everywhere?'

'Where exactly, for instance?'

The man unhesitatingly mentioned several place names. All these questions, however, were beginning to intrigue the rather naïve foreman, so Michel decided it was high time to clear off. Taking his precious wheelbarrow, he left the area without a hitch, picked up his bag and, with a sigh of relief, set off back.[2]

***

A room rented permanently in a little Parisian hotel opposite the Gare de Lyon served as headquarters, safe house and letter box for the head of the network and his associates.[3] Michel Hollard locked himself in there and spread a map out on the floor, placing his compass on it. What he saw was certainly not enough for him to think of anything more than the vaguest hypotheses. He did notice, however, that if he prolonged the string whose bearing he had taken, it passed right through the centre of London.

Chapter 2

Cradle of a Vocation

'Ever since childhood, I've lived in wonder,' my father told me in 1988. He was still alert and incredibly energetic at the age of 90. 'The universe that revealed itself to me has never disappointed me. So much so that when I wake up every morning, I often have the sensation of being the happiest man in the world!'

'Even after enduring all that suffering?'

'I had such a hard time that during the very sombre days, the enchanted vision of my early years abandoned me for a while. But I have always been able to pull myself together again by observing how beautiful life is, and that its best moments easily outweigh the worst ones!'

'Your optimism is nonetheless exceptional. Where did that come from?'

'I've always had faith in my lucky stars. But I can't deny the influence the family environment had on me. The world my parents made me discover gave me an abundance of happiness which is my most precious inheritance. And my home today continues to enchant me!'

***

Born on 10 July 1898 in Épinay-sur-Seine, a town in the northern suburbs of Paris, Michel Hollard was the second son of Professor Auguste Hollard and his wife Pauline, née Monod. A *Docteur ès Sciences*, Auguste Hollard was an eminent chemist and a colleague of Henri Becquerel, Pierre Curie, Marie Curie and Paul Langevin.

Michel Hollard's ancestry was partly Swiss on both the paternal and maternal sides. We will see shortly how the family's close links with the Swiss Confederation were of great help to him. Among his close relatives who distinguished themselves were the explorer and humanist Théodore

Monod, who was his cousin, as well as two future Nobel Prize winners in Medicine: Jacques Monod and Daniel Bovet. Apart from their respective abilities, all these men possessed the same virtues of generosity, courage and determination.

The family concepts of duty were undeniably austere. In accordance with these, the right to happiness could hardly be obtained without first helping or defending others. Honesty and civic responsibility would suffer no exceptions.

Even as a young boy, Michel's boldness aroused both admiration and worry among his entourage. One of his antics, worthy of Till Eulenspiegel,[1] gives an idea of his precocious bravery. Having decided to put his own courage to the test, he put on a 'special holiday show' for his five sisters. What he wanted to do was compare the pain bee stings caused with that of wasps. Watched by the terrorised girls, he let himself be attacked by the two insects he was holding in his hands!

From his childhood onwards, uncommonly, he was quite indifferent to the attraction of all things material. Like Diogenes, he despised ostentation and was quite content with a simple way of life.[2] Since material goods had limited appeal for him, his lack of interest in money and the value of things became proverbial around him. The people he knew socially and professionally took advantage of this all too often.

A devout Christian, he always had a ready collection of quotations from the Bible, and in the most tragic hours of deportation he would often quote verses to his companions that were best suited to their distress. Self-sacrifice had to be added to the exceptional blend of physical, practical and intellectual abilities he had shown ever since childhood. He was altruistic to the end of his days, denouncing the injustices he encountered in other people's misfortunes.[3] He was never to be found on the aggressor's side. He was averse to all forms of violence and he thought weapons as toys were not to be put into the hands of his children, as well as toy soldiers and other warlike symbols.

Under no circumstances did he ever feel hatred for his opponents. During two world wars, he did not fight the German people, as such. On the contrary, he was fascinated by the German intellect, especially its cultural and spiritual aspects.[4] The fighting in which he took part sought to overthrow not men, but doctrines.

The Scout Movement, created by Baden-Powell and recently introduced into France, exercised a lasting attraction and influence on him. Belonging to a group of scouts contributed to the young man's physical and moral education. Later, with nostalgic humour, he sometimes mentioned the scout's staff, parodying La Fontaine, 'I break, and do not bend!'[5] And throughout his life, he gave the most outstanding examples of how to follow the famous motto 'Be Prepared!'

Being a scout taught him to get by on his own materially, in all sorts of circumstances, foreseen or unforeseen. It also taught him how to use a compass; an instrument which turned out to be essential during his historical explorations and discoveries.

While still at school, Michel Hollard had hoped to be able to launch himself into higher literary or musical studies. Imaginative, gifted, with a refined, original poetic sensitivity, he had all the advantages you could want. But the declaration of war in 1914 took him by surprise on the eve of his sixteenth birthday and put paid to that dream. His sense of patriotism was already alive and he had the example of his older brother Vincent, a fierce patriot and future hero himself,[6] to persuade him to join the army and serve France. This early impulse was quite clearly at odds with his carrying on studying in the near future and he only went back to school after the Armistice in 1918, abandoning his earlier literary and musical aspirations once and for all.

However, he could not join up before he was 17. Having trouble controlling his impatience, like a thoroughbred colt, he got himself into the military Red Cross temporarily as an orderly. The time finally came when he was allowed to stand before the draft board. Sadly, they thought his virility was too underdeveloped and a lack of body hair contributed to his request being adjourned! The grounds for the refusal hurt his manly pride but the facetious would-be recruit successfully thought up a humorous send-up. When he stood before the army doctor for the second time, the latter nodded, smiling: the young man had adorned his private parts with a tuft of hair taken from one of his sister's dolls! More than three-quarters of a century later, the mischievous veteran was still pleased with himself when he recalled this schoolboy prank.

Michel's physical development was slow and he was convinced that this would assure him greater longevity. What was more, when he was young, he got his muscles used to daily exercise and throughout his life kept up this physical, but also mental, discipline. He thus became very tough, which helped him resist the catalogue of ordeals that both wars and deportation forced upon him.

Chapter 3

A Hero at 19

Once admitted to the armed services and invited to choose a military speciality, the new recruit chose the infantry. The future infantryman saw service in the frontline as the most direct way of driving the invading enemy out of his country.

But before being thrown into the fray, he had to be sent on a training course to be taught the rudiments of soldiering. From 1915–1916, with the war in full swing, this training was speeded up, but for the novice it was nonetheless long. The instructors were thoroughly tough and didn't show the recruit any particular indulgence, even though he was clearly younger than the others.

Right from the beginning, the would-be warriors were ordered to walk long distances carrying heavy loads: big sacks, Lebel rifles, cartridge belts full of mainly copper ammunition, and so on. In the early days, the teenager despaired of ever obtaining the necessary endurance and toughness. But this harsh system did have an effect and, through sheer willpower, the youngster of the group ended up outdoing his companions.

***

A real soldier at last, assigned to the 51st Infantry Regiment, it was not long before Michel Hollard distinguished himself. Promoted almost immediately to private first class, he showed a brilliant spirit of initiative during the fighting raging around Saint-Quentin; a martyred town in northern France where he saw a church burnt down. After a deluge of shells had fallen on the battlefield and caused a general rout, he refused to leave. All alone in the turmoil, he saved a position a few yards away from the enemy trenches. He was awarded the Croix de Guerre with bronze star for this act of bravery. Surprised, he declared he'd 'done nothing more than his normal surveillance job.'

His superiors deemed him worthy of joining a platoon of officer cadets. His brilliant success put him in command of a section whose men, mostly older than him, were generally more experienced than he was. He immediately noticed that the group's behaviour towards him could vary greatly depending on the situation.

During the training course, as the only volunteer among military service recruits, the young man ran into incomprehension, or even hostility, and his detractors played stupid tricks on him, accusing him of being overzealous. But his acts of bravery, added to the firm yet compassionate authority he now possessed, inspired respect and even devotion in his men. Recognising what the new cadet was worth, they accepted his command with good grace.

***

The death of his brother Vincent, the eldest of the Hollard children, brutally plunged the end of the war into mourning for his family. A cadet like his younger brother, Vincent Hollard had volunteered for the army and had drawn attention to himself by his acts of bravery, also earning him the Croix de Guerre. On 2 September 1918, a few weeks before the end of hostilities, Vincent addressed this letter to his parents:

> If these words reach you, it'll mean that I've been called upon to give my life for my country. I beg you not to give way to grief; as far as I am concerned, I have accepted this sacrifice for some time now. My time is the time that God has chosen.
> Life is only worth living if one perceives that supreme harmony for one instant which is its sole and rare beauty. I repeat what Henri Gounelle said: 'The beauty of life is worth more than life itself.'[1]
> So let us be dignified, let's be strong when the unique time comes.
> I hold you all close to my heart,
> Be happy, my loved ones, as you ought to be.
> Farewell. No, until we meet again!

***

Michel and Yvonne Hollard named their second son Vincent.

After the Armistice was signed on 11 November 1918, Michel Hollard decided to quit the army, despite an offer to stay on and make it his career. Peace seemed to be guaranteed at least for many years to come and with the fighting now over, the veteran thought that his being in the army was no longer justified. Coming back into society and finding his way in a world which had suddenly become almost trifling were new challenges for this man overflowing with energy.

The war had interrupted the development of a whole generation. The public authorities thought they were obliged to help the young men who had been driven out of classrooms by the events. The École Nationale des Arts et Métiers thus allowed a selection of former soldiers to take accelerated school courses. Thanks to these measures, Michel Hollard was able to attend the famous institution and obtain an engineering degree.

Then, in response to requests from the army, he served periodically with the military and was promoted successively to lieutenant and then captain in the reserve. After being an outstanding Resistance fighter and the leader of a network during the Second World War, he was promoted to lieutenant colonel in 1945.

Chapter 4

Refusing Defeat

With the general mobilisation of 1939, Michel Hollard was not assigned to a fighting unit, even though that was what he wanted. The army preferred to give him a job that corresponded to his engineering qualifications in the Centre d'Études de Mécanique, Balistique et Armement. This post was in the Paris region, whereas his family had joined his father-in-law in the Cévennes, a mountain range in southern France.

For several months, his desk-bound job prevented him from assessing the gravity of the situation properly. In May 1940, despite the continually advancing German forces, he still didn't want to believe disaster was on its way. Even the exodus of part of the population towards the south of France didn't cause him to give up hope.

But the day came when all the people in his department were called upon to withdraw to another factory in Tulle, located about 300 miles south of Paris. All available means of transport were soon taken by storm. The trains were completely crammed ages before they got going and many resourceful people didn't hesitate to cling to the outside of wagons or onto steps, ladders, buffers, and even sometimes hoist themselves up onto roofs. The roads were swarming with cars overloaded in the same way.

Michel Hollard had the impression he was witnessing an almost overall resignation which profoundly affected him. Refusing to imagine that the French Army had been routed, he only admitted that what he saw of the catastrophe was true when he witnessed military convoys fleeing in disorder.

When he was forced to leave, there was no more transport available, not even a bicycle, so he left Paris on foot. For luggage, he took his engineer's briefcase and a satchel containing several personal effects. The flight of refugees southwards from northern France and the neighbouring countries has been compared to the biblical Exodus. For Michel Hollard, this great journey on foot was more of a moral ordeal than a physical one. He was profoundly upset by the collapse of his country.

His only consolation was the certainty that his family was benefiting from the best possible shelter; an oasis of peace nestling deep in a Cévennes valley. For himself, he didn't fear the coming exertion or danger for the time being; he was only thinking of joining them so that he and his wife could decide what to do.

***

He made his way amidst hordes of uprooted people on foot. Seeing that most of these good people were more fragile than him, he was prepared to help anyone in trouble. But he soon found out to his cost that a panic-stricken crowd could turn out to be dangerous.

As the human tide approached Artenay, to the north of Orléans, an aircraft appeared in the distance. It seemed so small at first that it was taken for a reconnaissance plane, apparently harmless. Nonetheless three odd-looking objects dropped from it and the crowd threw itself to the ground. Two explosions echoed nearby, followed by cries, then silence. Out of the three bombs, one went off near a woman, killing her outright. Shrapnel from the second hit a young man who collapsed, losing blood.

Using what he could find, Michel Hollard, the former orderly, gave the unfortunate young man the necessary first aid. Laying him on the side of the road where everybody could see him, he tried in vain to attract the attention of passing drivers, who pretended not to see or understand. It was a long wait before a military vehicle stopped and accepted to take the casualty to a hospital.

That left the third bomb. It had fallen without exploding, but he had seen where it had landed. He got closer and decided to make a makeshift warning signal. For this, he made a flag of sorts using a rag he'd found on the ground and tied it around a stick. As he was putting up this simple warning sign, a group of overexcited oddballs came up, shouting at him. To them, the man could only be a traitor making signals to the enemy aircraft!

Beaten, insulted and stripped naked, he wasn't even allowed to explain himself. Grabbing his wallet, one of the men found the photograph of a relative who had a lock of hair unfortunately sloping across his forehead, a clearly regrettable similarity.

'Admire his master!' shouted the man, throwing him to the ground with the help of another crank.

Fortunately, an army patrol came up, intrigued by the kerfuffle. The accused owed his deliverance to the initiative of an NCO (non-commissioned officer) who said he was taking charge of the situation. The still furious civilians only started calming down once they believed their scapegoat was under arrest. The soldiers dispersed the frenzied crowd, enabling the unlucky prisoner to justify himself. As a reserve officer, he was now dealing with soldiers. Without losing his composure, he found the words to convince these men of his good intentions, while they stayed calm despite the ambient unrest.

Carrying on his way south, he entered Orléans, which had just been bombed. Several buildings were still engulfed in flames and some inhabitants were frightened of getting trapped. As he had spotted a possible evacuation route, he acted as a guide for several people in a state of shock. This involved walking back and forth through a stricken quarter.

His behaviour was such that it aroused the suspicions of certain clearly hysterical characters. Foreseeing a repetition of the Artenay incident, he slipped away in time and made his way into the countryside. These two experiences on the same day taught him that selfless acts could make people distrustful and that fearful crowds could misinterpret them.

***

During his eventful journey, Michel Hollard slept most of the time in barns or other improvised shelters. The weather was good and without any further incident he reached Tulle, where his colleagues welcomed him warmly and the company's management soon invited him to start working again.

'But what are we doing now, for work?' he asked.

'Well, since we depend on the military administration, none of us has anything to worry about as far as our professional futures are concerned,' was the answer.

He was disturbed by such uncertainty about the nature of his future career but was granted leave so he could join his family in the Cévennes.

He set off again but this time on a borrowed bicycle, an old contraption with a fixed pinion mechanism and no brakes. This picturesque and unpredictable mount enabled him to reach the village of Gorniès without too much difficulty.

Not far from Mount Aigoual and the Cirque de Navacelles is the old village of Gorniès, nestling at the end of the valley of the Vis, a tributary of the Hérault. For generations, Yvonne Hollard's family had rocked their children to sleep there. In this paradise, so isolated it seemed to be protected from the world's conflicts, three generations had been worrying about the traveller. Communication means had collapsed and the sources of information had almost dried up. The surprise reappearance of a husband, father and son-in-law caused considerable joy.

The announcement of the armistice confirmed that France had collapsed. Michel Hollard spent several weeks looking for a job in the so-called 'Free' Zone. Having obtained no satisfactory offer, he had to resign himself to returning to the capital with his family, despite the enemy being there. Meanwhile, the Centre d'Études de Mécanique, Balistique et Armement had settled back in Paris. Stopping by to see his manager, Michel Hollard learned he was to be honoured by being promoted to a new, prestigious and well-paid post.

'But who do we work for now?' he asked.

'Well, naturally we have to submit to the occupying authorities,' answered the manager, visibly embarrassed, nonetheless.

'Well, you've changed positions quickly! I'm afraid I'm not in the habit of swinging around like a weathervane. For the record, please note I've resigned!'

After this departure, Michel Hollard, now deprived of resources, recalled the lines of Rudyard Kipling:

If you can meet with Triumph and Disaster
And treat those two impostors just the same;
If you can keep your head when all about you
Are losing theirs and blaming it on you,

If you can talk with crowds and keep your virtue,
Or walk with Kings – nor lose the common touch,
Yours is the Earth and everything that's in it,
And – which is more – you'll be a Man, my son![1]

Chapter 5

Survival and Challenge

When it settled in a country it had just invaded, the German Army took over most of the local industries and tried to win over their personnel. Some people quit their jobs, just like Michel Hollard. Most, however, remained at work. They just buckled under, lost in despair.[1] The engineer risked penury because he had deliberately chosen to give up his job without hope of receiving the slightest assistance.[2] But he wasted no time seeking out another professional springboard.

When he started looking, he noticed that most of the job offers corresponding to his qualifications masked a veiled incitation to collaborate with the enemy. While talking with his family, he appeared confident and tried to reassure his wife. Stifling the anxiety he nonetheless felt, albeit secretly, he told her in front of the children: 'To survive, the French certainly need technicians and engineers in my speciality. Have no fear, my darling, the search I've only just begun is bound to lead to something. There'll obviously be some advertisers who are still honest. My references and enthusiasm are compelling and you know how tenacious I can be!'

After a lot of unsuccessful interviews, his determination was rewarded. An advertisement was put in a big Paris daily by a Dijon industrialist, Mr Durand, who specialised in making *gazogènes* (wood gas generators). These machines enabled internal combustion engines to use the carbon monoxide given off by burning charcoal as fuel, instead of petrol, which was now impossible to find.

Mr Durand had created the Société des Gazogènes Autobloc and was hoping to set up a subsidiary in the Paris region. The advertisement indicated that he wanted to recruit an agent with both serious technical skills and specific knowledge of the automobile sector. As this profile seemed to correspond to him, Michel Hollard prepared his application that same day. He was about to drop the envelope into the letterbox when he had second thoughts.

'I haven't got a minute to lose,' he said suddenly, 'I must catch the next train for Dijon. The letter risks getting lost in all the mail. A direct contact will give me a far better chance of convincing them.'

The next morning, as Mr Durand was going through the enormous volume of mail resulting from his advertisement, Michel Hollard turned up at the factory's secretarial office.

He was seen into the manager's office. As he'd thought, the competition was stiff. When he left his CV, he didn't forget to point out that he'd walked out of the Centre d'Études de Mécanique, Balistique et Armement, which was now working for the enemy. The reason for him deliberately quitting his job went down favourably with the factory manager and he went back to Paris with a temporary distribution contract in his pocket.

The results were not long in coming. The Autobloc brand quickly won the esteem of the capital's transport companies. Despite irritating quirks, the trucks fitted out with these strange devices worked almost as well as their petrol counterparts and they started operating again for the greater good of the population as a whole, mainly by distributing foodstuffs and medicines. Nobody seemed to miss the quaint handcarts originally used for this purpose.

After a few weeks, he was promoted to general agent for the Autobloc firm and ran into a new problem, or rather it was a foreseeable one: with the increase in the number of vehicles using the *gazogènes*, charcoal started to become rare. So, what had to be done now was to look after the fuel supply for the customers or the orders for installing new machines would dry up.

The usual charcoal suppliers, located for the most part far from Paris, had not been expecting to receive such an avalanche of orders. As a result, the users started fighting over the precious commodity. The market became fiercer and fiercer. Certain less scrupulous individuals didn't hesitate to go in for hijackings or even burglaries. A large load expected by the Paris branch of Autobloc was thus robbed, a rival fitter having succeeded in intercepting it and unloading it at his factory after bribing the transporter.

Pursuing its expansion, despite the challenges, the branch developed to include several assembly shops.

Now well established, Michel Hollard had to face another, more serious problem: the moment had come when the Germans in turn started running out of petrol. They were courteous but commanding; their technicians appeared at the Paris Autobloc offices. They were there to have a series of vehicles modified to *gazogènes*, and they paid well. Michel Hollard had to use all his skill and ability to turn them away. Never once did the First World War volunteer transgress the rule he'd fixed for himself: refuse all forms of cooperation with the occupying forces. Quite the contrary. Because of his family responsibilities, he couldn't even try to join the French combatants in London, but his wish to find another way of resisting was getting stronger and stronger every day, and going prospecting in the forest zones gave him the idea for a rather crazy plan.

Although the wooded slopes of the Jura Mountains were situated in a prohibited zone, they could be considered, at a pinch, as plausible areas for professional exploration. If he was able to get there, he'd try to cross into neighbouring Switzerland. There, in a country where he had so many ties, he'd seek out the representatives of Great Britain, a country still at war with Germany and an ally of the true France.

The business Michel Hollard had set up was already flourishing by the spring of 1941 and enabled him not only to meet his family's needs, but also to think about preparing such an expedition. At the beginning of May, he prepared the operation very carefully.

'Here at last are the funds I've managed to save so that I can try to carry out my plan,' he noted with satisfaction and a certain pride. 'A sum amassed month after month and entirely given over to my secret plan. Family expenditure has been taken care of for several weeks, as has that of the office; and Madame Boulanger, my secretary, has been paid until 15 June. I'm now at peace and free of my entourage for a fortnight or so.

'I've told people around me that I'm off for a meeting with the *gazogène* manufacturer, Mr Durand, in Dijon. I've announced that afterwards I'll be going to look for cuts of wood in the neighbouring forest regions so as to be able to meet my customers' fuel needs.

'The imperatives of my profession will therefore justify my absence. However, in case there's an unforeseen problem, my entourage can get through to me on the day I'm meeting the Dijon industrialist, whom my wife, my secretary and certain clients know. So I'll go and see him first and then, and only then, will I slip off, hoping that everything at home and at the office will be all right.

'I'll try to go through the prohibited zone and cross the Franco-Swiss border, then offer my services to the British representative in Bern. Our allies will certainly be happy to recruit a man of goodwill, ready to help them in France itself. I'll have to travel quite a distance in a country I don't know well. So I'll take my bicycle and a waterproof bag containing spare clothes, in case I need to swim across a river.

'Dijon is an excellent place to start my expedition. Placed as it is more than halfway along the way, I'll find good lodgings there. As I'm very fit, I could set off at dawn.'

Chapter 6

A Daring Undertaking

After meticulously studying the maps of Burgundy, Franche-Comté and Savoie, Michel Hollard started planning. He didn't say a word to anyone, especially not to his wife, whose anxiety he dreaded. But this veil over his intentions weighed on him, and this first trip and the next into Switzerland were the only ones he did without telling his family.

The personnel of the Autobloc *gazogène* factory in Dijon were indeed waiting for him to deal with several difficulties. The visit was also to give him the opportunity to tell the manager about his plan for forest exploration.

He made the first leg of the journey on the Paris-Dijon train on 15 May 1941. Everything went as planned and after a night at a hotel, he set off on his bicycle, feeling good. He headed for the village of Cusey, having chosen this route because the village was situated along the banks of the Marne-Saône Canal, beyond which extended the so-called 'Red' Zone, an area some 45–65 miles wide the Germans had delimited in eastern France. The chosen route also meant he had to make a fairly long detour to the north. This inconvenience had seemed unavoidable to him when he first examined the zone boundaries.

Entering this area was forbidden to anyone not holding a pass. Michel Hollard didn't have one, and for good reason. German guards patrolled unendingly, while others kept an eye on the crossing points.

When the cyclist reached the canal, he weighed up how difficult it would be to cross it. A lock spanned the waterway; it was lined with metal-tipped chevaux-de-frise[1] and signs warning of the presence of mines. Watching from behind a bush, he wondered if he'd not be better waiting until nightfall before getting into the water with his bicycle and dragging it across with the rope he'd wound to his luggage rack.

He was trying to put together a plan, which was not exactly very realistic, when a German patrol consisting of three cyclists came around the bend in the towpath. At the lock, the men calmly got down from their bikes. Through the leaves sheltering him, the onlooker was able to witness, without being seen, the exact movements the soldiers made so they could cross the footbridge safely.

Near the warning 'DANGER, MINES,' one of the blocks of barbed wire, which seemed set in the others, turned out in fact to be loose and of no use. The leading soldier moved it carefully so as to allow the men following, hampered by their bicycles, to advance one after the other. Once the device was put back in place, the patrol went on its way.

Captivated by what he'd just seen, Michel waited a long time before moving. Knowing what to do now, he repeated this magic 'open sesame!' After carefully replacing the steel hedgehog behind him, he crossed the little swing bridge on the lock without difficulty, his bicycle on his shoulder.

The relief he felt was mixed with pride at having discovered such a secret more easily than he could ever have imagined and without running into any difficulties. To boot, neither his clothes nor his bike got wet.

While watching again from the other bank, Michel Hollard had already spotted the lock-keeper's cottage, not very far away. It was obviously not impossible for a German guard to come out of it. However, it seemed relatively unlikely he'd encounter one. Indeed, he'd always known that running and looking after the locks was one of the 'reserved jobs' the administration entrusted to civil servants who'd been victims in the last war. The lock-keeper he might run into would most likely be a veteran like him.

In this he was not wrong. The man, middle-aged with only one leg, had watched him cross the canal from inside his house without revealing himself.

When the illegal traveller reached terra firma, the door of the building opened. Solidly built and lively despite his handicap, the keeper advanced along the terrace, staring questioningly at the bold newcomer.

'I don't have a pass,' whispered Michel, 'But I must get into the Red Zone.'

With a gesture, asking no questions, the official invited his unexpected guest into his office. He even offered to share the food spread out on the table with him. The traveller, who couldn't really hang about, declined but accepted a glass of wine, clinked glasses with him and expressed his thanks. As he left, he announced that he'd be returning.

Providence had just sent an ally Michel Hollard's way. A volunteer like him during the First World War, the lock-keeper was the first in a long line of such encounters. The Agir network[2] ('agir' is a French verb meaning 'to act') would be formed from relationships almost always forged by chance in the field.

Most people in provincial France had unambiguous patriotic sentiments. Michel Hollard's chance dealings often led to people joining him because of their instinctive mutual trust. The network leader's determination and charisma were sufficiently convincing. When questioning people he didn't know, his intuition about the sincerity of their beliefs almost never let him down. He placed his trust in countless people from all walks of life. Everybody was worthy until the day one rotten apple was discovered among them.

The cyclist left the lock and rode until nightfall, reaching Dole, where fortunately a hotel room was still available. The following morning, he reached Le Cernois, a hamlet situated near the border that was the home of a customs official recommended to him by one of his Paris acquaintances. The civil servant gave his visitor information about the German surveillance rounds, and agreed to keep his bicycle until he came back. Although well-intentioned, he actually passed on information that turned out to be wrong.

Michel had barely started walking through the thick Risoux Forest when he ran into the wrong sort of people and found himself in the German police station at Mouthe, where he spent the night lying directly on the floor. He was transferred to Pontarlier, where he appeared in front of an officer to whom he told his story about obtaining charcoal supplies for the *gazogènes*. The soldier seemed hesitant. Taking advantage of his indecision, the prisoner suggested he contact the French administration.

More than anything else, Michel Hollard was frightened of having to explain away his lack of authorisation for being in the Red Zone. Up until now, nobody had thought of checking if he actually had one of these special passes. Later, during the numerous trips he made into this forbidden sector, he was never asked to produce this document, which continually surprised him. No doubt, in the minds of the French policemen, it was clear that the Germans manning the crossing points had already checked him through. Perhaps some French employees also wittingly turned a blind eye.

After a moment's reflection, the German officer who'd been asked to get the French authorities to intervene seemed almost relieved. The idea of passing such a prickly case on to the local authorities calmed him down somewhat. Moreover, following the instructions given by Berlin, the occupying army had to try to create a suitable climate for persuading the French into collaborating in all sorts of ways.

Hollard's identity was checked at the French police station. He had to repeat his story about supposedly prospecting for trees. Nothing was said about being in the Forbidden Zone without authorisation and he was ordered back to Paris by the first train. Two gendarmes escorted him to a carriage where they found him a seat. Just before the departure whistle was blown, they courteously took their leave.

The traveller barely had the time to grab his bag and make his own getaway before the train got going. Using a door opening onto the tracks, on the opposite side from the departure platform, he made a detour and returned to the street, taking care not to run into the gendarmes he could see leaving the station.

Not far away, there was a bus leaving for Morteau. He climbed in almost by chance, knowing that its route ran alongside the border. For the next phase of his expedition on foot, he relied on his intuition, on his good luck, and on a map folded in such a manner that he could examine it discreetly along the way.

The trip enabled him to appreciate the pastoral charm of the Doubs Valley. The picturesque names of the border villages attracted his attention. His sense of the poetic as much as a look at the topography made him decide to head for the hamlet of Derrière-le-Mont, tucked far away from the main thoroughfares, right in the middle of the Jura forests.[3]

After getting off the coach, a cross-country walk through fields and forests enabled him to climb up to that faraway place, where he came across the worksite of pit-sawyer César Gaiffe. The sawyer declared that he certainly had the trees his visitor was looking for. They were almost at the summit of the mountain, on the slopes of Mont Châteleu. Michel Hollard asked if it was possible to examine them. A meeting with the *montagnard* (mountain dweller) Paul Cuenot was planned for the following day.

The traveller settled in the local farm-inn. Before going to bed, he had another look at his map and noted that the border passed near the site he was going to visit the next day.

The following morning Paul Cuenot was on time. He was a slim, athletic man in his fifties with deep blue eyes and a firm handshake. He held the bridle of a horse harnessed to a wagon designed for carrying wood. They followed tracks that wound steeply through the forest. Before going into the trees, the guide pointed to the summit of the mountain:

'That's where we're going.'

Conversation with this jovial, upright and direct man was established at once in a tone of familiarity. During the climb he couldn't stop pausing here and there to pick edible mushrooms that had sprung up during the night. Halfway up, the walkers stopped on the banks of a spring. Paul Cuenot had dammed it at an earlier period when its pure water used to disappear in a marsh.

A meadow of tender grass spread out now before their eyes. This was also the *montagnard*'s work, in a spot where, in earlier times, stones had been piled up with dead tree trunks and undergrowth. A majestic site was revealed to Michel Hollard. Over pine trees, sorbs and giant beeches, whose copses went down to the hamlet in steps, he could see behind him the sunny slopes of the Doubs River. As far as the eye could see, it zigzagged through meadows and spinneys, as it came out of the defile between sheer rocks.

In the course of their conversation, Cuenot suddenly alluded to the fact that there were undesirable occupiers around. Hollard seized this opportunity to reveal the real reason for his being there: to cross the border.

'I might have known! That changes everything, let's go another way. I'll show you the best way to cross the border. By the way, do you actually need our trees?'

'Perhaps we'll talk about that another time. At the moment, what I need above all is your advice as a guide.'

'All right, let's go! This way, it's safer.'

The two men and the horse-drawn wagon continued on their way for quite a while along the wooded paths without encountering anyone. In this countryside, to all intents and purposes isolated from the rest of the world, you could be led into a false sense of security. The last greenery broke out into a big field, spread out like a ravine with two slopes flanking a stream babbling at the bottom. The forest continued evenly over onto the other side, but the trees were irregularly planted with alternating thickets and clearings. An old barn, on the side of this little valley, was part of the forest tenancy that was Paul Cuenot's responsibility.

'Right across from us,' said the *montagnard*, pointing to the summit on the other slope, 'you'll come across a little wall. You can step over it and then you'll be in Switzerland. This is the right moment, don't hang around, because the Germans will be along in a short while. I know their routines.'

'Thank you very much. I hope to see you on my return.'

'So, you're coming back, then?'

'Of course! I have things to do here in France.'

'When do you think you'll be back?'

'I don't know exactly. Tomorrow or the day after, probably.'

The *montagnard* thought for a moment, and then warned him seriously.

'Well, wait a moment. It's dangerous! When you come back, before coming down the hill, look at this barn carefully. You can see it clearly from Switzerland. If I leave the door open, all's well, you can come down. If it's closed, wait! Now, you better get going, but don't hurry nor hesitate. Good luck!'

'Believe me, I'm very grateful. See you soon!'

Providence had just presented Michel Hollard with one of his most faithful and valued assistants. The *montagnard*'s unwavering look told of his earnestness. Without someone watching over him, he wouldn't have been able to head for the border without being in great danger. If he was arrested, he had no plausible reason for being there. There was no tree or cover to prevent him from being seen in broad daylight over a wide, completely open space, surrounded by shadowy areas where the Germans could lurk with their dogs. Safety depended wholly on Paul Cuenot's sound knowledge of how the enemy patrolled in the area.

Left now to his own devices, Michel walked down the glacis pretending to be calm. He crossed the stream and, hardly daring to breathe in anticipation, climbed up the other side at a measured pace. A certain feeling of relief allowed him to breathe more freely when he reached the edge of the forest, denser and wilder on this side. Hindered in his progress by the tangled undergrowth, he suddenly spotted a row of dry stones still quite some way off. With greatly increased energy, he hurried on up, over the interminable distance still to be covered, and stepped, breathless, over the little wall.

Chapter 7

Enchantment

The joy of treading once again the soil of his forebears, his second motherland, was combined with an instantaneous, revitalised sensation of peace. As soon as he'd lost sight of the border, the believer that he was stopped and composed himself for a moment to thank Providence.

Many of his relatives and friends lived in Switzerland. Two little streets in the centre of Lausanne perpetuate the memory of our family: an uncle who'd once occupied the post of first magistrate of the city; one of his sisters, Micheline, was the wife of Dr Charles Guisan, a doctor, musician and politician, well-known in the canton of Vaud. This brother-in-law's cousin was General Henri Guisan, the commander-in-chief of the Swiss Armed Forces.

Venturing for the first time on Swiss soil since war had been declared, Michel Hollard wondered how he was going to manage there without the help of influential people. Statements from his sister and brother-in-law, who lived in Mézières, in the Lausanne region, would've been enough to back him up. But during this first visit, he preferred not to reveal his presence to his local relatives. They would probably have considered what he was doing as mad. What's more, he was hardly very presentable after his rather eventful trip.

Money was probably going to be a problem for him because he was only carrying French currency and he feared it might be refused if he tried to use it. His needs, however, were very modest. Just in case, he'd brought along two hard-boiled eggs, a piece of sausage and a hunk of almost stale bread. The prospect of having to spend one or two nights under the stars, in a haystack or in a makeshift shelter, didn't bother him. He'd already had to make do with rudimentary living conditions during the First World War and during the exodus in 1940.

With the border behind him, he came across La Brévine, a mountain village with a reputation for harsh winters – hence its nickname 'Swiss Siberia'. On this Sunday in May, however, the weather was clement as the traveller, dazzled by the light at the edge of the forest, spotted the Swiss customs building bearing the famous white cross on a red background.

He had to get in touch with the Swiss administration immediately. Before presenting himself, however, he tried to improve his appearance, which left a lot to be desired. He started by shaking out his crumpled and dusty clothes. His shoes, especially, had come out badly from the long walks in the rain, along the muddy, stony paths. Using a piece of wire found on the ground, he succeeded in patching up one of the soles which was starting to gape open, making it more presentable.

The customs office he entered was empty. A little bell, placed where it could be seen, gave a strident ring when pressed. The head of the customs office appeared a moment later.[1] The visitor handed him his identity card.

'Monsieur, would you please allow me to come into Switzerland. I have some family business to sort out. Unfortunately, I don't have a passport.'

'You know that the border is closed, I trust.'

'Yes, I do. But I have a lot of relatives and acquaintances in the country, and I would like to go to Bern. I give you my word that I shall be back within forty-eight hours.'

He was expecting the civil servant at least to check by telephone. To his great surprise, however, authorisation was granted without any further ado. The customs officer hung on to the identity card, which Michel Hollard would be able to pick up when leaving Switzerland in a day or two. In the meantime, if anyone asked for proof of his identity, a border guard was at his post to provide it. Pleasantly, the head of the customs office gave him directions for the 9-mile or so trip he had to make between La Brévine and Le Locle, a town connected to Bern by railway.

No longer tired, the traveller felt euphoric as he set off along the road as though out on a victory march. It was Sunday. Clean-cut, smiling villagers and carefree young lads and lasses were milling around and talking animatedly. They even greeted the unfamiliar, rather odd-looking stranger as he passed on his way, just as if the whole population shared in his own joy. The morning church bells were ringing out loudly, as if to echo the elation he himself was feeling.

Suddenly, in the midst of the crowd, his eyes met those of a gendarme, easily recognisable by his specially shaped kepi. After several days of travelling in conditions a Swiss person could not even imagine, Michel Hollard could not go unnoticed. A law enforcement officer came up to him, greeted him and asked him for his papers. They then had to go along to the gendarmerie, where things were sorted out as the customs officer at La Brévine had said they would be.

The consequences of the police check were beneficial. With what he told them of his trip since he'd left Paris, the Frenchman drew sympathy and admiration from among his new listeners. The policeman who'd stopped him in the street telephoned his wife to let her know they'd be having somebody interesting round for lunch. At the same time, the duty patrol agreed that the Frenchman could go to Le Locle by bicycle, escorted by one of them.

While they were travelling, the two cyclists had the opportunity to exchange their views on the international conflict. Because his country was neutral, the gendarme felt he had to show a more reserved attitude, but it wasn't long before he was expressing his attachment to core values that were scorned by the Nazi regime. The Frenchman's determination impressed him so much that he wanted to introduce him to his superior. Michel Hollard felt that to refuse would've been tactless and discourteous. Although he was short of time, he couldn't disappoint the authorities who'd taken him in, so he agreed to meet the officer.

He wasn't to regret it. Despite its neutrality, Switzerland was obviously not immune to an attack. To be forewarned, it needed information from abroad, especially France, and information that was more serious than that handed out sparingly by the diplomats and the international press, which often had to be taken with a pinch of salt.

The visitor therefore met a member of the Swiss Army General Staff, who called himself Lieutenant André.[2] What seemed to interest the officer were some fairly vague indications concerning car building in

French factories requisitioned by the Germans, and also the occupation forces that the traveller had been able to note when going through the towns of Dijon, Dole and Pontarlier. He noted each detail carefully, even the apparently insignificant ones. The talk went on in such a cordial and frank manner that the Frenchman, now convinced of the upright nature of officer, ended up revealing the true reason for his presence.

The Swiss officer ventured a question, asking him if, in the case of his cooperating with the British Embassy, he would agree to inform him too. This question embarrassed Michel Hollard, who could foresee the risk of diplomatic difficulties he'd not yet thought about.

What's more, he'd taken part in the First World War, fighting in broad daylight; now, he would henceforth have to act in the shadows. His conscience instinctively disapproved of using ruse and dissimulation. If he had to answer questions from the German authorities, or even the French ones, he would suffer from having to disguise the truth, as he had already been forced to do in Pontarlier. But faced with an oppressive, ruthless enemy, he would obviously just have to accept playing an undercover role in order to carry on the struggle effectively, even though its secret characteristics made him feel uneasy.

Michel contented himself with just insisting on how uncertain the result of his trip to Bern was likely to be and therefore didn't reply to Lieutenant André's last request.

The lieutenant showed tact and discretion, respecting his visitor's reserve. Despite his disconcerting appearance in his worse-for-wear clothes, the Frenchman behaved with dignity and determination, which commanded admiration.

The soldier thought it was his duty to do something. After a brief aside with a subordinate, he decided to facilitate the continuation of his guest's journey right up to the meeting with the customs at La Brévine, on the return trip.

Without having asked or promised anything, and without having needed any help from his friends or family, Michel Hollard was seen onto the train to Bern by the officer, who gave him a return ticket. Moreover, he was able to benefit from a privilege he could appreciate materially, but symbolically too: being allowed to sleep in one of the barracks normally reserved for the troops during their manoeuvres. He was warned that the facilities would be spartan, but he had no doubt that they'd be quite satisfactory, as would be the quality of the rest he'd find there.

In the capital's railway station, he consulted a telephone directory and found the address of the British Embassy, located in a quarter that was some way off. The walk allowed him to admire the sights of a city where several of his forebears had lived, but which were for him a discovery.

Chapter 8

Rebuff

Thanks to the directions given to him by successive passers-by, all of them helpful, Michel finally spotted the escutcheon with His Majesty's arms decorating the façade of a beautiful, private town house. The door of a small building nearby was marked 'Military Attaché'. The sound of the doorbell brought a distrustful-looking porter to the door.

A visit from an odd-looking stranger at the end of a Sunday afternoon might have appeared out of place. Using what knowledge of English he had, Michel Hollard asked the employee to tell the official in charge that he wanted to meet him urgently. He was seen into a small room where he was kept waiting for a good hour, which might have seemed unpleasant but for a picture on the wall. It was a parchment reproducing four of Sir Winston Churchill's precepts:

In War: Resolution
In Defeat: Defiance
In Victory: Magnanimity
In Peace: Goodwill

These wise words quite matched the Frenchman's convictions and temperament, and were so relevant that he immediately took note of them and made a point of learning them by heart.

Then he heard regular footsteps in the distance on the street. After a moment, the sound of a key in the lock, followed by steps in the hall, brought the visitor back from the thoughts where Churchill's words had plunged him. His enthusiasm soon gave way to disillusion. A tall, thin man in his fifties with blue eyes and freckles opened the door and, barely greeting him, asked:

'What is it you want, sir?'

'I'm a Frenchman who has decided to fight against the enemy we have in common that has occupied my homeland. I intend to fight alongside those who've not put down their weapons. I've come from Paris by my own means to plan the fight alongside the English forces.' Far from the warm welcome he was expecting, unbelievably, he met with a rebuff. Expressing himself in correct French, the Englishman replied dryly:

'Monsieur, since the invasion of France, contacts between Switzerland and England have been suspended. Here we can receive nothing from home; nor can we send anything. Therefore, I regret to inform you that your offer cannot be taken into consideration.'

A cold shower would have been less disagreeable than this biting refusal. Michel waited in vain, aghast, for a few more cordial and encouraging words, but the other man considered his answer to be enough. For him, the meeting, just as needless as it was tiresome, was over. He even made a gesture betraying his wish for the encounter to be over and done with.

'If I understand you correctly,' the rebuffed visitor insisted, hiding his bitterness with difficulty, 'you don't trust me. You obviously can't know who you are dealing with. I shall therefore refer you to two of your eminent fellow countrymen. They are friends of mine who will readily vouch for me.'

On a page torn from his diary, Michel Hollard hastily wrote down the names and addresses of Robert Dudley Best, an industrialist from Birmingham, and Thomas Sturge Moore, the London man of letters. On the table he also left a sheet of paper bearing the names of the main French vehicle firms and several columns of figures. It was a summary of the activity in car factories requisitioned by the occupying army. He had obtained it through his good relations with a well-placed person in the ministry.

'I shall be back next month. I hope my efforts will not be in vain. Goodbye, Monsieur!' he said, abruptly leaving the building.

The Englishman did not, however, throw the papers into the waste-paper bin. He instead made enquiries with the two British men mentioned and the industrial data was put to good use; it was even revealed to the French population during one of the BBC's daily French broadcasts. Later, this untimely publicity was criticised as being dangerous for the informers in Paris. The BBC recognised its mistake which, fortunately, had no harmful consequences.

When he later recalled the uncomfortable meeting in Bern, Michel Hollard readily acknowledged that the English representative had had to show some reserve. Dubious individuals had no doubt come before him previously. He was unknown, badly dressed and not recommended, so he could only inspire distrust. When faced with the Englishman's coolness, he had no doubt been clumsy.

Such disappointment would probably have undermined the morale of anyone else. If he felt in any way hurt by the aloofness or disdainful impassivity of his first Allied contact, his resolve didn't falter. This eye-opener, on the other hand, put his determination to the test.

Thanks to the facilities made available by Lieutenant André, the traveller ended his return journey across the Jura Mountains under good conditions. When he reached the small wall on the border, he looked down at the barn for the pre-arranged signal. As if imitating a human gesture, the barn door was wide open, doing its job of signalling. Without the *montagnard*'s watchfulness, returning to France would clearly have presented an increased risk, because he now had to move back into enemy territory.

Paul Cuenot gave marvellous proof of his loyalty. Michel Hollard hadn't been able to tell him how long he was going to be away, so the *montagnard* had organised his work so as to remain in the danger zone as long as necessary. As soon as he spotted the walker at the top of the clearing, he went up to wait for him near where he entered the forest.

The horse had remained at the farm. Using forest shortcuts, they went down to Derrière-le-Mont, where Madame Cuenot, surrounded by children, was waiting for them. Dishes were being kept warm on the stove and their guest didn't have to be forced to do justice to them. The couple tried to persuade him to stay the night. Without saying anything of the nature of his business, he asked them to understand that although he was touched by their devotion, he couldn't afford to take a break and had to keep going on his way.

Despite his disappointing visit to Bern, he was determined to persist with his patriotic undertaking. Without making a drama of the

Englishman's rebuff, he was able to rejoice in the three solid friendships he'd made. He was associated with men whose activities were major pluses for carrying out his plans: the lock-keeper Arthur Vrignon, the *montagnard* Paul Cuenot and Lieutenant André Gagnaux, from Swiss Army Intelligence.

The return trip went through Pontarlier, but the bus going there had left a long time ago. So once again, Michel set off on foot. Without his bicycle, carrying on with his trip would become very complicated. If nobody had taken it, the valuable machine – a treasure in those days – should still be waiting at the Le Cernois customs building, for his return trip. But Michel Hollard's memories of the place weren't pleasant: it was controlled by the enemy army and above all he recalled the misadventure he'd had on the outskirts of the hamlet.

Overcoming his dread, he decided to try to recover his bike. To reach Le Cernois faster, he decided to alternate running and walking, but overworking himself for a week had cut his stamina. Moreover, the curfew, which was particularly strict in the border regions, was fast approaching. He had to stop somewhere. Fortunately, he met a local on the way, who told him where there was a guest house.

When he reached Le Cernois the next day, the encounter he was dreading indeed took place. On the road, he found himself face to face with one of the Germans who, a week earlier, had escorted him to Mouthe. But he had the right instinctive reaction: not without a hint of sardonic pride, he told the soldier that he'd been freed and had come back to pick up his bicycle.

His nerve paid off. However, once inside the building, nobody answered his call. On a clean page torn from his diary, he wrote a message, not without irony, to the 'French customs officials and the German occupiers of the building'. Expressing his surprise at not seeing them again, he was obliged to help himself, but thanked them for looking after it!

After leaving the note where it could be seen, Michel grabbed his bike and dashed off without running into anybody. He now had the means of getting around which to him seemed almost a luxury. In all weather, across all sorts of terrain, his trips had made him suffer a great deal. He didn't even try to estimate the distances he'd travelled. Such performances would certainly have been impossible without his regular physical training, which he'd kept up every morning, a little less than usual, but with as much energy since he'd left Paris. Just like Phaeton, he thought he was sitting at the reins of the chariot of the sun. The road to Dole, however, was long; he stopped there as he had done on the outward trip.

The lock-keeper's little house at Cusey, situated within the Red Zone, was now directly accessible before reaching the canal. In due time, he would be able to obtain information and advice. The employee, with his wife, welcomed him like a friend. As with the Cuenots at Derrière-le-Mont, Michel had to resist the touching insistence of the couple who wanted to prolong his visit.

While the three people shared an improvised snack in the lock's technical shed – a control tower where the surrounds could easily be watched – Arthur Vrignon remained on watch. When he announced that the coast was clear, Michel Hollard jumped up.

'Many thanks for your kindness,' he said going on his way, 'See you soon!'

Still, it was not without a certain anxiety that he set off across the footbridge. Before ascertaining with certainty that the barbed wire hedgehog was unmined, he quickly examined the layout. In the end, the rather forbidding gate let itself be moved easily in both directions. Under the Vrignon couple's watchful gaze, the cyclist set off again, waving gratefully.

He paid a short visit to the Dijon factory without causing much surprise, despite the signs of tiredness visible on his face, and his attire, which left a lot to be desired. The manager and even the personnel, who were increasingly concerned about the shortage of fuel for *gazogènes*, listened attentively to the information about the reserves of wood for carbonising he'd just explored.

Chapter 9

The Second Attempt

My mother, brother, sister and I lived in a state of increasing anxiety. The joy triggered by the return of the husband and father after an abnormally long absence immediately gave way to worry. We were struck by how unusually thin he was, and by the exhaustion he was just about able to overcome.

Believing that he was involved in some act of resistance was logical, at least in the mind of my mother. For a long time, family conversations had gravitated around the unfortunate fate that had struck not only France, but almost the rest of Europe and now threatened the world. All Michel Hollard's close friends recognised his desire for justice and humanity, and the way he rejected all forms of harmful politics.

Nine days had gone by since he'd left, without him being able to reassure his family as to his fate. A postcard he'd sent from Dijon, before heading off into the unknown, only reached us after he'd got back, and such a long absence couldn't be explained away by a simple business trip.

Aware of just how incoherent this was, my mother Yvonne Hollard lived in anguish. She could only approve of her husband's devotion to their homeland, but feared that the exalted vocation of the young First World War volunteer, when rekindled, would only precipitate their home and children into the turmoil. Even before he was able to start telling his story, she gave free rein to the distress that was gripping her. This lively and passionate woman, who was soon to give such precious help to her husband and the Allied cause, first and foremost obeyed her motherly and wifely instinct of self-preservation. Speaking first, she gave him her point of view to dissuade him, commenting vehemently on 'the foolhardiness and the irresponsibility of those who sought to thwart the force majeure.'

When my father was able to speak, he thought it better to say nothing of his true designs or of his trip's final destination. On the one hand, he thought, his wife wasn't ready to bear the shock. On the other hand, a second visit to the British Embassy in Switzerland could turn out negative once again, putting an end to his endeavours once and for all.

His eventful trek through Burgundy and Franche-Comté, allegedly limited to seeking out fuel in the Jura Mountains for *gazogène*-powered vehicles, provided him with a rather captivating story that he could use to keep his whole family spellbound.

We were therefore the first to be told about the secret the German patrol had unwittingly revealed to him, enabling him to get into the Forbidden Zone. As we knew and admired his powers of persuasion, we were unsurprised to learn that total strangers, like the Cusey lock-keeper, had unhesitatingly helped him.

My mother gave the impression that this partial account satisfied her, and everyone made sure my father was allowed to rest comfortably; he needed two or three days to regain his former bearing. And so life quickly resumed its former rhythm, favouring the development of the Autobloc *gazogènes*, which were now leading the Paris market.

At home, our parents tried to forget the moroseness of a country deprived of its liberty. They were full of sparkle and had the knack of keeping up a warm atmosphere. They could have been satisfied with material and social success, but as Michel Hollard was to say later:

> The ground had given way under our feet. Following a catastrophe which led to the loss of its sovereignty, our country had ceased to be our country. Although we still ate there, slept there, and lived there, the true joie de vivre had vanished. The French, for the most part, kept their dignity. But for them, life had lost much of its appeal, since they were no longer free. True, life continued, and the French carried on with their professions and jobs, and not only in the utilitarian sectors. Theatres, cinemas and circuses were open. Musicians and painters and writers were still able to express themselves. But the magic was no longer there: WE WERE IN MOURNING.

***

Michel Hollard had told the British diplomat he would be back. His will to serve the Allied cause was unshakeable and his decision to take part in the fight, in one way or another, was irreversible. As soon as he returned home, he began to prepare his second trip to Bern in secret.

The constant development of his business enabled him to make substantial profits and to continue putting money aside as a reserve to cover the expenses his patriotic endeavours would incur.

Strangely enough, as he set off again on his trip to Switzerland in June 1941, it was the ally he dreaded more than the enemy. He now apprehended the assistant military attaché's lack of comprehension and incredulity more than the mortal danger these forbidden crossings entailed.

Moral anxiety was what he felt above all. The immense effort he was getting ready to repeat would perhaps be in vain. As a generous idealist, he put all his intellectual, physical and economic skills into his commitment without being certain the assistant military attaché would take it into account. But for him, to give up was quite unthinkable.

'It doesn't matter!' he was to say later. 'A month earlier, I'd said I'd be coming back to Bern. It was almost a promise. I had to keep it!'

Since the route to Switzerland still went through Dijon, the city where the Autobloc *gazogène* offices and factory were located, Michel Hollard paid them another routine visit. When all the current technical and commercial problems had been dealt with, he said, as on his previous visit, that he was off prospecting for the precious combustible his clients were clamouring for.

A bike ride of 30 miles or so not surprisingly enabled him to reach an inn situated not far from Cusey. He had something to eat there while waiting for nightfall.

The sun was going down when he came in sight of the bridge where a sentry was on guard. To avoid him, he got off his bike and pushed it across the fields towards the canal. The fortified and mined layout of the lock still had the same hostile appearance with its spiky metal wall. Thanks to the familiar way of opening it, he easily got over the lock.

The hedgehog without any explosives, constituting the gate, noiselessly dropped back into its original position after he went through.

Despite the half-light, the lock-keeper was watching what he was up to from inside his little house. Madame Vrignon was immediately informed and started to prepare the small bedroom on the first floor. Indeed, his hosts assured him while serving him a drink that it would be very dangerous for him to be out and about near the canal at this late hour.

Their guest slept incomparably well in the picturesque room looking down on the canal reaches. At the first sign of daylight, he thought it more becoming to slip away discreetly to avoid disturbing the couple he believed were asleep, but the stairs creaked and betrayed him. He was then invited to join the Vrignons, who served breakfast a bit earlier than usual because he was there.

As with his previous visit, neither the lock-keeper nor his wife expressed even the mildest curiosity as to the purpose of his trip. The two former volunteer veterans, however, reminisced about the previous war, then talked about the present situation. As their points of view were similar, Michel Hollard declared, before leaving them:

'You and I, we are continuing the fight in which France is still morally engaged, despite its distressing situation. Thank you. See you soon!'

Rain nearly compromised the next part of his trip. Protected by his rather second-rate mackintosh, he pedalled for two and a half hours in pouring rain, reaching the town of Gray just as a bus was about to leave for Besançon along the same route. His bike was hoisted onto the roof of the vehicle and Michel, finally under cover, was able to offer himself an unexpected rest.

After reaching the terminus at Besançon, the rain was still pouring down when he set off again. As he got closer to the mountains the wind picked up, blowing in gusts and finally forcing him to dismount. He had to climb the steep hills on the French side of the Jura Mountains. Since the clouds and the rain obscured the horizon, he couldn't admire any of the sights he passed before reaching Derrière-le-Mont. The reward for all his trouble, however, was the warm welcome the Cuenot family gave him.

After twelve hours on the road, of which only two and a half were spent on the bus, Michel was soaked to the bone and exhausted. They lent him dry clothes and slippers, and he went upstairs to shower before being invited to dinner.

On both sides of a huge table, nine place settings faced each other, those of the parents and their seven children aged from 10 to 20, and they were all seated on very long benches.[1] The brood was creating a joyous hubbub, which suddenly stopped when the Parisian entered. He saw that a tenth place had just been laid for him in the middle of the assembly. He thanked the woman of the house and sat down, inviting the guests to resume their conversations. The plates were then filled with country cooking. He tasted it and said how good it was.

Eating and relaxing in pleasant company partly restored his strength. His impatience to forge ahead and his toughness would probably have encouraged him to set off immediately for Switzerland, which was just nearby, but the head of the family managed to dissuade him. On good grounds, too, for given his state of exhaustion, he was in no condition to make any further effort. Moreover, the late hour might allow him to think there was less danger.

The local farm-inn probably had a room, but in the Cuenot household everybody wanted their guest to stay under the family roof. A good bed was made available for him and he willingly accepted the invitation to stay.

The night before, the Cusey lock-keeper and his wife had offered him shelter in their picturesque accommodation. In the evening, after a rainy, windy day, the fraught cyclist could appreciate the charm and simplicity of the old mountain house.

As soon as it was light again, he was pampered once more by Paul Cuenot and his wife, who provided him with a substantial breakfast. The *montagnard* again went over the precautions to be taken to avoid enemy surveillance, but both men knew that no amount of advice could reduce the risk that any non-authorised person ran when moving around in the area. Indeed, the presence of the villager in the company of a stranger might even give rise to suspicion, without improving security.

The bicycle was stored in the barn and Michel set off alone along the paths leading to Mont Châteleu. For a moment, while he was climbing the slopes covered with giant fir trees, nature's beauty almost made him forget the danger. He even had the fleeting impression that he was off on a sporting outing. But this illusion of confidence soon vanished when he reached the little valley, at the bottom of which flowed the stream. He was aware that German patrols frequently crossed the site and positioned themselves in the half-light to keep an eye on the clearing. Through Paul Cuenot, he'd learned where to look to see if they were coming. He also knew when the most frequent rounds were made.

When the moment seemed to be right, he advanced calmly, like a peasant going about his normal business. His watch said 7.30 pm when he stepped over the little wall, beyond which lay Switzerland.

Once again, Michel Hollard felt the euphoria of freedom, albeit momentarily. Unfortunately, his enthusiasm was to be immediately cooled by another ordeal. The civil servant on duty that day at the customs post at La Brévine was inexplicably aloof and even asked him to turn round and go back! What had happened in the meantime?

My father never found out the exact reasons for this new attitude. In high places, orders had clearly been given to control the access to Swiss territory more strictly for people who didn't have their papers in order.

Chapter 10

Bienvenue

Preferring not to have any member of his family or friends living in Switzerland, who still knew nothing about his arrival in the country, intervene on his behalf, Michel Hollard obviously thought of getting a statement from Lieutenant André, the officer he'd met at Le Locle. Yet the current customs officer decided to ask first for instructions from his direct superiors. In reply, he was told to hold the Frenchman until another official could examine his case.

The visitor's wait was not too unpleasant. Taking in the sun on a carpet of green grass and moss outside the building, he ate a snack offered by the customs staff while waiting for a superior's arrival, who only turned up two and a half hours later. He then contacted Lieutenant André, to whom Michel Hollard had referred, by telephone. This turned out not to be so simple because the soldier had meanwhile gone home, to resume his civilian activity temporarily.[1] Lieutenant André confirmed the favourable impression he'd received during the previous month's meeting. His successor in the intelligence office, he added, would appreciate the French correspondent's worth.

A meeting was organised with the new official for the very same day, in the afternoon, at La Chaux-de-Fonds. This time, Michel was able to continue using the public transport system without any difficulty. On behalf of the army, the customs officers arranged the bus and train journey to the meeting point. He was met by a lieutenant who, like his predecessor, didn't immediately reveal his name. This soldier, Jean-Pierre Grandy, was to be just as a friendly and cooperative as his predecessor.

While waiting for Michel to arrive at the rendezvous point, the two officers had talked about him on the telephone. To ensure national security, the Swiss Army High Command needed information about any military movements made by the Germans, mainly in the areas situated near or in the direction of the border.

The Frenchman was able to make a report on several general observations he'd recently made on his way through Burgundy and Franche-Comté. Although it wasn't very much, his improvised report impressed the soldier, who probably appreciated the spirit it was made in more than its actual contents. On his own initiative, the Swiss officer decided to continue the assistance his colleague had instinctively given the Frenchman a few weeks earlier. Extending his permit to stay by forty-eight hours, he also took some practical measures on his behalf: an invitation to stay until the following morning at the Hôtel de la Fleur de Lys at La Chaux-de-Fonds, where they were staying and which already housed the headquarters, and giving him the material means to get to Bern and, from there, to return to the customs post at La Brévine.

During his first trip, Michel Hollard had understood that it would have been futile, and indeed improper, to wish to cooperate with the Allies on Swiss soil without the blessing of the Swiss authorities beforehand. As all the people he had met up until then shared the same convictions as him, and since they said they were prepared to fight to safeguard those convictions, he saw no reason to be reticent with his hosts. He believed in their sincerity. In the event of him being disappointed, he would naturally act according to his own conscience.[2]

All he needed now was for the English to go along with him, and for them to agree to such cooperation. The following day, rested, fairly well dressed and almost relaxed, he jumped onto the train for Bern.

***

Michel Hollard's second visit to the British Embassy in Switzerland started out a lot like the first one: a suspicious and fearful porter, an anteroom, then silence…but not for long. Three steps echoed in the corridor and the door opened, pushed by the assistant military attaché who was quite different.

Formerly haughty and disdainful, this time, although still a bit stiff, he was smiling. He held out his hand to the Frenchman and welcomed him.

The contrast with his previous behaviour was such that for a moment, Michel wondered whether he was dealing with the same person.

The Englishman invited him to leave the room and to sit in a neighbouring office on either side of a little table. It was now a matter of identifying the visitor.

'Please tell me where and when you were born.'

'What's your mother's maiden name?'

'What's your father's profession?'

'What are your parents' dates and places of birth?'

Further questions followed concerning various, more distant members of the family. During the interview, the diplomat consulted a document. At the end, Michel Hollard was invited to read the conclusion, written in English:

> If you are inquiring after Mr Louis-Michel Hollard, born at Épinay-sur-Seine on 10 July 1898, the son of Professor Auguste Hollard, *Docteur ès sciences*, and of Mme Pauline Hollard, née Monod, you are dealing with a true soldier who volunteered at the age of seventeen to fight in the First World War, and was awarded the Croix de Guerre.

To put an end to the ordeal of the questions, and to try to dissipate the malaise that his coolness on the first day had created, of which he was aware, the assistant military attaché explained:

'We often get suspicious characters coming in here. When you first came, I had to be cautious. Today I'm reassured. The offer you made last month – to serve British strategy – would be welcome, if it still stands.'

'My presence here today shows that my determination has not changed.'

'If you think it possible to come more or less regularly, how often would that be?'

After thinking for a moment, Michel Hollard answered, 'I hope to be able to make it every three weeks or so.'

'That would be the right frequency. But do you think that within that period, you'll have enough time to identify the big units based in your region with any certainty?'

Surprise, and even a little disappointment, could be seen on the Frenchman's face.

'Is the British General Staff really more interested in these details rather than in aerodromes, fuel reserves and ammunition stockpiles? Do you know that our enemies have started big military constructions and especially new lines of defence?'

'Naturally this information is important. However, what we need to know as a priority is where exactly the enemy's nerve centres are located. The way its forces are spread out changes all the time and we therefore have to keep ourselves up to date all the time about the movements of units: infantry, artillery, engineers, aircraft, etc., and to seek out where their HQs are situated. Here's a list of some of the divisions which until recently have been reported in the northern half of France. To begin with, you could check they are indeed there and identify them carefully. They're armoured units and at the moment they have to be watched carefully.'

Michel Hollard examined the document. He'd listened carefully but what was asked of him left him puzzled. He wasn't yet able to measure the importance of the information he was asked to obtain. When he'd arrived at the Embassy, he'd expected to be given a more precise assignment.

'I'll do everything possible to get you the information British intelligence experts want,' he concluded.

Before they parted, the two men talked a few minutes longer in an atmosphere that the Englishman was clearly trying to warm up even more. His initial aloofness had been partly feigned and probably necessary. Holding out his hand to the new agent, who still didn't know who he was, he introduced himself: 'Major Fryer'. As the Frenchman left, he cordially wished him good luck.

Without realising it, Michel Hollard had just been interviewed by a representative of the War Office[3] to become a military informant. He suddenly realised that, like it or not, he would now have to act in the shadows, rubbing shoulders with the enemy without ever being able to confront them openly. Previously, he would no doubt have considered that this dissimulation was incompatible with the Christian principles he'd been brought up with. Such scruples now seemed foolish. On several occasions, he'd already had to use imaginary forestry searches as pretexts for his presence in the Jura Mountains. To fight the enemy occupying his country, trickery was not only allowed, it was necessary.

'My work will be obscure and repetitive like that of an ant,' he thought. 'From now on, we have to lay the groundwork for the landing of Allied troops in France, even if this can't be envisaged for several years. The Germans are apparently very strong but it's only an impression of superiority. We have to make sure that success comes our way soon.'

As he made his way back through the rain, his trip was almost ended by a frightening incident. Just after crossing the border, he spotted a soldier lying in ambush behind a thicket not far away, rifle in hand. Luckily, the man was looking the other way. The fugitive knelt down, then slowly lay under the cover of the wet undergrowth. He had to wait a long time in this uncomfortable position before the enemy got up and left.

An hour and a half later, the whole Cuenot family welcomed their guest, now looked on as just another member of the family. They willingly squeezed up round the table to make room for him, and the bed he'd occupied the other day was made ready for him again.

With the coming of dawn, he wrote a thank you note for his friends, who were still asleep. His bike was waiting for him in the barn. He got on it quietly, determined to go as far as he could to the Cusey lock. The weather being good, his physical condition and his nerves of steel enabled him to complete the long trip, interrupted by short breaks to eat, before the end of the afternoon.

The lock-keeper Arthur Vrignon welcomed him like a brother and understood that once again it was useless to try to get him to stay. Whilst offering him the now traditional tot, he observed the soldiers guarding the canal. When he thought the moment was right, he went ahead of his visitor, with his acrobatic and skipping gait caused by his wooden leg, to move the unmined cheval-de-frise and enable his protégé to cross the steel barrier. From either side of the canal, the two men said goodbye.

Despite increasingly stiff and aching muscles, the cyclist found the energy needed to get him to Dijon, store his bike in the station's left luggage office, and jump on the night train for Paris. He was exhausted, but satisfied that he was a soldier once again.

Chapter 11

Amateur Secret Agent

At around 7 am, the apartment door opened quietly while my mother was getting breakfast ready. The return of the head of the family at this unusual time caused all-round happiness, enhanced by the element of surprise. Before leaving, he'd thought he'd be away much longer without being able to give or receive any news. Unable to foresee what his trip to the British Embassy would be like or how it would turn out, he'd carefully overestimated how much time it would take.

The secrecy with which he surrounded his real aims weighed heavily upon the heart of this man, normally so expansive and so strongly attached to his family.

Overcoming his tiredness, he tried to satisfy the curiosity of his wife and children before the latter went off to their respective schools. In a few sentences, he summed up his recent clandestine crossing of the canal and his amazing bicycle ride through the storm. His account, basically the same as the one that had intrigued us a few weeks earlier, temporarily stopped there. He promised to tell us more later.

It was clear he needed sleep. As it was time to go to school, our mother left at the same time as us three children and went shopping while he slept. When we returned at the end of the morning, we took turns butting in on our parents' lively discussion. They'd known each other ever since they were children and lived together in very close harmony. Despite the inevitable arguments, they'd virtually no secrets from each other. However, my father, up until then, had thought it wiser to say nothing about his struggle against the occupying troops.

My mother was very intuitive and could easily read her husband's mind. Pretending to believe his story to some extent, she wasn't really convinced by what he'd told her about his trip in the Forbidden Zone. She didn't question the events of his journey as he'd described them, but she couldn't help thinking that there was something incoherent about them. Did looking for *gazogène* fuel really justify him taking all those risks? There were some important parts missing in the story he told.

Until then, Michel Hollard had tried to gain time and reassure his wife. She also suffered from the occupation, morally just as much as physically. She was brave and strong, and dignified. She agreed with her husband's analysis of events and kept herself abreast of the situation by listening attentively to the Free French radio programmes broadcast from London.

Thinking the time had come to speak to his wife with no holds barred, Michel Hollard took advantage of a moment of relative calm to tell her about the real aims of his undertakings. After several months' discreet preparation, he'd succeeded in getting in touch with the British Embassy in Bern, a town from which he had just returned for the second time.

Yvonne Hollard, at first horrified, took hold of herself and listened to the rest of the account. A few weeks earlier, her reaction would no doubt have been more violent. When her husband finished his story by telling her about the mission given to him by the British assistant military attaché, she was unable to stifle a cry of anguish. Hoping to calm her down a bit, he told her that despite everything, the type of mission required of him would hardly put him in jeopardy.

***

Unlike what the new agent had been expecting, the information that Major Fryer wanted at first didn't concern targets that were to be bombed. The British secret services no doubt already had informers whose job it was to guide air raids. But it was also possible that the officer wanted to try out the newcomer by giving him missions thought to be less dangerous.

In the hive of activity that was Paris, the inexperienced agent was quick to realise he'd underestimated the difficulty of the task. London radio often spoke in veiled terms of French groups up in arms against the occupier. Since Michel Hollard hadn't been able to get in touch with any network, he could only count on himself to think up a plan of action.

Countless German soldiers from all services and ranks were constantly going up and down the capital's streets. To the simple observer, this uniformed crowd was just an anonymous amalgam. In contrast, the very varied enemy vehicle pool sported easily recognisable distinctive signs.

Indeed, at the time – June 1941 – the different units were all marked by figurines and silhouettes, evocative symbols on little panels generally fixed on the rear of the vehicles. These clues could be a squirrel, an elephant or even a star. They were found on the car park gates or warehouses and on pennants hanging over the entrances to headquarters. As the cars, motorbikes, lorries and other such vehicles went past, it wasn't impossible to work backwards to their home bases, or even to the headquarters of their units.

French Army buildings were all occupied by the enemy. Michel Hollard knew most of these buildings well, where with despair he now saw the swastika flying. When he went to observe some of these centres in Paris, he noted the descriptions of the large number of vehicles going in and out of them. But there was such a variety of distinctive signs and symbols going past that this preliminary investigation turned out to be in vain.

The first useful leads he managed to follow were those he found among the lorry mechanics he frequented when installing the *gazogène* apparatuses. These specialists, with whom he'd had business dealings for several years since before the war, liked him as much for his professional competence as for his human qualities. Most of these men openly expressed their dislike of the occupier, even though some of them did allow themselves to be tempted into carrying out well-paid repairs on German Army materiel. In reality, you had to be driven along, like Michel Hollard, by an unconditional determination to resist the constant pressure, or even threats, the enemy made if you refused to collaborate.

The most notorious acts of this type of collaboration were indeed committed by people of lesser character. They silenced any scruples they had by saying to themselves that compromise was inevitable and, most often, didn't even try to hide the fact. One of the mechanics thus revealed, rather naively, in the middle of a group of technicians, that he was working on a series of big military vehicles. Michel Hollard, who was there with them, waited until he could talk to the man alone. Without giving away his underground activities, he had no trouble carrying on chatting with him and getting to know where the vehicles in question were being kept; they were being garaged in one of the big suburbs he knew well.

Luck was indeed smiling on him when he got there. It was a huge pool and the centre of intense activity.[1] A short while earlier he'd noticed an unceasing coming and going of soldiers, many of whom were of higher ranks, all around one of the most beautiful hotels in the neighbourhood. A quick check enabled him to note that, near the two sites, most of the vehicles, big and small, all bore a common insignia. The same sign could be seen on the entrance to the building. He'd just flushed out one of the biggest motorised units in the Paris region, as well as the address of its senior officers. Encouraged by this first result, he started thinking up a travel programme that would reconcile enquiries of this type with his professional obligations.

The locals had no hesitation commenting on troop movements. Thanks to chance conversations he had with them, he was able to find the whereabouts of other enemy units spread throughout the Île-de-France region fairly easily. Having memorised the reference symbols painted on a lot of vehicles in different places, he set off to observe the first-class hotels and chateaux in the neighbourhood. He found the same figurines without any great difficulty, embroidered on the famous command pennants showing the colours of Germany.

Indeed, to house themselves with their advisors and sometimes large teams, the senior officers always chose chateaux, prestigious residences or grand hotels requisitioned for them, preferring these to their barracks (why should these gentlemen deprive themselves of the comfort and the splendour they could find locally?). When preparing for the Liberation of France, it was vital for the Allies to know where these people were billeted.

By attaching pretty, apparently innocent little insignia to the rear of their vehicles, the Germans gave their enemies precious information. What a strange lack of perspicacity! In the end, they did realise it. A short while after Hollard, who had become a great amateur of these picture hunts, had learnt their meaning, the nice little animals, flowers and other so easily identifiable signs vanished from the vehicles forever.

My father spoke openly to his family of his activities. What trust this man placed in his children aged between 11 and 18! The idea that any one of us could betray him even unwittingly with untimely chatter never even crossed his mind, and he never thought he needed to insist on how confidential what he told us was. Any appeal for discretion would have seemed superfluous to him.

No matter how charmingly useful they were to the French Resistance, when all the little decorations disappeared from the German military materiel, Michel Hollard was at a loss for a moment. His first reaction was to think that the situation was irremediably compromised, but he very quickly changed his mind.

'Now it's time to show them I can manage! I must inform our Allies at all costs because their other sources of information, in the same situation, risk drying up. Everybody knows that senior enemy officers laze around in the luxury hotels. What if I went discreetly round all the most luxurious residences in the Île-de-France?'

So he came up with the idea of making his enquiries the other way around, starting by seeking out the most attractive places to live. Obviously, this new method was more dangerous than the previous one. Now he was venturing very close to the wolves, daring to taunt them right inside their lairs.

Having drawn up a list of a few big hotels and chateaux that were accessible by public transport, he was soon able to check if his intuition was right, which it was; most of these prestigious establishments were haunts for the 'big predators'.

His reasoning was as follows: these important people, living like princes, no doubt ruled over troops who were billeted locally but more summarily, so logically, the German units must be occupying the buildings abandoned by their French counterparts. As neither men nor vehicles could move around without attracting their neighbours' attention, gathering any observations made by the French locals ought to enable him to find the locations and even to reconstruct the units' chain of command.

Michel Hollard's contagious conviction and his persuasiveness had already opened up frontiers for him. Men and women he met for the first time gave him all the help he needed without holding back, even though they knew almost nothing about him and had no proof he was sincere. The secret of building up the Agir network lay in its leader's zeal and charisma.

Chapter 12

Reinforcements

In the beginning, Michel Hollard acted by himself. Despite his inexperience, he amassed a harvest of information about the armoured units based in the Paris region. He went back to Bern; there, with satisfaction, Major Fryer received this information which until then the London headquarters were only partly aware of.

The new files he'd brought the officer obliged him to keep up a hellish rhythm if he was going to make a visit more or less every three weeks. He couldn't reduce his business activities; they not only provided for his family, they also financed his continuous trips, both professional and secret.

With typical selflessness, he didn't even think about mentioning his expenses to the English. After a few months they simply offered to pay his expenses of their own accord. It would never have occurred to him to make any money, no matter how little, from his activities in the Resistance. Later, his discoveries became so important that the British asked him to give up his private job entirely and made up for this by paying him the equivalent of an officer's salary. Nonetheless, he never gave up his job with the *gazogènes* and the excellent cover it represented, though it did end up becoming wholly fictitious.

Meanwhile, Michel Hollard carried out his activities only by his own means. The Swiss authorities, it is true, continued to provide him with transport and hospitality. Pursuant to a confidential, friendly understanding with the British Embassy, they granted the Frenchman wide-ranging privileges which allowed both countries to benefit simultaneously from the same information.

His main military correspondents were the Swiss officers André Gagnaux, Jean-Pierre Grandy and Pierre Huser (alias Thévenaz). In order to protect him from any action the German secret services might take on their territory, the Swiss authorities issued false identity papers for him in the names of Jacques Rolland then André Gilles.

Michel Hollard realised very quickly that he could only obtain a certain amount of information by himself. He needed to create a team to deal with the scope of his mission and it wasn't long before the first recruits were found, as the development of his *gazogène* business allowed him to keep in touch with the lorry drivers' milieu.

Louis Villette, an old business acquaintance, used to drive his lorry constantly all around the north-western region. Because of a professional authorisation he had, he was allowed to conduct transport jobs all along the coastal zone. This earnest and spontaneous man didn't conceal his patriotism. He accepted at once to act as an observer and the information he collected went beyond what Michel Hollard could have hoped for.

In answer to requests for clarification from the secret services in London, the lorry driver managed to identify several German units established in northern France, accurately locating them together with their command posts. But he didn't stop there. Every time he went through Paris, he collected a great deal of information on the attack and defence equipment the occupier had installed near the coast:

- Complete and accurate surveys of the anti-aircraft batteries situated between Abbeville and Calais.
- The discovery of a submarine base being set up at Boulogne-sur-Mer.
- A new map of Abbeville Aerodrome and its approaches.

Very clever camouflage concealed this aerodrome. From the sky it looked like a group of farm buildings. The biggest building, a huge hangar, was disguised as a church complete with tower!

A short while before this base was bombed, the British broadcast the following strange announcement: '*La bière est bonne !*' (The beer is good!) This was the agreed signal warning Michel Hollard and Louis Villette that an RAF air raid was imminent. Luftwaffe[1] aircraft, especially fighters whose job it was to prevent British air raids, were destroyed on the ground and in the hangars.

Louis Margot, another lorry driver, came to the Autobloc offices for the first time as a customer who wanted to convert a used vehicle he'd just bought so it would run on wood charcoal. The visitor was a former soldier with a glorious record; a war wound had returned him to civilian life. He and Michel Hollard didn't talk long about everyday subjects because they both quickly realised they had similar views on the catastrophic condition the occupied country was in.

The mechanical conversion was relatively complex, meaning it took several days before the lorry was back in action, giving the two men the opportunity to meet several times. When the vehicle was ready, Michel Hollard, whose opinion of the driver's integrity had increased during their talks, decided to speak to him openly before he left.

Alongside a mechanic, the lorry driver was examining the vehicle carefully to get the hang of the new, rather delicate and uncertain system, when at the end of the initiation session, Michel Hollard asked him to follow him into his office.

'I think you know that I'm a former soldier like you,' he said. 'The ideas you've been airing these last few days lead me to think we could act usefully together, just as we did separately before.' Louis Margot's face barely showed any surprise.

'But how can we carry on the struggle if the battle is already lost?' he asked.

'The disaster in France must not be considered separately from the European or even world situation. Only recently the Nazis were boasting that they could carry on with their conquests. Yet I know from a reliable source that their armies are starting to get bogged down. Their propaganda is trying to pull the wool over our eyes and all official information is a pack of lies. I'm an optimist by nature and I want to believe that freedom and justice will triumph one day. But until then we will most likely still have to go through long periods of suffering. Our allies are carrying on the fight without the French Army. Luckily, General de Gaulle and a few French units are saving our honour. Family responsibilities have prevented both of us from trying to join them. However, in occupied France, men like us can take part in the fight. Don't we have a duty not to stand idly by?'

'Of course we do!'

'So, since we both share the same convictions, what I'm asking is whether or not you would be willing to take part in the activities I've started without giving up your job.'

'I was expecting something like this. What would you like me to do?'

'Well, while you're driving around, you run into a lot of enemy convoys, don't you? You could perhaps locate their billets. Whether they're tanks, artillery or other vehicles, as you're a soldier you'll know what they are. The officers will probably have taken up residence and established their command posts in the most luxurious residences near to the vehicle pools and other assembly areas. These stately homes are often not exactly discreet. These occupiers can hardly resist the lure of luxury and splendour so we can almost thank them for drawing attention to themselves and even for making the Resistance's task of spying on them easier..! Do I need to remind you not to get too close to these wasps' nests?'

'Don't worry! I'll try to be careful.'

Louis Margot quickly backed up his words with actions that showed how determined and devoted he was. Following Michel Hollard's instructions, he started by carefully locating and observing several enemy units billeted in the Paris region.

What he came up with was so pertinent that Hollard gave him an assignment to which the Allied air forces attached great importance: the very dense network of tethered anti-aircraft balloons the enemy had installed all around Paris. It's not difficult to picture how concerned pilots were about the treacherous, invisible cables holding down the balloons and how much it helped them once these moving obstacles were accurately located. Louis Margot carried out this essential task right up until the end of the war, regularly noting where the winches were moved to, the changes in altitude and when the balloons were released.

Originally, the British military correspondent seemed to be interested almost entirely in how enemy troops were spread out in the occupied territory. The reports he received went way beyond what he was expecting. When he received them, the diplomat was a bit indifferent to begin with. Maybe he thought some of the details were a bit fanciful, until the day when the secret services in London had been able to check them and realised just how reliable they were. With the exactness of the information now proven, Major Fryer was instructed to give Michel Hollard carte blanche to extend his research to include anything he considered to be of military use, and over as widespread an area as possible.

To fulfil this greater demand, however, he needed to recruit more people. Many years later, the former Resistance leader expressed how surprised he still was when he recalled how he built up his network:

'The way people were recruited,' he declared at one of the Agir Association reunions, 'no doubt illustrates how original our organisation was. The process was, in fact, quite unbelievable, unless it was some miraculous experience which both inspired and protected us..!'

'But,' one of the association's members reminded them, 'in the overall atmosphere of despondency prevailing in France at the time, people needed a man of your mettle to lead them by his exemplary conduct and influence!'

'You were all filled with patriotic zeal. All I did was awaken your indignation against the tyranny you were putting up with in silence. Before that, you were holding back these underlying feelings which were grumbling in your hearts. Recall the circumstances in which we met for the first time, one after the other. None of us ever doubted the good faith of the still unknown person they were talking to.

'As for me, when forming the network, I didn't need to make any indirect approaches and nobody needed to prove they were acceptable. Does that mean we were foolhardy? Certainly not. When we met for the first time it was most often by chance; we just looked each other straight in the eye and our frankness was enough to know we understood each other. By using this method, we admittedly risked making a fatal mistake every time. But we created amongst us a climate of total trust which exalted us and sealed our friendship.'

***

The examples of Louis Villette and Louis Margot, energetic and discreet Resistance workers, demonstrate how simply the Agir network was built up. They joined the list of the names that included of the lock-keeper

Arthur Vrignon and the *montagnard* Paul Cuenot. Never once did these two allies from the early days fail to protect Hollard from the German patrols and their dogs when he ran the gauntlet of coming near the border.

When the first members of his team went into action, Michel Hollard was still far from imagining how big his group was going to be. But along the way new Resistance workers, carried away by his infectious zeal, added their efforts to his. Among the very first was Gaston Ségur, a loyal friend who had already fought by his side during the First World War. Now a senior public finance official, he used his successive positions in Brittany (Guingamp and Lorient) to report on the enemy in this region close to England.[2]

Chapter 13

The Olivier Giran Tragedy

Michel Hollard's parents were friends with the family of the pastor, philosopher and historian Étienne Giran. His son, Olivier Giran, had been to Saint-Maixent Military Academy. At 21, he was an NCO and very unhappy with France's debacle; he joined a group that was preparing to leave Marseille for England. But it all went wrong and he was arrested. He was released after several weeks in prison and at his parents' home he heard admiring talk about Michel Hollard's activities.

Despite the difference in their ages, the two men shared several character traits which made it easy for them to understand each other. They were from the same social background and felt the same need to devote their energies to their country, despite the dangers involved.

Olivier Giran wanted to meet the Resistance leader. 'Was it possible,' he asked himself, 'for one Parisian, all alone in a world cowed by the enemy, to manage to think up a serious plan for resisting the enemy?' If so, he was ready to offer him his help.

One day in the autumn of 1941, we saw this young man arrive at PPP,[1] our Parisian home. Even though he knew Michel Hollard wasn't always in Paris, he knocked at the door on the off chance. My father arrived shortly afterwards. He realised intuitively that here was somebody of the same calibre as himself. The visitor said he knew about the struggle in which his host was involved, in the name of freedom. As a soldier himself, he wanted to take part in it.

Dutifully, Hollard thought it better not to encourage the young man to follow in his footsteps without thinking seriously about it first. He warned him firmly that if he relaxed his vigilance or self-control, be it just for an instant, he ran the gravest risks. Olivier Giran concurred, stating that he felt he was ready to take certain risks but that he would always think before acting.

Then he told him how well he knew the Jura Mountains near Pontarlier. Before the war, he regularly used to spend his holidays in the Swiss border village with the enchanting name of La Côte-aux-Fées, and he knew all the paths used in the region for crossing the border.

Hollard then remembered that at Verrières-de-Joux, not far from there but on the French side, he'd be able to count on reliable help. A small mechanical parts factory in this town had a Swiss production manager he knew was favourable to the Allied cause. This was Mr Albert Grandy, father of Jean-Pierre Grandy, who'd met and helped Hollard during his initial secret visits.

After the young man had listened approvingly to his warnings, he ended up being convinced. Impressed by the earnestness and the obvious resolve of the man who was to become his agent, Hollard decided to send him to the assistant military attaché at the British Embassy in Bern, with the express mission of passing on the latest operational reports in his stead.

On his way to the Swiss capital, Olivier followed the same route and used the same transport as his boss (train and bicycle), via Dijon then Cusey. To access the Forbidden Zone, he was naturally helped by the lock-keeper and Madame Vrignon. When he got close to the border, he turned off towards Verrières-de-Joux and reached the factory where Mr Grandy worked.

With the help of this Swiss citizen, he was easily able to get round the German guards' watchfulness and was welcomed into Switzerland by the customs and police authorities, who had been instructed to grant him an entry permit and an authorisation to travel.

The contact with Major Fryer in Bern and his return trip took place in the same good circumstances. Indeed, Olivier Giran carried out his mission so well that Michel Hollard thought he had found the assistant he'd been needing.

For months, my father's undercover work took up most of his time and energy, but he also managed to continue running his business. The financial records of the Autobloc agency confirmed how good his management was. With the family budget thus assured, together with all the expenses incurred by his hectic activity, and still without any financial backing from the English, or from anybody else for that matter, Hollard was also able to pay Olivier Giran a salary. With no other source of income, Giran became the network's first full-time employee.

Although he'd never done any work for Autobloc, the company agreed to issue the young man with a business card, as it did later for other members of the network. In case he was taken in for questioning, he could claim he was a commercial representative. Alert, intelligent, and tenacious, the new recruit showed that he was keen and clever, beyond all expectations.

He had barely returned to Paris when he asked his boss to give him an area where he could watch and classify the enemy's big units and strategic installations. After the success of his first journey to Bern, he was the right person to complete the trip again. Since this second trip made him go through Dijon and Burgundy, on the way there and back, he was told to start prospecting systematically in that area.

His initial investigations were appreciated not only by his boss and the English but also by the Swiss Army High Command, who very understandably paid particular attention to any military activities near the big centres situated along the routes leading to its borders, such as Dijon.

During the winter of 1941–42, Giran thus carried out a great deal of work as an informer and liaison agent, to the entire satisfaction of his correspondents and of his superior, whom he replaced for several trips between Paris and Bern without any noteworthy incident. All went well until May 1942.

The Giran family had lived in the Netherlands for a long time and they kept up close ties there. During a visit he made to the Dutch Chamber of Commerce in Paris, Olivier Giran learnt that a group of seven young Dutchmen were running from the German police. Altruistically, and without telling Michel Hollard, he relented and agreed to be a guide for the hunted men to help them reach Switzerland. The little group achieved its goal without incident.

Three weeks later, the dutiful guide once again didn't obtain his boss' permission to escort another group, bigger than the previous, along the same route. As the group was moving along stealthily in the mountains, suddenly, a German patrol appeared nearby. Luckily, the fugitives were neither seen nor heard by the inattentive soldiers and got away with just a big fright.

When Giran received a third request of the same type, it took a long time before his generosity made him agree. This time, however, he decided to inform his superior but, foreseeing an unfavourable reaction, he waited until the last minute before telling him about it. Hollard was against the trip even more due to learning of it too late. However, he was assured it would be the last time, which indeed it was.

Until the end of his days, Hollard was to blame himself for not having been able to temper the young man's enthusiasm or calm his excitement, and for not having opposed such an unsound undertaking more successfully.

Among the Dutchmen was an individual who'd succeeded in winning them over with lively patriotic statements. In fact, this base and corrupt character had already sold the lives of his comrades to the enemy secret services. Using his information, the fugitives were 'picked up' by a sinister 'welcoming committee', who arrested them in Dijon station.[2]

The news came as a bombshell to Agir's boss, for in the space of a few weeks Olivier Giran had become not only a valued associate, but also a true friend. Dropping everything, and despite the dangers he risked by going to look for the prisoner, he went to the Dijon prison. There was a repulsive-looking soldier on guard, a real Cerberus. Next to him was a no less typical 'grey mouse'[3] who assisted him as a bilingual secretary.

'I've come to see if you have one Olivier Giran locked up in here.' The woman translated the question for the guard, who indifferently went through the pages of a large register. Suddenly he stopped looking. He looked for a long moment at a paragraph in the big book with a frown. Addressing the interpreter, he asked her to tell Hollard that the next morning a more specialised service would be able to answer him.

Hollard preferred not to give away the fact that he understood German. After the secretary had translated the sentence, he left them with a brief nod. To his great astonishment, he was able to leave the place without being asked any questions, even though the guard had stared at him suspiciously during the exchange. This obviously not-so-subtle man, who was used to seeing lots of people with hostile feelings go past him, had become aggressive. However, when he'd consulted his register, his awkward behaviour had unwittingly given the answer as to Olivier Giran's fate: it was certainly here that he was being held, at the bottom of some nearby cell.

The unfortunate Giran was not involved in anything to do with the Dutch partisans. Thanks to the traitor, the Germans knew that he'd already been to Switzerland illegally. In his defence, he made up stories, claiming he'd organised a lucrative smuggling business, and pleaded guilty at once. In this way he admitted to a whole series of imaginary common law offences, no doubt fairly serious where the French administration was concerned, but which, in the eyes of the occupying authorities, had nothing to do with acts of resistance. At the beginning of the case, this explanation seemed plausible enough and was not rejected by the military judge.

There was increasing hope that the trial would end with a moderate verdict until another bombshell was dropped. A new act of treachery, this time from a phoney friend, or rather a true villain, turned the nightmare into torture.

A short while after his first trip to Bern, Giran had believed the sincerity of patriotic statements by an individual living at Morteau, near the Swiss border. He claimed he wanted to fight the army of occupation. Hollard's assistant had neither his boss' experience nor intuition and made the mistake of trusting this character, whose declarations were affected; this alone should have been enough to set alarm bells ringing.

This dubious individual had started an illegal operation, was arrested at the border by the German guards and was handed over to the Gestapo.[4] To force its prey to spill the beans, this organisation resorted to all means of coercion, including torture. To the individuals who fell into its clutches, it offered to give them back their freedom in exchange for an attitude it described as 'understanding'. This meant the unfortunate people had to agree to reveal any secrets they had, to 'grass on' their friends and often to pretend to pursue their previous activities so they could occupy positions that would better serve their new masters.

After the first interrogations, this character accepted the deal. But he wasn't happy with just satisfying his captors; he went even further and denounced even more people.

Fortunately, he was not in a position to harm Hollard directly since Giran had not mentioned his name. Unluckily, among this criminal's first victims was the young Resistance worker's own father, whom he had naively introduced to the would-be traitor. A respected man of the cloth, whose followers extended well beyond his religious environment, the Reverend Étienne Giran was highly respected, especially after having had the courage to denounce openly the notorious handshake between Hitler and Pétain at Montoire.

The German judges considered him as a danger; he was already a suspect after his public declarations and, in their eyes, he was now seen as the accomplice of a dangerous terrorist, his son. Arrested a short while later, then condemned for deportation, Reverend Giran was imprisoned at Buchenwald, never to return.

As for Olivier Giran himself, the traitor accused the young man of the most terrible acts, denouncing him as an informer who'd passed on information to English diplomats in Bern.[5] He was tortured for nine months, his prison warders hoping to get details of his organisation from him. He was grilled according to the usual techniques without his giving anyone away. Sentenced to death, he was shot on 16 April 1943 at 9 am on the Angers firing range.

Olivier Giran had drawn up a farewell letter for his parents, a few lines of which follow here (he was writing the last words as the guards came to get him):

> I'm quite calm, but death is already pressing and I've so much still to tell you! First of all, certain things must be said once and for all.
>
> I shall stand before God conscious and confident. I believe in Him, I believe in the life of the soul, in a spiritual life where it seems to me, where I'm even sure – because my sad heart assures me of this – that I will be at one with you in spirit in all that is beautiful, noble, and just, which I will be a part of. Before men, I did what I thought was my duty, with elan, joy and, at times, enthusiasm. It was war. I fell, as others did and as many more must do…
>
> I'm happy with my fate, happier than most who vegetate and are bored…Forever keep a picture of me as smiling, happy and alive, a son who, thanks to you and conscious of the profound love that unites us, can die happy…

> Yes, long live France! Men are cowards, traitors or bastards. But France is pure, clean, alive and well.
>
> I'm happy, I'm not dying for any faction or man. I'm dying for my own idea of serving Her, my country, for my heritage, and for both of you, whom I adore.
>
> I'm happy, I love you.
>
> The door is opening,
>
> Farewell!
>
> I hug you both,
>
> Olivier.

A German Army chaplain, Pastor Hermann Hühn, accompanied Olivier Giran until the very end. When he returned to civilian life at the beginning of 1946, the clergyman told Madame Giran of the feelings that her son's attitude inspired in him at the moment of death. In a letter dated 4 March 1946, he expressed his emotion:

> I was crying for him myself, he whom I had learnt to respect and love in two hours, and I am crying as I write this letter to you. I repeat what I told you earlier...: you can be proud of your son who knew how to die strong and free. I was certain that he was full of the thought that in death he was reaching the fullness of his life and that he could never achieve more.

Then Pastor Hühn admitted to Madame Giran that he'd delved into the memory of her son to find subjects for his sermons which were striking enough to move and edify his churchgoers:

> Often when I speak of the certainty of the afterlife, I tell the congregation about the last days of a man called Giran, who went so superbly through death to go on to eternal life. And every time, once again, I see that the account of his sacrifice touches the hearts of my listeners. You see, his death itself moves a lot of men who never knew him and acts as an example which will lead them into everlasting life.

Chapter 14

Hide and Seek

Michel Hollard never got over this loss. The anniversary of the death of his first assistant, 16 April, became a day of mourning for him every year. The emotional shock was quickly followed by concern the German police would necessarily work backwards to the Autobloc company. But its personnel, forewarned that the young man had been arrested, had given the enemy investigators suitably evasive answers.

The name of the firm's Paris manager was not on the sales representative card the Gestapo had found on Olivier Giran. However, they had no trouble finding his name, which was well known to car industry professionals and administrative services. In theory, Michel Hollard didn't need to be unduly worried since no clear evidence up until then had permitted the enemy police to link an engineer, whose good reputation was confirmed everywhere, to any subversive activities.

Meanwhile, another group of Germans, vehicle mechanics, insisted on trying to get Michel Hollard to supply them with *gazogènes* so they could equip a large number of vehicles, since petrol was becoming increasingly rare.

In the hope of persuading him, they made tempting financial offers. This game of hide and seek went on for so long that the German technicians ran out of patience and got angry. As neither persuasion nor the lure of profit had worked, they slammed their fists down on the table. To the officer who came to hand over a requisition order for almost all the apparatuses he was going to receive, Hollard replied calmly, without comment, that he took note of the order. Thereafter, he used a series of clever tricks to ignore it and to make sure he continued to satisfy only his French customers by roundabout means.

One of his lawyer friends warned him of the risks he was taking dragging his heels; he would probably be given a prison sentence. If he made amends, however, and agreed to correct his mistake by supplying the precious *gazogènes*, not only would he get off lightly but there was a good chance he'd receive no sentence at all.

A short while later he indeed received a summons from the German court. He naturally refused to turn up before his enemies and to start playacting the guilty party seeking forgiveness. He was therefore condemned in absentia to six weeks in prison. This sentence was passed when the preparation for Olivier Giran's trial was taking place. As the prisoner was supposed to have worked for the Autobloc agency in Paris, there was the disturbing possibility of the courts making a connection between the defendant's behaviour and that of his boss. The threat obliged Hollard to quit both his home and his office, and the Autobloc assembly stations. From then on, he was on the run, like a hunted animal.

Yvonne Hollard kept her cool; she managed to avert the danger with brio, for the time being at least. Through the local tradesmen, in the centre of the Latin Quarter in Paris, she learnt that from time to time mysterious people were prowling around the neighbourhood. Her concierge warned her that a strange person had been asking around about the people living in the building.

In order to stay in touch with his family and secretary, Hollard organised meetings in different places, usually at relatives' or friends' homes. With the complicity of various café owners, he also set up a system of telephone meetings so that his main associates could contact him quickly in case there was a problem. This turned out to be a good idea. The day following the concierge's warning, Yvonne Hollard was visited by two German policemen in uniform. They wanted to see her husband.

'I'm afraid he doesn't live here anymore,' she said regretfully.

'We must have his new address.'

Showing surprising presence of mind, Hollard's wife declared that he'd left home and the Paris region. As he was getting increasingly disturbed and unstable, the couple had decided to separate. However, from time to time, she added, he got a terse message or two to her. In the event she received such a message, she saw no problem in telling them!

They didn't insist. More or less convinced by the story they'd been given, they formally said goodbye and left the flat. From the window, she watched them leave and then went out herself, looking all around her to make sure that she wasn't being followed. She headed for a nearby bistro to use the telephone procedure her husband had set up.

When the connection was made, they organised a meeting, away from indiscreet ears. Hollard began by warmly congratulating 'Yvonnette' (the private nickname for his wife) for getting rid of the unwelcome visitors. It was obviously high time for the whole family to leave the flat. The very same day, the couple arranged to meet up with the Autobloc secretary, Madame Boulanger, who knew all about her boss' activities.[1]

This meeting was given over to winding down one company and setting up another. The Paris branch of Autobloc had to be officially dissolved because its manager had supposedly left. At the same time, the two women were given the task of finding new premises and setting up a new business, similar to the first one but with a different name.

Before leaving his wife and his secretary, Hollard advised them that he'd be sending letters informing them that he'd decided to stay out in the country permanently. These letters would soon be dropped at the post office in Foix. From several sources, we knew that both commercial and private mail was being opened before it was distributed to the two Paris addresses. We hoped that the Gestapo agents would be put off, thinking they were picking up information secretly which, for once, was indeed intended for them…

As the Office Technique du Gazogène de France took over from the former Autobloc agency, the Hollard family left their home, Place Paul-Painlevé, where there were signs of it being under renewed observation.

In looking for a safer refuge, Hollard was helped by a member of the Saint-Rémy-lès-Chevreuse municipality, which at the time was still just a big village less than an hour from Paris by train. There he rented a beautiful villa, nestling on the edge of a wood, which seemed to offer relatively good protection, first for his family, but also for himself during his rare, brief visits. This building was also occasionally used as a strategic base during the most tumultuous period of his activities.

Chapter 15
Kaleidoscope

The distribution of occupation troops on French soil was like a vast, constantly turning kaleidoscope. Movements depended on the unpredictable strategy thought up by Hitler's headquarters.

In response to London's requests, Michel Hollard's mission, and that of his team, at first mainly consisted of not only providing a rough map of the French-based enemy units, but of keeping it constantly up to date. The network leader quickly realised that in order not to miss any of the enemy's main movements, he needed men he could trust that were available all the time.

A few weeks after Olivier Giran appeared, another young man, Joseph Brocard, turned up of his own accord. Driven on by a similar calling, the two men acted independently of one another and never met. Fate, which had been fatal for one, kept on dogging the other without, happily, succeeding.

In the regions bordering eastern France, wild rumours were going around of a purported route enabling people to reach England from Switzerland. Joseph Brocard, living in Pontarlier, managed to cross the border near his home with the intention of reaching London and putting himself at the disposal of General de Gaulle.

In despair at having to return to France empty-handed, he was received by Lieutenant André Gagnaux, one of the Swiss Army officers who regularly met Hollard and, unofficially, made his contacts with the British easier. On the advice of this soldier, Joseph Brocard managed to reach Paris, where he met up with the leader of the Agir network.

Hollard was quickly convinced of the young man's seriousness and capabilities and promptly decided to put him through his baptism of fire. As soon as a false identity card had been made for him in the name of Bart, as well as a work certificate saying he was a *gazogène* salesman, the untried agent set off to go around Brittany. His mission there was to locate the divisions the enemy had deployed in the area.

Although inexperienced, Joseph Brocard set off tracking down the enemy installations, which were particularly dense in this region, separated as it was from England by only a stretch of the sea. He provided such a detailed, accurate report that his superior immediately suggested carrying on and extending his enquiries. Just as with Olivier Giran, but with other territorial assignments, this second assistant was now employed full-time, his expenses also being covered by Michel Hollard.

Soon after he was taken on, he made an inconsequential mistake; the account of which may help the reader to get an idea of the tense atmosphere in which these men were living.

To limit any underlying danger, being punctual for a meeting was de rigueur. One day, Joseph Brocard turned up to one such meeting three minutes late. Hollard calmly removed his wristwatch and gave it to him without saying a word, except the friendly order to keep it.[1]

At the head of an increasingly large team, Hollard continued his struggle without contacting other 'patriot' movements. This expression, like the others (partisans, dissidents, rebels, resistance fighters, mavericks, etc.), designated all types of secret soldiers fighting the invader before the term 'Resistance' was coined once and for all, together with the abbreviation FFI (Forces Françaises de l'Intérieur – French Forces of the Interior).[2]

Most members of the Agir network operated independently of each other, in different regions, and didn't even know each other. They knew nothing of the way the organisation was made up. At more or less regular intervals, each of them handed Hollard their information and he gathered and collated everything that had been harvested during his rounds. He alone made sure that everything was overall coherent.

Acting alone was the best way of protecting all the agents against the risks of careless talk, indiscretion, and denunciation. Although the network suffered other losses after the Olivier Giran tragedy, which were just as painful, none were through betrayal.

To be simple, the way the team functioned was to use none of the technical advances whose development had been accelerated by both world wars. Thus, though trained as an engineer, Hollard never envisaged using telegraphic and radiotelephonic equipment to send messages and secret documents, even though the English wouldn't have hesitated to supply him with it, had he asked. Although he was at the origin of a lot of decisive air activity, he never once thought of asking the Allies for help transporting people, parachuting, kidnapping or escaping by plane. At no time did he or any of his team ever carry weapons.

With his simple methods, he had to make considerable physical efforts and it took longer to communicate. To make up for these drawbacks, he never hesitated to set off at once, and whenever it was necessary, spend uncomfortable nights in packed trains, go across the mountains in winter and summer, trudge through snow or storms, and withstand fatigue and cold thanks to his stamina and willpower.

In a despairing period of dejection, during which there were no signs to foretell what the outcome of the conflict was going to be, his energy and his courage astounded his comrades. His example revitalised those who were impatient and those who were becoming demoralised.

With varying results, everyone tried to react to the ever-urgent requests from the English to keep the map of occupied France up to date by indicating the location of enemy units and their headquarters. Moreover, some made a point of honour of adding certain enemy dispositions to their list: aviation facilities, anti-aircraft batteries, weapons factories and depots, fuel reserves and distributors, and various other military buildings.

By constantly expanding his field of action, Michel Hollard noted that most of the population still had patriotic feelings. His constant travelling led to many impassioned discussions. During chance meetings, his powers of persuasion continued to sway supporters, so much so that soon all the regions he'd visited had their Agir sympathisers.

There were a good number of these among the SNCF personnel. Henceforth, with these observers constantly on the lookout for movements of troops and materiel, no suspicious convoy could get by unnoticed. A few months later, this silent vigil enabled some of those based in Normandy to sound the alarm bells.

Chapter 16

A British Entreaty

At the beginning of November 1942, during one of his visits to the British diplomats in Bern, Michel Hollard was received for the first time by the military attaché in person, Colonel Cartwright, who welcomed him warmly, a glass of whisky in his hand. An event of considerable importance, which enemy propaganda was trying to conceal in France, had to be celebrated: the Allied landings in North Africa. To celebrate this doubtlessly promising, though still fragile, success, they raised their glasses.

The welcome Michel Hollard received that day was not prompted by this good news alone. Colonel Cartwright informed him of the high esteem in which he was held by his administration, and then added that because the conflict was spreading, the Allies would certainly be needing more information about the way the enemy forces were disposed in enemy-occupied France.

As far as he was concerned, Hitler was going to have to send large numbers of reinforcements to fight on the other side of the Mediterranean. Fearing the Allies might attempt something along the southern coast, he would most likely grab hold of the so-called 'Free Zone'[1] and spread his troops throughout mainland France, quite unscrupulously neglecting the agreements concluded with the Vichy government.

Events soon confirmed the English officer's prediction; the enemy did indeed cross the demarcation line and occupy the whole country. Its forces were not only reorganised, they were suddenly deployed over a surface area almost twice as large as before. For what the French informer was doing, the news of the invasion had a considerable impact because all of a sudden, he had to extend his network into the Southern Zone.

Amidst the jumble of relatively reliable information reaching London from all over, the military authorities had long preferred the reports from Michel Hollard, whose thoroughness and seriousness had been quickly recognised. After making an initial assessment, they tried to ascertain from their colleagues in Bern what material means the Frenchman had for informing them. The English diplomats in the Swiss capital answered that because of his reserved nature, their partner quietly overcame the inherent difficulties of his dangerous activities, without complaining or asking to be paid. The information he provided, however, had turned out to be so precious that the War Office decided to ask him if he was now prepared to work for the Allies on a full-time basis.

One day, when he was expected in Bern, an officer who was already set up in Switzerland was hurried to the Embassy. This person was entrusted with top-secret missions in Switzerland by the Secret Intelligence Service in London, which was active throughout the country from its base in Lausanne. Although his activities were discreetly tolerated by the federal authorities, as a precaution, he called himself rather enigmatically 'O.P.', simply because of the discretion his work required. With the passage of time, I can now reveal the name of this gentleman, James Kruger, who soon became Michel Hollard's case officer.

The two men hit it off almost immediately, and continued to do so right up until the end of the war. O.P., however, only gradually revealed the scope of the tasks the administration wanted my father to undertake. An industrialist in peacetime, he had that distinction of the cultured and refined Englishman. He already knew about his partner's worth from the testimonials reaching him both from England and Switzerland and, thanks especially to his subtle psychological sensitivity, he quickly foresaw that their budding cooperation would pay dividends.

His colleagues at the Embassy, overcoming their natural aloofness, also painted a glowing picture of their guest, which reinforced what he thought. From the beginning of the interview, O.P. promised his new contact he'd do his best to make his task easier. From then on, their meetings would no longer necessarily take place in Bern, but at points more easily accessible from the border. The traveller would thus save time and effort and at the same time thereby benefit from faster relays for sending urgent messages to London.

The Englishman was aware that his partner was acting through idealism and in very dangerous circumstances. He was surprised, however, to learn that up until then, the money needed for running the network came entirely from its leader's personal finances!

'Mr Hollard, what you do for us is an essential contribution,' declared the officer, 'and until recently your *gazogène* company's good results have enabled you to bear not only your personal expenses but also the remuneration of several members of your team. I would consider our action irresponsible, petty and negligent if we didn't intervene financially on your behalf. As far as the London authorities and I are concerned, the circumstances in which you act are precarious and a source of worry.'

'But,' the Frenchman replied, 'Europe and no doubt the rest of the world are going through a very critical period. Mankind is sitting on an inferno which has to be put out at all costs. Goods and material possessions are of no use to us if we lose our freedom or our lives.'

'We admire your commitment and we are very grateful,' said O.P. 'Your information has turned out to be so useful that I've been instructed by my administration to ask if you'd be willing to cooperate even more closely with us than in the past. For this you'd have to be prepared to give up your professional activities and, as compensation, you'd be given the equivalent of a military salary.'

Michel Hollard was expecting almost anything except a proposal like this.

'I'm honoured by your offer,' he answered, 'but I'll need a fortnight to think about it. I'd like to discuss the situation with my wife. In the meantime, can you wait until my next visit for my answer?'

'That's quite understandable and we can wait. However, please know that whatever you decide, you won't have to worry any more about paying your agents. In any event, the money you need for them will be taken on by our services.'

Back in the Paris region two days later, Michel Hollard explained to his wife that what London proposed confirmed brilliantly how valued he was. Why refuse such an offer that would most likely not affect his strategy?

The young woman wasn't entirely able to hide her frightened reaction to this news. Her husband was already leading the life of an outlaw and constantly playing cat and mouse with the occupier. She knew he would never give up taking part in the fight for freedom with all his strength. His cooperation with friendly countries was based on trust. Drawing up an agreement or an alliance for something that was already tacit would have no other effect but to ratify what existed already and would scarcely have any effect on the course of action this relentless warrior had chosen.

'I must have the courage,' thought his wife, 'to accept that the danger that threatens him will continue for as long as the war lasts. As in the past,' she concluded, 'the only thing I can do is my utmost to help and protect him.' She therefore didn't try to get involved in the conditions of his engagement with the English.

However, they did need to decide on what was to become of the Office Technique du Gazogène de France. Michel Hollard brought together his wife and Madame Boulanger, his secretary, to examine the situation caused by his imminent and almost total withdrawal from the business for an unspecified period.

The secretary, who'd always shown how cooperative and discreet she could be, thought unhesitatingly that her duty was to stay at her post. Both ladies declared that together they were prepared to make sure the company continued, at least in theory. Indeed, even though the captain was leaving the helm, it was important not to scuttle the ship, even if it was making a loss, since the fictitious activity of a company representative was far too valuable a cover story for certain members of the network!

Chapter 17
Extending the Network

When Hitler extended the military occupation of France to the whole country, in defiance of the terms of the June 1940 Armistice, Michel Hollard had no agents who could tell him anything about the territory which, until then, had been considered as the Free Zone. If he wanted to discover how the German units were now spread out, he'd have to expand his circle of agents quickly. He started by going to the Portes-lès-Valence marshalling yard; a point along the valley of the Rhône through which most railway traffic passed on its way to and from the Mediterranean.

'When I approached the stationmaster, Louis Jouanen,' Michel Hollard later recalled, 'he was examining certain technical facilities. He agreed to stop and listen to what I had to say:

'It seems that not all the trains going through your sector are very friendly!'

'Unfortunately, we have to put up with the law of the strongest. It's hopeless!'

'The situation will probably change soon!'

'Do you think so?'

'I hope so. The enemy has started falling back on several fronts. We can make a contribution to that struggle. That's why I wanted to speak to you.'

'Do you think I can be of use to you?'

'Indeed, you can. You work on a very important strategic site here. Most enemy trains heading for the south of France and Italy pass right in front of you. If you can give me information about them, you'll be serving the Allied cause effectively.'

'I'll try and keep a careful watch.'

'Be discreet! I'll be back next week.'

A week later, Louis Jouanen gave him a complete rundown on the German convoys that had recently gone through the Portes-lès-Valence sector. The new recruit went on with his watch until the end of the war, becoming one of the most active SNCF intelligence agents.

Other contacts were made in circumstances similar to those of Louis Jouanen. In the presence of someone new, a few minutes' discussion was usually enough for Michel Hollard to judge whether he could trust the person or not.

***

From time to time, the German Army High Command ordered the SNCF management to transport big units across France and even beyond. Under the secret initials TCO (*transport en cours d'organisation* – transport being organised), concealed instructions were sent to high-ranking personnel. Indeed, in a lot of cases, it was possible to deduce where each division or army corps was leaving from and where it was arriving. Because a unit was usually replaced at once by another where it was billeted, well-directed enquiries made by astute railway workers enabled the schedule of enemy forces to be kept up to date continuously.

The importance of such information, if correctly interpreted, prompted Michel Hollard to increase his visits to the railway yards. Just like Louis Jouanen, most of the railway people recruited in this way turned out to be devoted and determined until the Liberation, and some of them played a key role in discovering the secret V-1[1] weapons.

For a long time after the end of the war, Agir's founder still marvelled at the perfect loyalty of his team members, most of whom he'd come across along the way, almost by chance. These meetings, always improvised, sometimes took place in chaotic conditions. There were two mishaps: one ended well, while the other was almost a disaster.

Taking advantage of his previous experience with the railway workers, he decided to have a closer look at those working at Tarascon station. The railway junction near this station seemed to him to be well placed enough to keep an eye on the railway traffic, provided it was an experienced eye. He therefore repeated the method of approach which had proved its worth several times. Relying on the comments which, when asked, an employee from Tarascon had made about his own superior's patriotic inclinations, he organised a meeting with the deputy stationmaster. After a few minutes' conversation, the man promised to collect information about transiting enemy convoys and a meeting was arranged for the following week.

Meanwhile, the Vichy government decreed that it was going to oblige the SNCF personnel to make the occupation army's movements easier, reminding them of the professional secrecy to which they were bound.

On the day of the meeting, the deputy stationmaster stood Michel Hollard up, thinking he was getting out of his engagement by leaving the station before the agreed time for the meeting.

Michel Hollard asked around and found the man after a long walk along the railway lines. He was supposed to be carrying out a technical inspection. Embarrassed and pretending to have forgotten, he was unable to escape being told off. Michel was so determined that the man relented, pulled himself together and became one of the Agir team's most regular informers.

As a precaution, Michel Hollard often donned a railway worker's garb before he went out enquiring in the railway world. When mingling with the workers, he could easily pick out a person whose face, general look and behaviour inspired trust. He'd get closer and risk this type of question:

'Between you and me, does your boss like the *Fritz*?'[2]

'Hell no, thank God!..' was the reply he usually received.

Such a declaration would reassure him as to how the department head would react to his approach, which is how he'd done things before meeting Louis Jouanen.

He was informed by one of his agents that there was going to be heavy military railway traffic in the Toulouse area, so he went there. However, he made the mistake of asking for the town's deputy stationmaster without taking the usual precautions. He'd perhaps subconsciously become used to making contact too easily up until then. High-wire acrobats are constantly playing with danger and accidents happen when they forget to follow the safety rules.

As soon as the deputy stationmaster understood why the newcomer was there, he stood haughtily behind his desk, raising his voice angrily and threatening Hollard with denunciation.

'Sir,' said Michel Hollard very calmly, 'I sincerely hope you don't obey our enemies mindlessly. It would be the last straw if you denounced me to them!'

He said goodbye abruptly to the furious, stupefied man, who was perhaps a bit ashamed deep down. Then he turned on his heel and left, trying not to rush, despite the shouting. However, once outside, he quickened his step and vanished as quickly as possible.

As he was unable to obtain any further information in Toulouse on the troop movements he'd been told about, he had no misgivings about taking the next train to Nîmes where his friend, André Rauzier, another railway worker, could perhaps enlighten him. He wasn't to regret the detour because the news he obtained, which was immediately confirmed to him, concerned a vast operation of which he learned the dates and other important details: an army corps was about to transit via Toulouse on its way to Italy.

After a difficult train journey and a long walk over the mountains, Michel Hollard transmitted the information to London via Bern. The General Staff received the dispatch just before the transfer started, but the German police learned that the leak came from an SNCF official in Nîmes. A few days later, to try to catch the guilty party, they surrounded Nîmes station and occupied it by surprise.

André Rauzier managed to get away with flair thanks to his astonishing presence of mind, his resourcefulness and sheer luck; a steam locomotive[3] and its tender, ready to leave, were waiting for their crew at the platform. Without a moment's hesitation, he jumped into the cabin, turned up the pressure and left the station at full steam in the most fantastic way. Amid the deafening din of the puffing and whistling engine, he allowed himself the luxury of taunting the soldiers who were gesticulating, powerless and dumbfounded.

His mad dash for freedom ended at Lunel station, in the neighbouring town. He lived in hiding for a while until a well-placed friend in the SNCF administration organised a change of residence for him.

There was another setback for Michel Hollard when he went to consult one of his closest childhood friends, who was responsible for the Saint-Brieuc civil defence. In their youth, the two boys tried to outdo each other in being fearless. He was hoping for assistance from a man who had immense privileges available to him in this strategic coastal region, which was off-limits to the general public. In particular, his childhood friend could move around freely, day and night, even on the shore and during alerts. He was therefore in an ideal, albeit dangerous, position to help the Allies in the event they landed on the Brittany coast.

'My former friend has categorically declared that for his family's sake, he's unable to help, which of course was his right,' admitted the network head.

A lot of enemy convoys, in steady streams, also moved around by road, so Hollard decided to set up a chain of surveillance points along the main roads. He started with the famous Route Nationale 7, the great road that links the north and south of France. He remembered that before the war, while travelling down that road, he'd stopped at a beautiful hotel-restaurant at Pierrelatte (Drôme department), run by a woman of great character.

'With a bit of luck,' he said to himself, 'she'll still be there. But because of where it's located, the hotel will most probably be frequented by customers in greyish green uniforms.'

When he got there, a pack of young and old wolves of the officer class was indeed eating and drinking in the large dining room. Madame Simone Boirel, the hotelkeeper, was still in charge and recognised her former customer. In one sentence and in a low voice, she spontaneously expressed, without any other precaution, 'her regret at having to inflict upon him such an unpleasant and overcrowded spectacle, from which she was the first to suffer.'

Hollard thought her attitude and the bold remark she'd made revealed quite clearly where her loyalties lay. Taking advantage of the opening, he answered that he'd like to carry on with the conversation somewhere else. In a neighbouring office, their talk confirmed his initial impression of the hotelkeeper's way of thinking. However uncomfortable it made her, she had to accept a lot of wearisome guests courteously. Her loveliness sometimes attracted some risqué remarks, forcing her to 'play a part in order to stay pleasant and dignified, whilst at the same time discouraging any vulgar advances'.

Without beating about the bush, the Resistance leader said:

'You're in a position here which could enable you to help the Allies boot the enemy out of our country. Underground activity inevitably has its risks, and I would quite understand if you didn't want to take part.'

'How can I make myself useful?'

'You're involved indirectly in the constant movement of senior officers who find good cheer and lodging here. Because of its good reputation, your restaurant was probably recommended to them before they left. They usually stop here on the way from their previous strategic posting to their next one. I'm sure that with all your feminine wiles you'll be able to find out where they come from, where they're going and maybe even what their names are.'

'You're probably giving me credit for skills I don't really have, but I'll do what I can!'

Madame Boirel kept her word. The quality of the services her inn offered and the atmosphere she managed to create often enabled the customers to forget why they were there. Under these circumstances, quite a few officers gave themselves over to saying interesting things in confidence. At the end of a good meal, the hotelkeeper would take advantage of the overall feeling of euphoria to get close to the important customers. She would then open her visitor's book, which had already been signed by a lot of well-known people. Flattered, these gentlemen almost never refused to write a few lines, followed by signatures, which were often quite revealing! When the travellers were leaving, their attractive hostess said how nice it'd be to receive a few words when they got to where they were going. They felt obliged to comply and often kept their word. In this way, the probable location of their new assignment was identified!

The watchfulness of the military police in civilian clothes also had to be taken into account. They were all the more redoubtable as a lot of them spoke perfect French and could blend in anonymously with the population. For Madame Boirel's own safety and, of course, so as not to expose himself needlessly, Michel Hollard no longer showed up at the hotel.

His rounds now regularly took him to the departments in the south, where military movements were stepped up. With Madame Boirel, he decided their meetings would take place on the train during the less than half-hour trip between Pierrelatte and Montélimar. This moving meeting place had the double advantage of saving the traveller quite a lot of time and of being relatively safe. Without getting off the train, he could pick up all the reports from his informer, who then left him at the next stop, Montélimar, and jumped almost at once into the next train going the other way, returning home as quietly as possible.

A lot of top brass were identified in this way and located thanks to the shrewdness of the lovely innkeeper. This little game carried on for a long time without any problems, until a traitor betrayed the network.

Michel Hollard's agents, who were becoming more and more numerous along his circuit, would bring him their information, which he then added to his own findings. His destination was now Lausanne, where he was welcomed by both his new British partner, O.P., and a Swiss Army officer going under the name of Thévenaz. This was officer Pierre Huser, who offered him his warmest support. The three men were to remain close friends for the rest of their lives.

***

The luxurious French buildings and palaces where the occupation army's bigwigs took up residence often looked like impregnable citadels. A lot of heavily armed guards prevented anybody who could not show their regulation laissez-passer from gaining access. Alone among the French were a few collaborators who were duly accredited with the enemy; the hotel personnel also held the indispensable *Ausweis* (ID card).

Any attempt at investigating such an inhospitable place was folly and seemed suspect. Michel Hollard overcame his apprehension, however, and took on the seemingly overwhelming difficulties, succeeding in carrying out a reputedly impossible mission right under the enemy's nose.[4]

In July 1943, the Swiss and Allied secret services were convinced that Generalfeldmarschall von Rundstedt was the supreme commander of all the German forces deployed in the south of France. Surrounded by his staff, it was believed he was still living in the Hôtel Terminus in Avignon.[5] Alerted by various signals, and especially by all the unusual bustle going on in the area, Agir's boss wasn't so sure. As he had nobody present in Avignon, he stopped off there on his way back from a tour of the south.

A square chequered pennant floated in front of the hotel, meaning an army group headquarters was there. The approaches to the hotel were protected by white barriers, behind which was an imposing guardhouse. Outside, several disillusioned-looking French policemen made up the watch.

Michel Hollard caught sight of the Café de la Bourse on the other side of the street and entered. While the boss was serving him a drink, he tried to gather information discreetly.

'Between you and me, do you know if the main resident over there has been replaced recently?'

Instead of answering, the landlord just picked up his change and left without a glance in his direction. Being snubbed in such a manner was hardly likely to discourage Hollard. On the face of it, there was no reason for him to fear the French policemen on guard, even though their job was to assist the Germans. Why not just ask them outright?

'Indeed, the general in the hotel was replaced a fortnight ago,' answered one of the men, without seeming to be surprised by the question.

'Do you know the new guy's name?'

As though the question was totally artless, the policeman consulted his colleagues, but they didn't know. One of them suggested:

'If you want to find out, why don't you go and ask Pierre Pamard, the hotel manager? If he knows the answer, he'll most likely give it to you. He's a good lad.'

'Yes,' added a colleague. 'He's a real Frenchman who puts up with the difficulties of his delicate position admirably.'

***

Michel was encouraged by the policemen's short answers. Despite the impressive military set-up, he decided to try a short visit at once. Thanking the police officers, he headed for the hotel entrance.

To the guard who asked for a pass and then to the NCO who, at his request, took him aside, he explained in German the reason for his unexpected visit: to give Mr Pamard an urgent message.

'Without an *Ausweis*, you can't get in,' the NCO repeated, explaining what he himself risked if he allowed him through despite the restrictions. Asserting in a low voice that he had an accreditation for the hotel, Michel secretly slipped the most compelling of arguments into the German's hand: a packet of deluxe cigarettes, a rare product appreciated everywhere, even by non-smokers, as they could gainfully replace banknotes in all sorts of transactions.[6]

Making his way through the vestibule crowded with officers, he approached a young blonde woman coming out of an office, no doubt a secretary.

'Could you announce me to Monsieur Pamard?' he asked.

'Certainly. Who shall I say wants to speak to him?'

Off the top of his head, he made up a rather spur-of-the-moment excuse which, despite everything, apparently satisfied her.

'Tell him it's an old army friend. Monsieur Pamard has most certainly forgotten my name!'

The hotel manager, notified, appeared with a big beaming smile, which quickly vanished when he saw a man he'd never met.

'Please forgive me for using such a ploy to speak to you,' Michel Hollard declared to the tall, dark-haired man of 35, who was visibly taken aback. He asked him in a hushed voice to listen to what he had to say, but somewhere else, further away.

'I used this manoeuvre to get to you because of the situation,' he continued when they'd reached a more isolated area. 'I have to know the name of the man who's settled in here, replacing Generalfeldmarschall von Rundstedt, and I can't find anybody who can tell me.'

The answer sprang forth without hesitation, and was precise and even more informative than he had hoped for:

'Before it was General von Felber, but he left two weeks ago. If you want his replacement's name, I'll have to ask my wife. Would you like me to go and ask her?'

'Please!'

The master of the house's speech, as well as his overall conduct, revealed frankness, apparently confirming the French policemen's assessment, but waiting right in among the enemy turned the minutes that followed into an eternity.

The manager reappeared carrying a card on which the visitor could read 'General von Sonnenstern'. With this precious information, he thanked his informer who promised to meet him again in a more reassuring place.

Pierre Pamard declared with a mischievous smile that he knew the best place for any future meetings. He gave him the address of a brasserie, whose boss was known in the area for belonging to the pro-Nazi militia! The enemy police naturally thought it was quite unnecessary to keep an eye on it. Paradoxically, no other meeting place could guarantee better protection. This den played its part perfectly, almost under the protective gaze of the duped owner.

The senior officers in command of enemy troops spread throughout southern France met periodically at the Hôtel Terminus. Although their names were, as a rule, confidential, they were often on letters and even sometimes bandied about the corridors. Every time the hotelier identified one of them, he got into the habit of ingraining it into his memory. He managed to discover gradually who most of these figures were.

Naturally, Pierre Pamard suffered from the ambiguous situation in which he got himself ensnared, before suddenly becoming its victim. He had been known for a long time and was regarded sympathetically by most of the Avignon population, who felt sorry for him and the way his lovely establishment had been invaded; he was neither worried by his troublesome guests nor by the local Resistance movements until the enemy armies began to be routed.

A misunderstanding made a martyr of him in the confusion caused by the highly charged atmosphere of the Liberation. Persuaded he'd been in collusion with the enemy, an uncontrollable group of overexcited people enticed him into a trap and killed him.[7]

In other regions, Hollard managed to establish ties in the hotel world and in households with people who were obliged to live in close proximity to the occupier and were able to observe them at leisure. Hired in an authoritarian manner (not everyone had the means or the strength to resist the enemy's requisitions), most Frenchmen nonetheless remained patriotic at heart with a civic sense, like Pierre Pamard. They felt they

The seven Hollard children in 1907. The happiness evident in their faces would soon be disrupted by the outbreak of the First World War. *From left to right:* Michel (hero of this book), Jenny (grandmother of Philip Sandt, co-translator of this book), Mireille holding Irène, Noémi, Micheline and Vincent (killed in action in 1918).

The First World War. Michel Hollard waited until his 17th birthday to be able to join the French Army. Enlisted first as a volunteer orderly, he was soon promoted to volunteer infantryman, first class.

Yvonne and Michel Hollard at the beginning of the Second World War with their three children: Francine, Florian and Vincent.

Thanks to the help of Paul Cuenot, who lived nearby, Michel Hollard regularly crossed the Franco-Swiss border guarded by the enemy.

A barn door was used as a signal. Paul Cuenot would close it to warn Michel Hollard that danger was lurking.

Dr Charles Guisan (cousin of General Guisan), a doctor, musician and member of the Swiss Parliament.

Micheline Guisan, wife of Dr Guisan and sister of Michel Hollard.

General Henri Guisan, commander-in-chief of the Swiss Armed Forces.

Olivier Giran, a great Resistance fighter. He was betrayed by a double agent and died a martyr.

The invasion and annexation of French territory by Germany and Italy during the Second World War.

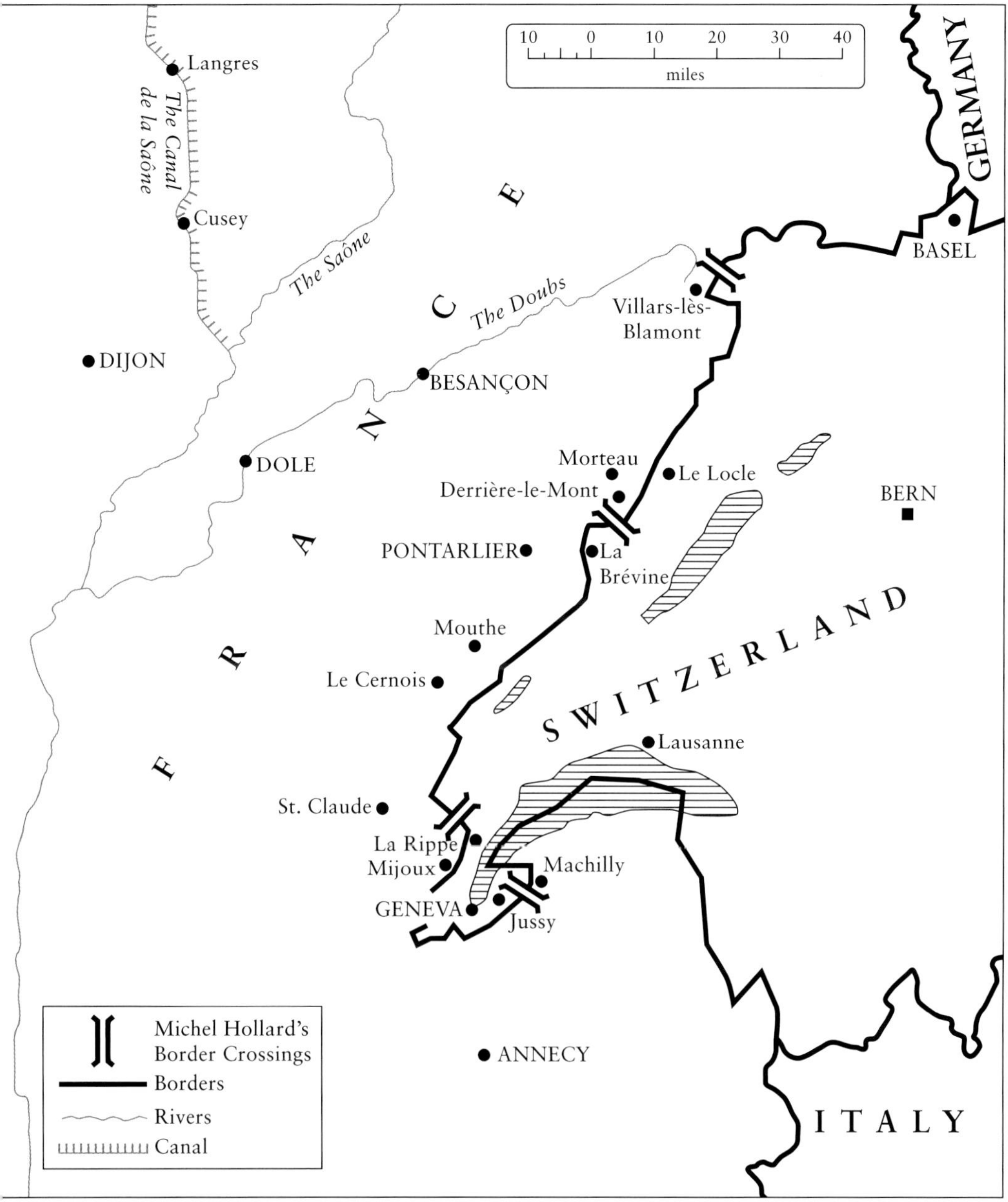

Illustrated above are the four locations chosen by Michel Hollard to cross over into Switzerland illegally.

François Paccot, Michel Hollard and Claude Neury reunited in peacetime at Machilly (Haute-Savoie).

The commemorative stela, on the Charlemagne Bridge at Mijoux (Ain), in which pictures of Michel Hollard and his protectors Denis and Alice Poncet are sealed.

Joseph Brocard in 1944. Seriously injured while escaping from the enemy, he was taken by Michel Hollard into Switzerland where army doctors cared for him as one of their own.

Robert Rubenach, one of Michel Hollard's assistants.

André Comps, who managed to copy the secret map of the V-1 launch site at Yvrench Bois Carré.

Diagram of the secret V-1 weapon.

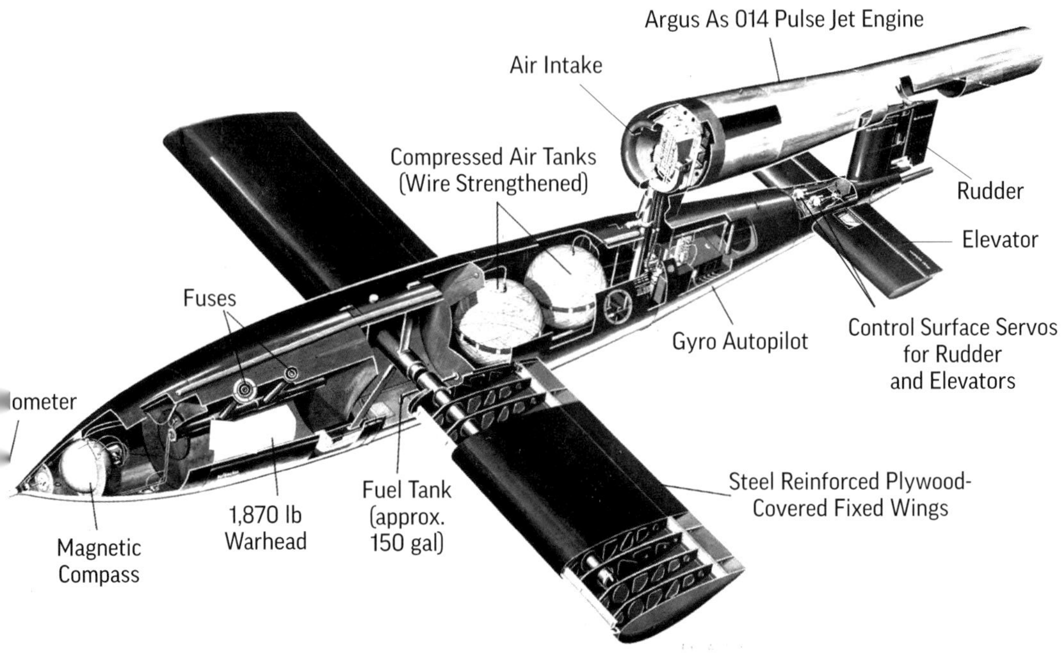

The V-1 after takeoff.

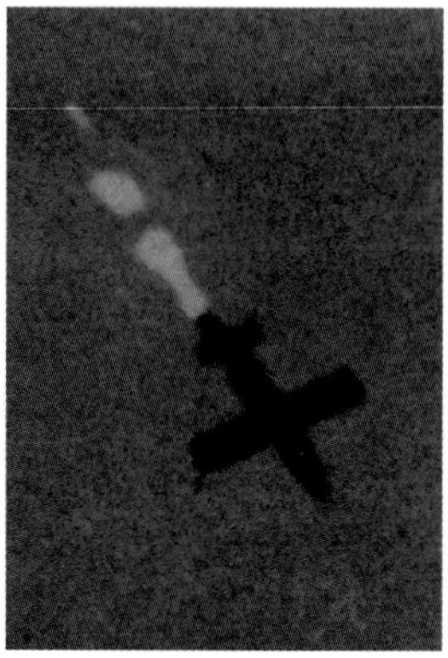

The Guards' Chapel in London after being hit by a V-1 flying bomb on 18 June 1944. There were 121 killed and 141 seriously wounded in this tragedy. (Crown copyright)

were condemned to serve the enemy and were bitter; if the opportunity to get their own back arose, they took it. When Michel Hollard took the risk of approaching them, these porters, valets, electricians or maîtres d'hôtel were in fact surprisingly cooperative.

'So you couldn't avoid revealing your clandestine activities to them,' I said, quite surprised, while he was reminiscing one day. 'Was this inside that dangerous place or near it?'

'I never concealed what I was asking from these men.'

'Even when you were talking to someone you didn't know?'

'After looking for a moment at the guy I was talking to, who was himself in an awkward position, I either questioned him or refrained from doing so.'

'And if the person became outraged and refused to answer?'

'It almost never happened.'

To make identifying the senior officers easier, Agir's founder asked for and obtained an infallible tool from O.P., his English correspondent and friend: an excellent little collection of photographs showing the faces and giving the names of all the enemy bigwigs in their pecking order.

'Hey, that's the bloke living next door!'

'I've found my oddball!'

'There's my weirdo!'

This sort of cheeky way the employees had of reacting when they saw the photographs of their customers revealed their satisfaction at having passed on, albeit in a little way, information to the Allies.

***

Despite all its efforts to disinform, censorship was not able to keep the population in the dark of how operations on the various fronts were really going. Millions of radios managed to break through the jamming daily regardless of the ban. In perfect and often derisory contradiction to the German-controlled media, the BBC announced the enemy armies' first setbacks.

In 1940, while an unfortunately not insignificant part of French public opinion had allowed itself to be taken in or impressed by Nazi propaganda and demonstrations of strength, the number of citizens with wavering, fickle or go-getting opinions was steadily decreasing. And you couldn't trust those who collaborated out of self-interest, conviction or because it was an aberration. All the more reason for avoiding the Vichy Milice like the plague.

***

In order to extend the Agir network over the whole of France, its leader had to speed up the already frantic pace of his railway trips to remote regions. He travelled most often at night and was thus able to meet his agents fairly regularly. When they handed the information to him, he gave advice and encouragement to those who might need it, constantly strengthening the warm bonds without which the organisation would have quickly caved in. These exhausting rounds enabled him to keep his organisation in focus without ever losing control of it.

At the beginning of each trip, the traveller's uppermost worry was finding a seat in the generally overcrowded trains. There was smoke everywhere too and to crown it all, there was the lush orchestration of clanks, roars and pathetic whistles given off by the gasping locomotives. A little space where he could nestle, often in the corridor, was enough to make him happy. Miraculously, the surrounding chaotic environment never stopped him from dropping off into the sleep of the righteous.

From time to time, he was helped by the train conductors. Seeing him making the same trip time and time again, some of them made it easier for him to get hold of a better seat. One morning, one of these Good Samaritans, worried at seeing him still asleep as he was getting close to his usual station, woke him up just in time to prevent him missing it.

***

His network of agents soon stretched out to cover all regions. Those busy in the north, east and in the west of France were often recruited in the railway sector, and even more often among the lorry drivers, his professional partners in the car milieu whom he had recruited in Paris.

With the occasional exception, they met up with him one by one in the capital to hand over the results of their observations.

He was not only given the usual, essential type of information on how enemy units were spread out and what their chain of command was, on fuel distribution centres and aviation facilities, etc., but also more unconventional information. Among other discoveries, he learned that trenches were being dug about 2.5 miles from the shores of the North Sea, the Channel and the Atlantic. This was a defence system with buried power lines, which would set off a barrage of mines in the case of an Allied landing. On his bike, Joseph Brocard was able to survey all the maritime areas, and noted his observations on maps.

When meeting his agents in the centre and south of France, Hollard usually had to go to the very place where they were carrying out their missions. From Paris to Nice and Toulouse, via Dijon, Lyon, Valence, Montélimar, Pierrelatte, Avignon, Tarascon, Arles, Aix-en-Provence, Toulon, Marseille, Nîmes, Montpellier, Carcassonne and other places, he went tirelessly to collect from each of them the results of what they had done over the past few weeks.

The trip started in Paris, near the Gare de Lyon, where he could rush off to the Rhône Valley, the Jura Mountains or the Alps, and down to the Mediterranean. Before setting off on each journey, he dropped into the safe house he had set up close to his departure point. The room, rented on a permanent basis in the old Hôtel d'Annecy,[8] included a large wardrobe whose upper cornice was used as a hiding place for documents which had accumulated since his previous trip. This undetectable space, accessible only after carrying out a fairly acrobatic balancing act, was almost out of reach for the personnel in the building. Half an hour before setting off on his rounds, he removed the dossier and placed it carefully in his briefcase, which expanded with each phase of the trip. After the last meeting, he would round off his circuit by heading for Switzerland with the precious and compromising information.

Chapter 18

Record Number of Illegal Crossings

Michel Hollard's very first route via Mont Châteleu and La Brévine, with the help of Paul Cuenot, the *montagnard*, had been very easy during the summer months, but when winter came, each step he took in the snow could betray him. As he didn't know any other way of crossing the border, he tried out various tricks.

On his first attempt, he became a tightrope walker on a barbed wire fence to avoid leaving tracks on the ground. The result was painful and humiliating. With his hands and legs all covered in blood, he turned up at the Swiss border post wearing tattered trousers. He discarded this idea as not very practical so, for the next crossing, he tried attaching a set of old soles and heels pointing backwards under his shoes, but putting this into practice was very awkward. He persisted nonetheless with his rather naïve idea of tricking the soldiers as to which way he was walking. When he crossed the border the next time, he was able to test how uncomfortable snowshoes were, likewise worn backwards.

With the help of Providence, these rather erratic experiments all ended safely, despite the mountains being increasingly dangerous in winter. In the end, however, such challenges would have turned out badly. The Resistance leader therefore thought it time to find other routes into Switzerland that were less frequently covered in snow. He headed at first towards the Montbéliard region where Vincent, my brother, was a boarder in a school near the frontier. In case he ran into a problem in the area, where the enemy had reinforced its surveillance, having a son nearby was a plausible reason for being there.[1]

Looking at the lie of the land, he first selected the village of Villars-lès-Blamont, between Montbéliard and Porrentruy. As usual, he wasn't afraid of going up to strangers whose appearance seemed honest, and a young country couple offered their help to the newcomer wholeheartedly.

Émile and Geneviève Mathiot lived on a small farm separated from Switzerland by a partly bare hill. They set up a signalling system using gestures to help the traveller cross this treacherously open zone.

As soon as he got there, the friendly peasant woman went off to put her goat out to graze high up from where she could keep an eye on the movements of the enemy guards. By means of a series of previously agreed gestures, she was able to guide Hollard. If the young woman walked forward one or two paces when facing the farm, he knew he could head for the border. The woman, making doubly certain the coast was clear, confirmed this by waving her handkerchief. A meeting at a very precise time had to be arranged for the return into France, which was codified by gestures similar to those for the departure. This outward and return scenario caused its participants a lot of anxiety. Indeed, patrols sometimes appeared at unexpected times, but the woman always spotted them in time and knew how to distract them long enough for Hollard to get away.

In this countryside the walker only needed to make a moderate effort to go from one country to another, but Michel started thinking that this last barren stretch was too dangerous. By himself, in the middle of the wide, open space, he was just as frightened as he was on the snow-covered slopes of Mont Châteleu.

***

Without giving up on the crossing point at Villars-lès-Blamont, Hollard started looking for another route which he could use all year round. A Swiss customs officer, who knew both sides of the Franco-Swiss border, gave him the benefit of his experience, showing him zones the Germans had cordoned off which seemed less secure. In particular, he recommended two places near Geneva, one to the east and another to the north.

When coming from France, the first of these points was in the middle of a wood and was fairly accessible, between the villages of Machilly (France) and Jussy (Switzerland), to the south of Lake Geneva. Coils of barbed wire were stretched some 20 inches from the ground and fixed to the trunks of a row of trees, following the border between the two countries borne out by a stream. The German guards didn't prevent the local population from moving about in this zone but they were there patrolling all the time. With the help of several friends, among whom were some railway workers, Michel Hollard thought up a series of ingenious ways of approaching people, some of which were quite amusing.

On his way from Annecy, he left the train for a moment in La Roche-sur-Foron station, where the person in charge of the station buffet promptly handed him his bag, which she kept for him when he didn't need it. It held a railway worker's complete gear (jacket, trousers, a cap with the SNCF initials, leather bag, red cloth pennant, armband and lantern). When he returned to the wagon, the traveller used the lavatory to put his railway uniform on, his supposedly professional clothes slipped over his normal ones. All he had to do then was to stuff the unneeded items into the bag.

When the train halted in Machilly station, where gendarmes checked the travellers' identities, the fake railwayman went off, ignoring the exit. Walking along the railway line, he strode into the open countryside until he reached a ditch a few hundred yards away, under the ballast embankment. Pushing aside the tangled vegetation at the entrance of the obscure hideout, he got hold of an agricultural tool (axe or pickaxe) he'd left on his previous visit.

After hiding his SNCF employee disguise in the same place, all slipped into a big bag, he put on a beret. In one hand he took the tool he'd just recovered, in the other a coarse canvas bag slung over his shoulder. This rustic pack completed his transformation into a Savoyard peasant. It didn't contain products of the land, but rather strategic documents.

The farming couple Joseph Paccot and his wife, their sons François and André, the farming families Neury and Lionnet, living near the border, all occupied good vantage points to watch the enemy guards' movements. Without fail, these patriotic people took it in turns to help the Resistance leader who'd become their friend.

As soon as he was dressed up like an occasional farmhand, he headed for the Paccot's home. These vital helpers who'd been anxiously waiting soon lavished attention on him. Now that he knew about the enemy's presence in the area from the best sources, he waited for the right moment to set off into the bordering wood and climb over the forbidden fence.[2]

At the Swiss customs post where, as usual, he turned up unannounced, the Swiss officials had begun by smiling at the way he was dressed. But they soon bowed before the man in this attire and as a special favour made an individual locker available to him.

***

The Swiss customs officer, who'd advised him so well as to which border areas were least guarded by the German police and to the traps they'd laid, also showed him, among other ways of getting from one country to the other, a place near Divonne-les-Bains (Ain department), to the north of Geneva. When Hollard found the spot on the map, he noted that to get there, he'd have to go a long way on foot, partly on steep and frequently snow-covered paths. His first reaction was therefore not to use it, but he quickly changed his mind.

'How can I be so foolish as to neglect the disinterested opinion of someone who knows the frontier so well? Since I have to make such an effort to get there, why wouldn't it be the same for others? Enemy surveillance can't be so thorough there.'

Experience confirmed the customs man was right, but there was another reason why he preferred the route; halfway along it was an enthusiastically patriotic farming couple, Denis and Alice Poncet. These farmers, living near the village of Mijoux, close to the Col de la Faucille mountain pass, welcomed and pampered him as though he were one of the family.

Afterwards, when he used that route, the Resistance leader donned his farm worker's gear in the train between Morez and Saint-Claude. Never did either the enemy soldiers or the French gendarmes notice this character tirelessly climbing the mountain and crossing the river, rather aptly called the Valserine. This charming tributary of the Rhône is spanned by the famous Charlemagne Bridge, a strategic point from time immemorial. It was through this same place, which in 790 marked the limits of the Holy Roman Empire, that the demarcation line passed in 1940. The Poncet couple's loving care gave him excellent protection when they put him up on each of his trips. Rested, fed, and reassured, he was always confident when he set off on the hazardous road which led him to the border, then the first Swiss chalet in La Combe-du-Faoug and the village of La Rippe.

For the return trip, which he tried as much as possible to time within an hour, simple signals similar to the ones which had been so effective at Mont Châteleu were used. As an outbuilding of the Poncet's farm was visible from the other side of the danger zone, a large wooden panel leaning against the building would warn him, if needs be, that a German patrol was in the area nearby.

His various crossing points ranged over a distance of more than 90 miles between the Franche-Comté region and Geneva. In almost three years, Michel Hollard carried off the exploit forty-nine times in each direction, a total of ninety-eight crossings.

This impressive feat could not have been possible without the help of the following families in their various locations: Cuenot (Derrière-le-Mont), Mathiot (Villars-lès-Blamont), Paccot, Lionnet, Neury (Machilly), Poncet (Lajoux-Mijoux) and also others. In the rural sector, as elsewhere, Michel's strength of character and natural leadership inspired respect before friendships formed. Since they were unable to get rid of the danger entirely, these brave and dedicated farmers used all their resources to divert or delay the enemy and watch over and guide the steps of the heroic man.

His travels were extensive. From Saint-Claude to La Rippe, via Mijoux[3] and La Combe-du-Faoug, the uneven route was no less than 25 miles long. His plans forced these interminable walks on him all throughout the year over steep, muddy and snow-covered ground. In almost three years of underground war, Michel Hollard covered thousands of miles, regardless of any latent danger.

Now that watchful minders protected the most dangerous points, he nonetheless took the risk, thanks to unforeseen difficulties, of frequenting critical zones without any help. During the winter of 1942–43, he left Saint-Claude one evening rather rashly, despite a snowstorm, setting off in the direction of Mijoux with the intention of stopping there and continuing on his way to Switzerland the following day.

When he took this regrettable step, he disregarded his normal safety principles. The terrible weather prevented him from making any unpleasant encounters but his wanting to save time at all costs made him waste a lot of it. After walking for four hours in the increasingly deep snow, he hadn't even reached the halfway mark along his trip. With the raging weather giving him a rough time, he was forced to give up and retreat, quite furious with himself. In even worse weather, this retribution reached its height as he made his way back. At Saint-Claude, he took the train again for Machilly, his other crossing point near Geneva where, with the help of François Paccot, the undergrowth along the border was ideal for crossing. He had wasted fifteen hours and slept very little for three nights in a row. But this stubborn optimist considered all this running around as an excellent opportunity to measure his staying power.

***

Such a misadventure did nothing to prevent him from doing it again. During the same 1942–43 winter, and once again on the route from Saint-Claude to La Rippe, he took the usual paths covered in a white blanket about 8 inches thick. All went well up to Mijoux, where his friends Denis and Alice Poncet offered him dinner with their usual generosity. He didn't give in to the temptation to sleep under their hospitable roof, and despite the experienced *montagnards'* warning about all sorts of dangers, he left the farm at sunset without a compass. The night was soon very dark and as the walker's feet sank deeper into the snow, he quickly lost track of the paths. Continuing to forge ahead blindly under a starless sky, he could no longer count on his instinctive flair. He ran uncontrollably into various hard obstacles hidden under the powdery snow and even the icy bottom of a stream he couldn't see. After advancing hazardously for three hours, he couldn't recognise the slope down to Lake Geneva which he should have come across ages ago. His glow-in-the-dark watch told him it was 10.30 pm when he stopped to take stock of the situation.

'The border most likely runs somewhere nearby,' he thought. 'But where? On which side?'

Choosing a very big tree which dominated the others as the starting point for his search, he visualised four directions from the tree in the form of a cross. He started to explore the branches of the cross methodically over a distance of 1,000 paces each time. The first two were in vain. Returning with relief each time to his tree, he set off in the third direction.

'While thinking my chances were dwindling, I counted out aloud the paces before the fateful 1,000,' he recounted, still surprised, when he got back. 'I made out a large rectangular stone partly covered in snow right next to me. Having cleared away the snow, I saw by the flame of a match that it was well and truly the Swiss boundary marker, emblazoned with its sculptured escutcheon! Not believing my eyes, I advanced 50 or so yards into Swiss territory and stopped a moment to thank God for having saved me, once again.'

***

With these trips back and forth increasing, such emotions didn't prevent him from seeing the crossing of the borders and of the demarcation lines as a sort of athletic contest. A long period of regular trips without any incidents gradually allayed the sportsman's vigilance and increased his boldness. But the day came when overfamiliarity made him forget the danger he was running.

Near Geneva, the undergrowth on the Machilly border offered dark shadows that were too welcoming so as not to hide any pitfalls. The clandestine traveller often used this route, however, especially when the mountain was snow-covered.

There was a narrow escape once when he was making his now routine approach. He was about to start climbing the last barrier, bristling with barbed wire, behind which flowed a little stream, the Hermance, when he was taken completely by surprise after a big police dog rushed at him, bit him on the knee and tried to immobilise him, waiting for his masters to catch up. A savage, merciless scuffle broke out which had to be ended at once, before the soldiers arrived at any minute.

The farmer's garb he was wearing helped to save him. As was often the case when he was going through a danger zone, he was wearing two garments, one over the other. The top pair of thick corduroy trousers together with those they covered made quite a compact, substantial mass.

The animal dug its teeth into it but only its fangs were able to penetrate through to the victim's flesh.

The fight was in full swing. Michel Hollard was still struggling but managed to grab a broken stick lying on the ground. One of the ends was sharp. He managed to get this makeshift sword into the narrow space between the lips and the corner of the dog's mouth. With a desperate effort, he gave the stick a sharp twist at an angle in the hope of opening the vice-like grip of the jaws. The improvised sword entered the dog's throat, and it released its prey before dropping to the ground lifeless.

A moment later, Hollard was already on the other side of the barrier and about to touch Swiss soil when a guttural command rang out in German:

'*Waffen nieder!*' (Put your weapons down!)

Looking in the direction where the order seemed to come from, he saw a Swiss border guard, standing a way off, ready to fire his rifle. He seemed to be aiming at somebody beyond the boundary fence. Turning his head again, Michel Hollard saw two German soldiers – most certainly the dog's trainers – ready to shoot. Given the circumstances, it's doubtful these men would've given the regular warnings before firing if the Swiss customs officer hadn't intervened.

Exasperated and furious, they lowered their weapons. Out of rage, they let out streams of crude and lively abuse at the Swiss border guard who pretended impassively not to hear their rantings. Hollard rushed up to meet him crying out:

'Monsieur, you saved my life. How can I thank you?'

'Don't. I've only just stopped those foreigners from violating Swiss sovereignty. On no account must their bullets cross the border! Who are you and what are you doing here?'

Taken aback, the newcomer nevertheless kept his head and declared carefully:

'I'm French. Your country's authorities are expecting me.'

'Show me your papers.'

'With your administration's permission, I come into Switzerland without any official documents.'

'Follow me!'

The incident took place at a time when the instructions to allow Hollard to enter and to come and go as he wished on Swiss territory hadn't yet been passed on to all the officials likely to come across him.

The visitor reached the customs post under escort. To the border guard's great surprise, he was welcomed warmly. The person in charge of the post gave orders for the leg bitten by the dog to be bandaged.

***

On another day, the overconfident traveller dropped his guard once again and ran into a German patrol, whose route crossed his near the border at La Combe-du-Faoug. Any ungainly movement on his part, the slightest sign of hesitation or panic, would have betrayed him. The make-believe peasant, walking resolutely and almost larger than life in his makeshift garb, went up to a grazing cow. With ad hoc orders, and the help of a stick picked up from the ground, he got the frightened animal to move forward, reluctantly at first, then more or less submissively. The soldiers were clearly amused by the comic spectacle of the clumsy cowherd struggling with his stubborn animal and continued on their way, quite oblivious of any hoax.

After this inconsequential misadventure, Michel Hollard had at his disposal a false document which enabled him to justify his being in the Forbidden Zone. His friends the Poncets had no misgivings about protecting him and compromising themselves. With their help, he got hold of an official identity card which made him a farm labourer called Sylvain-Adrien Regard, born in Mijoux (Ain) and living with his employers at Lajoux (Jura department).

***

Normally a non-smoker, he'd recently given in to temptation and started smoking, ever since his London correspondent O.P. had brought light cigarettes 'made in England' – a rare luxury at the time – to Lausanne for him and which he thought were harmless.

During a return trip into France through La Combe-du-Faoug, he made the double mistake of crossing the border at night while smoking. He jumped when he heard '*Halt!*' shouted by a German-sounding voice at a distance in the forest. The order echoed in the distance gloomily.

Perfect self-control and instant reflexes gave the reckless smoker the means to correct his mistake. As he was foresighted and crafty, he was in the habit of sticking pins and needles into the lapels of his travel jacket. In seconds, the cigarette was fixed to a tree at eye level and clearly visible, the glowing tip fanned by the wind. As he moved away hurriedly, he heard the distant warning shouts, followed a few seconds later by a series of shots…

***

In the border wood near Machilly, the fight between Hollard and the police dog prompted the construction of a second barbed wire fence parallel to the initial barrier, which was much more of a deterrent. With a height exceeding 2 yards, this metal wall made the clandestine traveller take considerably greater risks, which flayed his hands and legs and tore his clothes.

Yet these additional drawbacks didn't put him off. He always preferred using this route whenever weather conditions prevented him from taking one of the mountain ones. The Machilly site and its two barbed wire fences became so familiar that after thinking up a particular approach, he was even able to play the role of guide during two tricky relocations.

After the death of my grandfather Auguste Hollard in July 1943, our scattered family had a lot of trouble giving my grandmother suitable living conditions in Paris. Distraught, my grandmother particularly suffered from malnutrition and insufficient heating. The impact of the occupation was felt more rigorously every day.

During one of Michel Hollard's visits to the Swiss village of Mézières, near Lausanne, at the home of Doctor Guisan and his wife, his brother-in-law and his sister Micheline, the latter suggested generously, without realising how unrealistic it was:

'If it were possible to get "Mamaman"[4] to travel and bring her here despite the border being closed, she'd obviously be our guest for as long as she wanted and we'd love to look after her…'

'I'll think about it. It's a daring idea, indeed. But it doesn't seem so far-fetched!'

When he returned to France through Machilly, the traveller examined the metal barrier closely. He concluded that if needs be, two or three suitable tools would probably enable him to make an opening in it and put things back as they were after his mother had slipped through. He then went to consult his friend, the neighbouring farmer, Joseph Paccot, who could only give a rather negative opinion but did say that if, despite everything, the plan was carried out, he and his family would do everything they could to help.

The expedition meant that those taking part had to be rather crafty; a character trait that dear and revered Mamaman, in all her candour, was quite lacking. She did know, however, that an unknown friend, claiming to be a cousin, would be there to meet her with unexpected outbursts of enthusiasm when she got off the train.

The scenario imagined by the Resistance leader came off marvellously. When the train arrived in Machilly station, Mamaman saw one of the Paccot sons coming up to her. My father had signalled to him through the window before the train stopped completely. Watched by the soldiers on border guard duty, the villager very ostensibly hugged his supposed relation and showed his affection for her whilst guiding her to the horse-drawn cart. Nobody was surprised to see them trundling off together towards the farm where Madame Paccot gave them a meal.

Meanwhile, Hollard, who to Mamaman's surprise had donned his special garb for the occasion whilst on the train, set off by himself to the foot of the metal fence. With wire cutters, he cut through the twisted barbed wire in such a way as to clear a path 5 feet high by 1 yard wide. He'd almost finished when the horse-drawn carriage arrived. Mamaman got down all perky, thanked the make-believe cousin and went through the gap without even noticing how strange this route was. He quickly realigned the wires back to their original positions, after which they continued their trip in the country by crossing the Hermance. The son carried his mother over the river and placed her gently on the other bank, in territory that was at peace. She was quite unaware of the tour de force that she'd just been the star of.

André Gagnaux, the Swiss Army officer and Michel Hollard's friend, was there to meet them at this far-flung point of the country. He invited his guests to climb into his car and without a moment's delay, drove them to the Geneva-Cornavin station to catch the train to Lausanne, where several members of the Guisan family, impatient and marvelling, were there waiting for them on the platform.

***

Michel Hollard later used the Machilly route to play the role of smuggler once again. This time it was a question of saving a woman and her child wanted by the Gestapo. The enemy border guards, though usually routine in their patrols, did carry out unexpected ones from time to time. Such was the case on this particular day, and things could have turned out very badly indeed for everyone, especially for the guide.

He was pushing apart the last bits of barbed wire on one side of the breach, already half-open, when he spotted some soldiers. He grabbed his axe without getting flustered and, making powerful and precise movements, started to chop down a tree some yards away from the boundary. François Paccot appeared in turn with his workers and had seen from far off that his friend had suddenly turned himself into a woodcutter. This unexpected change revealed how serious the situation was.

While the fugitives, hiding terrorised behind their impromptu shelter, were waiting for the guide's instructions, the German soldiers passed on their way, quite easy-going and indifferent, right next to the make-believe logger doing his job. The damage caused to the fence had also escaped their attention, leaving the path to freedom open.

***

After the creation of the Office Technique du Gazogène de France, of which Agir's leader was still in theory the boss, Hollard was able to obtain an access card for southern France, even though his professional justification was fictitious. But he was unable to use it for very long because the German police were making enquiries about him. After the Wehrmacht invaded the Southern Zone, the old demarcation line remained operational using another system of inspections, which was more irregular and most often took place unexpectedly in the railway carriages during the journey. This reduction in surveillance, imposed upon the enemy by the shortage of personnel its military setbacks were causing, was applied everywhere in France, including the access routes to the Forbidden Zones. Several railway workers in the Agir network strived to inform their boss regularly so that he'd be able to get around in trains that would be free of military control.

The preventive measures his agents took were obviously not always enough to guarantee him absolute peace of mind all the time. Twice he experienced the throes of the outlaw caught in a trap by inspectors from the flying squad. After other dangerous misadventures, he was only able to avoid capture thanks to his lively imagination.

When returning from one of his customary trips to Switzerland, during a discussion with an SNCF conductor aboard a train, he learnt that in the station at Auxonne (between Besançon and Dijon), a team of Gestapo inspectors was getting ready to scrutinize the train's passengers. In his distress, his initial reaction was to jump off the train, but a glance outside made him dismiss this suicidal idea. Walking with difficulty along the corridors all crowded with passengers sitting on their suitcases, he carried on thinking about jumping off as soon as the train slowed down. After moving along slowly, he was able to reach the last passenger carriage. Beyond that there was still a goods wagon, but no corridor with concertina vestibule to get to it. By means of the outside ramps and steps, he managed to get into the wagon, which an SNCF employee was keeping an eye on, with relative ease.[5]

'Monsieur, the Germans mustn't see me at Auxonne, my papers aren't in order. Can you hide me somewhere?'

Forbidding, and obviously not keen to get involved, the man turned a deaf ear. The traveller, now ready to jump off as soon as the train slowed down enough, opened the door again without heeding the employee's protests. He then noticed that the goods wagon was fitted with a sort of square transverse pontoon just over 2 feet high and wide. Built into the floor, this long caisson had two locked access hatches, one at each end.

'And what if I disappeared in there?'

As luck would have it, he'd come across a special model of an old wagon, perhaps designed for a hunting association and whose original purpose had been abandoned a long time ago.

'Well, if you want to sit in the dog kennel, I've no problem with that!' answered the man.

The clandestine traveller had to crouch down and lower his head to get inside the disused shelter. In Auxonne station, unseen behind one of the doors pierced with air holes, he took pleasure watching the soldiers doing the checking, gesticulating all over the place. When the danger was past, the employee who'd been haughty and taciturn up until then laughed mockingly when he saw Hollard crawling out of his hiding place. Recalling the event made my father happy:

'I must admit the railway worker's laughter was rather called for. After staying in that mud-spattered and sooty cubbyhole for almost an hour, I came back out looking like a coalman or a chimney sweep!'

***

During another railway trip, he escaped from the German police in even more dire circumstances. Aboard a crowded train, coming back from his usual meeting with his English correspondent, the only room he could find was a corner of the vestibule. As for his bag, which was full of compromising documents, he simply hung it up on the wall.

Two German inspectors turned up to examine some of the luggage. Chance or intuition guided their choice. Unfortunately, the bag caught the attention of one of them, but he wanted to find out who the owner was before checking the contents.

Somebody, most likely without any harmful intentions, answered his question by pointing to Michel Hollard with a vague hand signal. For the time being he wasn't under suspicion, so he made a gesture to say it wasn't his and moved away, avoiding doing anything hastily. As soon as he was out of sight of the agents bending over their discovery, he sped up, jumping over obstacles, hedging along the corridor between travellers and packages to try and reach the end of the train. A distant voice shouted an order rendered unintelligible by the noise of the train. To escape the clutches of his pursuers this time, there was only one extreme solution left: jumping off the train into the countryside.

The train suddenly slowed down noticeably as it came to a bend and the fugitive did not miss his opportunity. Despite vehement protests and shouting from people who witnessed the scene with dread, he opened the door and threw himself out. The track ballast was a rough surface on which he rolled and skidded harshly. Multiple bruises and grazes on his hands didn't prevent him from getting right back up, more or less in one piece, but with his clothes in a pitiful state.

Seeing the train stopping a bit further on, he realised the danger wasn't over. Luck smiled upon him once again, however, when, on the other line, a long goods train was coming towards him slowly, going the other way. Screeching and wheezing, its varied wagons went past him endlessly. For the good sportsman that he was, hoisting himself up aboard the wagon of his choice was child's play. The last one was a brake van with a lookout cabin. Hidden on top of this moving vantage point, he had fun watching the soldiers in the distance having to give up their searches.

***

Another dangerous episode had a happy ending thanks to the devotion of Denis and Alice Poncet, the farmers in Mijoux. At home, my father often mentioned this adventure, calling his friends the snow angels. When returning to Paris after one of his usual missions to Switzerland, he agreed to help some acquaintances by taking a personal letter. This was a private matter between a wife and her husband, from whom she was separated because of the war.

Before the train crossed the demarcation line, he hid a package containing the letter in a corner which he thought wrongly to be inaccessible. Unluckily, the parcel didn't escape the enemy inspectors who got hold of it.

He apologised to the unhappy husband. A priori, a letter containing only private remarks ought not to be a problem for anyone. But when Hollard was once again back in Switzerland a few days later and told the sender about the incident, she revealed the contents of the letter. Among other revelations, she mentioned a French *montagnard* by name living near the border. He was getting ready to send certain compromising documents from Switzerland to Paris, as well as food supplies.

The matter suddenly took a preoccupying turn for the worse. The Germans would certainly soon question the man living in the country and try to discover all the links of this secret chain. The only way of reducing the danger was to get hold of the person as quickly as possible and stop him from sending the package. Fearing it might already be too late, Michel Hollard set off at once.

Despite a thick blanket of snow, he walked all night in the mountains, crossing the border near Mijoux without the help of his usual protectors, who were unaware of the situation and not expecting him. After falling down more than a hundred times and chilled to the bone, he arrived within sight of the Poncet farm in the early hours.

He wanted to settle down in the barn and wait for them to wake up, but his presence didn't go unnoticed. Although it was still early, a grog was prepared for him, together with a charcuterie plate, which he thoroughly enjoyed in front of a big fire. He told the Poncets the reasons for his surprise visit and his hosts invited him to settle down to sleep, which he accepted without any hesitation. He begged them, however, to wake him two hours later because he still had several more miles to cover before getting where he had to go.

Like a jack-in-the-box, he woke up in a panic…in the middle of the afternoon. The farmer's wife, waiting for him to wake up, gave him no time to complain. 'Don't worry,' she announced, 'all's well. My husband left this morning on skis, as soon as you fell asleep. The route was long and difficult, but he's just telephoned me at the post office where I was waiting for his message, as agreed.[6] The man hasn't sent the package yet and up until now no unwanted visitors have turned up. They can ask all the questions they want; the answers are ready…'

Chapter 19

Harbour Graveyard

The presence of Allied troops in North Africa at the beginning of November 1942 forced Hitler to strengthen the forces he had in the Mediterranean. After ordering the south of France to be invaded, the Führer wanted to get his hands on its navy, whose Toulon docks sheltered its most beautiful jewels.

When the German troops broke through into the port, only four submarines were able to clear off hurriedly with a series of complicated manoeuvres and join the Allies. Refusing to hand over the naval forces to the enemy, the crews chose to scuttle their own ships – battleships, cruisers, torpedo boats, destroyers, submarines and numerous escort vessels – on 27 November 1942.

The news caused general consternation.[1] In Lausanne that day, the Agir network boss was asked by O.P., his correspondent sent by the War Office, to try to obtain information as quickly as possible. What was important to assess was the extent of the damage, boat by boat, and to estimate how much could be salvaged and used by the enemy.

Not knowing anyone in the Toulon region and despite having few skills in naval matters, Michel Hollard decided to make some enquiries at once. Two days after the event, he reached the suburbs of the city whose access was under guard. An inhabitant of the outskirts showed him a roundabout way he could use to avoid the watchfulness of the enemy police.

The population, reputed for its joyful and expansive temperament, seemed to be overwhelmed in an atmosphere of mourning, and even groups of men from the Kriegsmarine[2] were walking along the streets looking almost as sad as the people of Toulon. Having rushed to grab hold of a splendid fleet, they'd suffered the affront of being invited, as helpless witnesses, to a sort of pitiful requiem mass.

Michel saw the roads for the first time at nightfall; lines of motionless silhouettes whose ghostly appearance was accentuated by the darkness. Leaning to one side, three-quarters submerged, the wrecks revealed part of their superstructure, funnels and masts pointing obliquely skywards.

There would've been no point starting to explore anything properly at this late hour. Finding somewhere to sleep for the night risked being difficult, so without further ado Michel Hollard entered a nearby hotel.

'Our establishment has been entirely requisitioned for the occupation troops,' he was told at the reception. 'Besides, practically all the hotels in town have been requisitioned. You'll most likely have a lot of trouble finding a room.'

Thus turned away, Michel was about to leave the premises empty-handed when a German NCO came out of a nearby room and asked:

'Why are you in Toulon, Monsieur?'

'I'm a technician. I've come to repair equipment.'

'Would you be able to get my personal radio working again? It's damaged.'

'Probably, if none of the parts are out of order.'

'Then please come with me.'

In a neighbouring room, after a few minutes of looking at the defective radio, the impromptu repairman was certain the breakdown was minor. He said nothing about what he'd diagnosed, however. Turning towards the soldier, he proposed a deal outright.

'Monsieur, the receptionist here has refused to put me up. If I succeed in repairing your radio, can you get them to give me a room here?'

'I'll see to it.'

Alone, he easily got the faulty radio to work again. The NCO was so happy with the result that he invited the Frenchman to finish the evening with him at the bar. Politely, Michel Hollard turned down the invitation.

'Tomorrow morning,' he assured him, 'I've a particularly delicate job to do and I must be fit and ready!'

Appreciating this sign of professional conscientiousness, the NCO didn't insist. He was even courteous enough to accompany Hollard along the corridors to show him to the room he'd been able to make available for him, one of the most comfortable in the establishment.

At the enemy's expense, therefore, Michel Hollard was going to be able to sleep properly and consequently be in the best physical condition to carry out his enquiries at daybreak.

He woke up early, feeling refreshed. The dining room, where he was invited to have an excellent breakfast, already echoed with the laughter and jokes of a gathering of sailors sitting at a table. They disappeared once their meal was over.

Fifteen minutes later, as he approached the Harbour Zone, he found himself up against an enemy patrol. Although in this case the danger was no greater than it usually was, he hesitated for a moment before deciding to push onwards toward the wharfs. To his great surprise, not only was he not turned away, or even questioned, but he was greeted with deference as he went by. Those responsible for checking had most likely recognised the privileged guest from their hotel. At any rate, Michel Hollard didn't run into any obstacles.

Whereas earlier they'd been given over to bustling and gladly mischievous crowds, the wharfs were now deserted and seemed under a spell. On the surface of the basins they delimited, glistening multicoloured slicks made up a nauseating cocktail of oil, grease and tar. A great deal of solid debris was floating around, as wreckage continued to escape from the hulks of certain ships, some of which were still smoking.

An ironic detail in the middle of this disastrous scene drew Michel's attention. The statue of Le Génie de la Navigation, facing out to sea, was playing with a yo-yo while scanning the horizon! Some practical joker had succeeded in placing the derisory object on the finger of the allegorical figure. This facetiousness cruelly evoked the rise and fall which even the most formidable strongholds can't avoid sooner or later.

Near the monument with its incongruous accessory were two onlookers. Visibly overwhelmed by the sight of the engulfed fleet, two men of different ages were commenting on the tragedy they'd witnessed. The leader of the Agir network watched the two unknown men for quite some time, but he was too far away to catch what they were saying. However, their attitudes were expressive enough for him to decide to take them into his confidence. Once again, his intuition helped him. Without hesitation, the two men gave him the names of the most important ships that partly emerged from the water around them. They told of how one ship, before she was destroyed by her crew, had held at bay a powerfully armed enemy unit on land. The confrontation lasted long enough for the remainder of the French ships gathered in the port to be scuttled. During this incident they lost several friends who were among the sailors.

The men spoke with dignity but were unable to entirely conceal their distress. The older of the two, Alexandre Roman, could barely control his bitterness. He'd dedicated his life to serving the French fleet as a foreman at the arsenal workshops; he could now see the result of his work reduced to nothing.

Michel Hollard, a determined optimist, tried to placate him by insisting on the positive aspects of the ordeal. He praised the French sailors' courage and spirit of sacrifice, and remarked that Hitler had just suffered a stinging setback. If he'd got hold of the Mediterranean fleet, the balance of power in the world would have been greatly altered.

When Michel suggested carrying on the conversation elsewhere, the three men went into a café. Introducing himself as a travelling engineer in charge of developing and maintaining the *gazogènes*, he told them he was intending to return soon to Toulon. His trips unfortunately ran into the restrictions imposed by the Germans. To enter Toulon and the Coastal Zone, anyone who was not a resident had to have a very good reason for being there. So, if his Paris agency were to receive a written request to repair a faulty machine, he might be able to obtain authorisation. The officials in charge of the passes would no doubt accept an interzone postcard, provided it was worded properly and posted from Toulon. Could he hope to receive such a request for repairs from one of these two gentlemen?

Although they were surprised and puzzled, they didn't react negatively. Michel Hollard understood their hesitation and anticipated their answer. On a regulation pre-stamped postcard, he drew up a service request to be sent to his own company. Then he wrote down the company address dictated by Alexandre Roman in the box reserved for the sender. A mutually convenient despatch date was also written down. The three of them went their separate ways after the future correspondent had taken the card.

As far as the Resistance leader was concerned, there was no doubt that the two men from Toulon were serious, and it seemed unlikely to him that his expectations would go unmet. Indeed, the postcard sent on the agreed date reached its destination at the right moment. Having thus received a request for repairs the administration thought plausible, the *gazogène* expert obtained the pass he needed to enter the port of Toulon, officially this time.

The next time Michel Hollard saw Alexandre Roman, he told him about his underground activity. This confidence was almost superfluous. The arsenal foreman had gathered at once that the engineer was more interested in the wrecked ships than in his *gazogène* business. The man from Toulon, having already given the Parisian a brief account of how the fleet was scuttled, agreed to continue working within the Agir network.

Beginning in early 1943, at a rate of almost fortnightly meetings, the new partners worked at keeping the Allies informed of any main naval activities deemed suspicious, not only in Toulon, but along the entire French Riviera. Firstly, the new agent responded to the initial request from the English about the exact state of the scuttled ships. He described and precisely evaluated the partly submerged units the enemy navy might think about getting back in working order.

Meanwhile, he revealed the specifications of a new, French-designed torpedo, kept secret until then, which he'd helped to develop. The enemy had unfortunately been able to get hold of several of the weapon's components when they took the arsenal's test centre.

While battle was raging around Sicily, the enemy sent some damaged motorboats to the Toulon dockyards. When each boat came in, Alexandre Roman worked out how long it would take to repair it so he could estimate the date it would probably be leaving. These forecasts enabled the Allies to watch out for the boats when they left, several of which were surprised and sunk.

In a well-sheltered creek near La Seyne-sur-Mer, the Germans set up a secret naval supply base. When he learned about this new development, the Agir agent wanted to have a look at it from a nearby cliff. As he was taking notes, a soldier who'd been hiding close by surprised him.

The suspect made up a rather implausible story which got him out of the tight spot: he claimed he was sketching the layout of his future house, looking at it from the clifftop!

During all his constant running around, Michel Hollard was generally able to follow the timetable he had carefully set up before setting off on a trip. However, on several occasions, unforeseen circumstances caused him to be delayed, which prevented him from completing some of his travels within the conditions and deadlines as planned. A case in point was in Provence, where one of the local agents offered his services to make up for the lost time. As the man had already drawn attention to himself by his ill-timed zeal, the network leader hesitated but, not without warning the man, Hollard ended up taking the risk of entrusting him as the intermediary.

The man first met with Alexandre Roman in the Toulon region. Then he went to Nice to contact two other members of the network, Jean Maiffret and his son Louis. Intending to speed up and simplify future intelligence gathering, he announced he'd organised a meeting for the regional informers; an initiative that broke one of Michel Hollard's security rules.

Hollard sensed danger as soon as he learned of this. He returned to the French Riviera in a hurry, to cancel the arrangements made without his consent, but arrived too late; the Gestapo had just picked the three of them up.[3]

This catastrophe deeply affected Agir's leader. The memory of his missing agents was to accompany him until the end of his days. His responsibility in their fate tormented him. In the spring of 1941, at the time he was carrying on the underground struggle by himself, he hadn't envisaged bringing anyone else into his undertaking. Now as the head of a constantly growing team, he was carrying an increasingly heavy moral burden.

He was haunted by the Olivier Giran tragedy, but that had been caused by something outside the network's activities. A lucky star had been watching over the other team members for a fairly long time, but the evil eye was now falling on several of them, and the list of the group's martyrs was to become even longer.

In northern France, the Gestapo surprised Gaston Brogniart and Paul Moreau, SNCF workers and members of Agir, who were busy collecting information concerning German troop movements. Sentenced to death after a summary trial, they fell to the bullets of a German firing squad before their leader was even informed of their arrest.

Chapter 20

The Joseph Brocard Odyssey

Many people modelled themselves on Michel Hollard, and sometimes he had to temper their recklessness. One of them was the young Joseph Brocard, who had drawn attention to himself by drafting a remarkable report on enemy installations along the Atlantic, the Channel and the North Sea coasts. On another occasion, while carrying out a mission for the Allies, he paid dearly for his daring but managed to avoid the worst.

Comparing debriefings made by its bomber pilots with reports from the photographic services, the RAF was certain the Germans were making changes to the Pontoise-Cormeilles-en-Vexin airbase. This airfield, near Paris, occupied a very large area on which new runways and taxiways had now appeared.

However, only one third of the carefully hidden tarmac seemed fit for use. Another part of the layout was marked out better, lit up at night and lined with most likely fake anti-aircraft guns acting as a decoy. Allied aircraft, tricked by this lure, had bombed it heavily. But up until then, the deluge of bombs hardly seemed to bother the Luftwaffe aircraft still sheltering there, thanks to the careful camouflage.

It was therefore urgent to give the misinformed bombers the information they needed to get their bombing right. Joseph Brocard, alias Bart, had already proved he was brave and ingenious. Having examined the lie of the land as it had been beforehand, he took on the investigation.

On 19 July 1943, he started by cycling round the airfield to fill in and make notes on a map of the site he'd dared to obtain. At a fair distance from the entrance and the official, fenced-off and guarded sites, he reached a deserted, unprotected zone. He went past a sign reminding the public that entering was strictly forbidden, at the risk of severe punishment. As there was no guard, he concealed his bicycle in a bush and entered the restricted area.

His mission was to spot any buildings that were hidden from the air and to note any set-ups that were decoys. A series of buildings located a few hundred yards from where he entered caught his attention at once. From a distance, these constructions looked like genuine aeronautical structures. Moving closer despite the increasing danger, he came across more and more token and excessive constructions, resembling a big game for kids.

Seen from the air, the installations no doubt created the necessary illusion; the whole thing was undeniably conceived with great skill. Strange-looking aircraft which were quite incapable of flying were parked around the make-believe hangars and workshops. They were just imitations made up of a series of boards.

Reaching the edge of the set-up, he noted down what he'd seen on the map, using signs and abbreviations for the big toys he'd just realised were innocuous. Excited by his discovery, Brocard was intent on discovering more. The idea of turning back while he still could never even occurred to him. He continued walking, advancing across apparently vacant land which gradually brought him to the square of a clearly fake church that seemed to conceal some sort of aeronautical equipment. Not far away he spotted a group of buildings that looked like a farm and no doubt concealed some other technical or logistical function.

Believing the place was unoccupied for the time being, he carried on advancing resolutely and then went beyond the point of no return. He understood this too late. As he was noting things down on the map of the fictitious village, the door of the make-believe building was pushed open by a soldier ready to use his gun. The prowler caught in the act had no choice but to obey the soldier's orders. Prodding him in the back with the gun barrel, the soldier forced him into his superior's office.

Before setting off, Joseph Brocard had made up something to say should he be arrested, so all he had to do was tell his story, that he'd found the map at the station where he'd got off the train. It contained handwritten information he thought might be interesting about the recent developments in country living conditions and he wanted to check out how true they were. He'd known the area for a long time, but he'd just come across a hamlet he'd no idea existed! How could he not resist visiting it? He'd been caught while simply out walking…

The officer didn't believe a word of what he was saying, believing the story to be odd and too ingenious. He responded by hitting him and said the incident would have to be dealt with by the Sicherheitsdienst (SS Security Service). The agents of this organisation, known for their ruthless cruelty, grilled the prisoner with their usual brutality. Stoic and stubborn, the Frenchman put up with the violence and clung to his unlikely story.

After several hours of interrogation and beatings, the exasperated but conscientious German police chief had a sheet of paper placed in front of Joseph, who was ordered to write down some of the handwritten phrases on the map as they were dictated to him.

The prisoner's fate depended, therefore, on a handwriting analysis. If the two handwriting samples turned out to be similar, there was no doubt he'd be executed. Despite his efforts to change his writing, Joseph Brocard thought all hope was lost. But luck was with him. The handwriting expert was absent for twenty-four hours. The military police took him and put him in a building it occupied at Houilles, to the northwest of Paris, to await the expert's return.

They made him climb four floors then threw him into a cramped, dark cell. What lay before him the next day didn't destroy his morale. As a ray of light shone through the cell, the prisoner's hopes rested upon it since it came in through a small window near the ceiling. Two vertical bars and thick wire mesh blocked it off.

As soon as the guards had locked the door, the prisoner, far from being downcast, found enough strength to study the situation objectively. He put the bed frame up against the wall and used it as a ladder to investigate the window on the off chance. The bars on the small window were spaced just enough to let his slender body slip between them. As for the mesh frame, when he had a close look at it, it revealed several signs of weakness. Some wires lent themselves, given the right action, to being twisted in all directions. Although he had no tools, he managed to break one of the fixations on the frame after a lot of effort and wounds to his hands.

He had to put his bed back when he heard footsteps in the corridor, and as night had fallen, he dropped onto it hurriedly. It was just a routine inspection. As the guard had not spotted anything abnormal, Joseph went back to work. He kept going at it for a long time, interrupted by repeated rounds.

The metal ended up giving way, but his success didn't give him much hope of succeeding in breaking out. The opening he'd just made looked down on the ground from a dizzying height and a night watchman did his rounds regularly.

But zeal and instinct for survival greatly increased the prisoner's efforts. Now that he'd partly made an opening, he had the illusion of freedom. A railway line ran along the building. While he'd been working on the opening, he'd noticed that the trains went by fairly regularly. Now it was getting late and there were far fewer of them. If he dared to jump, the noise of his fall and his shouts of pain if he hurt himself wouldn't go unnoticed. The only way to avoid attracting the guards' attention was to drop down as the next train went by. Dry ground with a few stunted blades of grass was 40–50 feet below him, waiting.

To try to lessen the impact of his fall somewhat, he thought of making good use of the blanket from the bed. In the hope that this rectangular bit of cloth would more or less play the role of a parachute, he grabbed it. After a lot of effort, he got himself through his makeshift exit and waited, all hunched up, for the next train to go by.

The minutes passed, interminably. A late train, approaching more and more noisily, made him feel a mixture of hope and dread. Sensing that the brief moment of time needed for him to try to regain his freedom was almost upon him, he started a series of contortions. First he forced his legs through the bars, then his body, and finally, with barely a millimetre to spare, his head. He lost his balance and, kicking his feet against the wall, pushed himself clear of the building. At the same time, he stretched his arms out, opening his derisory parachute as much as possible.

Before crashing to the ground, the fugitive seemed to resemble an acrobatic figure. The din of the train drowned out the cries that were forced from his throat despite himself. His body partially dislocated, he writhed in pain but remained conscious.

'I heard the sound of boots,' Joseph Brocard was to say later. 'I managed to roll over. I could make out a guard coming to the foot of the hedge under which I was hiding. A minute went by. I saw the German, whose silhouette stood out against the moonlight. He remained motionless and then urinated…almost all over me, then he left. After a moment, I started checking if my arms and legs worked. I was aching all over. The pain in my back became overwhelming. Like an animal on all fours or crawling, I managed nonetheless to get across several little gardens and reach a house where there was a light flickering…'

The poor man dragged himself to the door. Staggering, he managed to grasp the handle, enabling him to keep his balance. The people inside had heard strange noises. Someone opened the door unheedingly and the man in need of help suddenly lost his support and fell into the doorway.

Stunned, the residents Jean Menguy and his wife rushed to the stranger's aid, but there was no way that they could know that the man had fractured his spine! Their first efforts were therefore harmful. They tried to lift him, but he passed out. Panic-stricken, they laid him gently on a bed and wanted to call the hospital but the patient came to, early enough to stop them:

'Please don't do anything!' he cried out. 'No matter how bad my injuries are, I must get back to Paris at once. I've escaped from the German police and they'll soon see that I've disappeared. If they capture me, I'll most certainly be shot. What's more, I've implicated you.'

In spite of the danger they also faced, the Menguys did their utmost to help Joseph while they listened to his story. His chest and back were seriously injured and they wrapped them up tightly in an old sheet. Without further ado, the two men left taking infinite precautions, with Jean supporting Joseph. By a roundabout route, they reached the station where a train for the capital arrived a short while later.

The German gaolers had relaxed their watch during the night, but when they saw that the cell was empty, the bird was long gone.

'That chap's a real hero,' Michel Hollard was to say many times, evoking his trusted assistant's exploits. 'When he arrived at my HQ near the Gare de Lyon, I naturally asked the question, "Did you talk?"'

'He answered me, "No, Michel, I didn't, I swear!"'

'I was sure you didn't. I'll look after you and you'll be all right.'

Joseph Brocard admitted later with terrible honesty:

'After what I'd gone through, I could understand that those who sometimes couldn't hold their tongues had an excuse. If I'd been tortured any longer and if I'd been able to choose between death and a betrayal, I'm not sure I'd have had the strength to stick it out. They were real brutes!'[1]

Michel Hollard immediately telephoned his cousin, Professor Raoul Monod, a surgeon practising at the Hôpital des Diaconesses. As there was a risk that someone was listening in, he spoke in a roundabout way. The doctor nevertheless understood that his relative needed him for a fast and discreet meeting concerning a third person, and he organised things so that he could give him an appointment at the end of the afternoon.

By x-raying and examining him, the specialist was able to determine the extent of the injuries. The young man's first three lumbar vertebrae were crushed and displaced. The reflexes and sensations of his lower limbs had partly disappeared. For the time being, the surgeon put him through a series of painful, yet essential, manipulations, then wrapped him in a plaster cast.

The German police had a description and photograph of the fugitive and regularly checked the health services, as they did the hotels. Taking a huge risk, the management of the infirmary and the doctor decided to keep him in hospital secretly for eight days. After that, it was imperative for him to disappear, even though his fractures and lesions were still not consolidated. The safety of the hospital, as much as that of the patient, meant he had to be evacuated quickly to another place where he could convalesce.

Agir's boss looked for a suitable place to shelter him, first in the Paris region and then in the provinces. But none of the addresses offered Joseph Brocard both enough protection from police investigations and the medical facilities he needed.

Michel Hollard then offered to take him into Switzerland, if he felt strong enough to take on such a trip. After his terrible ordeals, the patient felt he could put up with the problems of a journey which, when all was said and done, was just routine. Despite unremitting pain and being a bit wobbly on his feet, he accepted this new undertaking.

As it was summer, the young man preferred to use the Jura route, in the region he came from. He knew the Cuenot's welcoming farm at Derrière-le-Mont and the Swiss customs officers at La Brévine.

The troubles started on the platform in the Gare de Lyon, fifteen minutes before they left. A conductor wanted to see their tickets, which the two men evidently didn't have. Michel Hollard was still counting on the railway workers' understanding and spirit of cooperation. He explained that the doctors had ordered the young invalid to convalesce out in the country. The conductor asked them to prove this by showing him the prescription. As an answer, the invalid unbuttoned his shirt and revealed his plaster cast. On it was a big Croix de Lorraine, between the bars of which had been written:

1er RÉGIMENT DE PARACHUTISTES
(1st Parachute Regiment)

The picture, made by a patient in the hospital, alluded to the prisoner's escape using a makeshift parachute. Joseph hadn't told his friend Michel Hollard about this imprudent drawing, so he was just as stunned as the SNCF conductor. Although he found the prank hilarious, he did make a disapproving face. As for the zealous conductor, he opened his eyes wide and, with a discreet nod, indicated to the two travellers they could board the train.

In 1994, on the fiftieth anniversary of the Liberation, Joseph Brocard took part in a France-Télévision programme shown by the FR3 channel as a tribute to Michel Hollard. In it, the fugitive evoked his trip to freedom:

> In those days, to get to the Jura Mountains from Paris you had to take a steam locomotive. No high-speed trains like today! The wheels continually vibrated and knocked on the disjointed rails of the period – knock knock…knock knock…knock knock – forcing me to lift myself up constantly with my arms to relieve the pain in my vertebrae and lighten my infernal plaster frame. At Besançon, a small local train was waiting to take us to the little station of Grand'Combe-Châteleu, some 6.25 miles separated us from the

> refuge at Derrière-le-Mont. It was an immense area which I walked across by a miracle, thanks to Michel's help. I thought it was the end of the world! I lay down on a bench. Our friends the Cuenots wanted to give me something to eat, but I couldn't swallow anything. They got a bed ready for me but Michel said: 'No, no, no, we must carry on at once while he's still warm. If we stop, he'll not be able to move any longer!'...So we kept on.

As soon as he returned to Paris, Michel Hollard told his family about the expedition:

> In this border zone, coming across any soldiers would have been fatal. Normally I only used the narrow and steep shortcuts. But, as my friend could only move with great difficulty, we had to take the paths that were easily passable, therefore more frequently patrolled by the Germans. There were still some miles to go through the woods and rocky areas. The slightest obstacle required such efforts from Joseph that he couldn't manage without my help. Exhausted and parched, he got some of his strength back by drinking at the source tapped by Paul Cuenot, towards the middle of the trip. The *montagnard*, always available when times were difficult, had gone on ahead to scout out the most dangerous part.
>
> From afar, we finally spotted his barn. The position of one of the doors, either wide open or shut, indicated whether he thought we could risk it or not and approach the border. At first, we were very anxious because the door was closed, but then I realised we were ahead of the agreed time. Sheltering under a thicket, we went through a long stressful moment until the reassuring silhouette of dear Paul arrived and opened the door in the right direction!
>
> In order to tackle the final leg, my companion drew on his last ounce of strength. He was worn out when we reached the border. I had to support him first on one side, then on the other, for the last few dozen yards. He became so weak that in the end I had to drag him backwards with my hands under his armpits. After a

> considerable effort, we got near to the little boundary wall. Although I too was exhausted, I had to lift him on my back.
>
> Weighed down by this dead weight, I had the greatest trouble making the final climb. A German enemy appearing now could still turn out to be fatal, even though we were in Switzerland. We only felt safe when I had lain him down, out of sight of the border. Thick fir trees protected us. We were surrounded by branches which made up a splendid backdrop conducive to contemplation.

A few moments to relax and meditate in this enchanted area restored some energy to the fugitives. Half an hour later, the Swiss customs officer on duty at the La Brévine post saw the two exhausted but euphoric men arriving.

The officer, André Gagnaux, the faithful partner and friend, was not long in joining them. He quickly had them accommodated in Neuchâtel. His brother agreed to take the wounded man into his own home temporarily while they waited for the military medical authorities to take over.[2] Until the end of the war, various Swiss specialists came to look after Joseph Brocard. They succeeded in considerably diminishing the consequences of his dramatic escape.[3]

Chapter 21

Eureka!

Rescuing Joseph Brocard, followed by getting him settled in Switzerland, had led to a nearly three-week delay in the schedule of investigations Michel Hollard had organised for himself, but a new, unforeseen event was soon to disrupt his schedule once and for all.

Madeleine Boulanger, the secretary of the now fictitious *gazogène* company, handed him a letter from Rouen. It came from an SNCF engineer working in that town, Jean-Henri Daudemard, who'd joined the Agir network a short time earlier. The letter was worded in such a way as to indicate that recent strategic observations in the area had revealed something that made the overall situation concerning, and what this was had to be found out urgently. As usual, when it came to something of the utmost importance, Michel Hollard personally took charge of the matter.

Rumours concerning new German inventions in the armaments sector were rife. People conjured up all sorts of fancy weapons. Some people even talked rather prematurely about a rocket.[1] Others alluded to composite projectiles and to various types of revolutionary bombers, huge cannon, or even new, supposedly invulnerable submarines. There was also talk of a mysterious 'death ray' intended for aerial defence. It was announced that this invisible beam would soon be capable of bringing down planes by paralysing them in the air.

Somehow, no one knows for sure, a man from Luxembourg managed to obtain O.P.'s address in Switzerland and barged into his office one day. His appearance was somewhat colourful but not without a certain dignity. The Englishman was disconcerted by the person's originality and had to make an effort to take him seriously. As for the visitor, he was a little wary at first, fearing the person he was talking to might suspect him of telling tall tales. He wanted to be absolutely certain that the important information he had would be passed on to the authorities in London.

After a long discussion, the atmosphere became more cordial. Then the visitor asked for some tools and, removing one of his shoes, took off the heel. A piece of paper appeared, folded several times and covered in dust, revealing a careful sketch with explanations. The document's author revealed that residents along the Baltic Sea coast had had the time to observe a curious winged, powered machine in flight. After a long trajectory over the water, it suddenly ran out of fuel and fell into the sea.

This information was corroborated by a spectacular discovery made on the island of Bornholm (Denmark). On 22 August 1943, while walking along the shore, a local inhabitant thought he could see the wreck of a plane far away, standing out against the skyline. He was bold enough to go near it and saw it was a sort of self-propelled flying machine weighted with cement. It was stuck in the sand and its original shape still seemed to be almost intact. The identification sign 'V83' was on the rudder. The crash must've taken place recently, but nobody in the neighbourhood had apparently noticed it yet.

Hasager Christiansen, a Danish naval officer who lived nearby, was alerted and came over to have a look at the strange kite. He sketched it, took pictures of it, wrote down some comments and somehow contrived to get all the information over to the secret services in London.

The English specialists at once noticed there were similarities between the machine that had fallen on Bornholm and the one described in the message brought earlier to Switzerland by the man from Luxembourg. Although both descriptions were rather simple, there was no doubt they depicted the same type of projectile.

***

The Peenemünde Centre, created in 1936 on Hitler's orders, had already been working for several years on new weapons without anyone knowing about it.[2] Indeed, even most Wehrmacht officers had no idea this research was taking place. However, the extremely secret installations in this veritable citadel took on such proportions that rumours ended up leaking out, and the Intelligence Service managed to get hold of some of the results of the experiments carried out in the rocketry domain from this supposedly impenetrable stronghold.

The two craft that had flown along the Baltic coast were not rockets, but unmanned planes. But how had these machines taken to the air and become lost? They were no doubt part of a prototype testing programme. The experts in London thought that to launch them, a fairly complex installation would have had to be set up either aboard powerful planes or on the ground, perhaps at the nearby Peenemünde base. Although it was premature to establish a definitive link between the flying machine seen on the island of Bornholm and the construction site at Auffay explored by Michel Hollard, the latter's report did create a sensation among the British.

'It may be that you've come across the preparations for the most terrible attack ever mounted against England. The outcome of the war may even depend upon it,' declared O.P. intuitively.

At the same time, the Allies were looking at a variety of strategies for their landings in Europe. However, the rumours announcing the appearance of apocalyptic weapons were spreading quickly. If the enemy had mastered some avant-garde technology and suddenly managed to spread death and destruction in the British capital, any plans to land and deploy Allied troops on the continent would be thwarted. The balance of power between the belligerents would suddenly be altered, running the risk of tipping in favour of the enemy.

London HQ's answer to the Frenchman's message was not long in coming, though he didn't know about it until he arrived back in Lausanne ten days or so later. He was asked to consider his investigations into the new enemy weapon as a priority over all his other intelligence leads. He was asked to start searching systematically for all the new installations.

But Michel Hollard hadn't waited for his contacts on the other side of the Channel to ask him to extend his investigations. At the Rouen social services department and on the site of his initial discovery at Bonnetot-le-Faubourg, he'd been given the names of several places where other buildings of the same type were springing up. Without hanging around, he'd gone to the vicinity of each site, all of which were closely guarded.

He held off from tempting fate needlessly and didn't try to enter any of the forbidden areas. By walking round each site on the outside, he quickly recognised that the layout was similar to the one he'd seen during his initial investigation. Nonetheless, he repeated his most risky move several times: taking a bearing of the launch ramp. Positioning himself parallel to it, he quickly looked down at his little scout's compass. The bearings he noted down were all directed at London.

These checks dispelled any lingering doubts he may have entertained. Despite all the mystery still surrounding these installations, he was now sure that a gigantic attack was being prepared.

To start searching for similar sites, a methodical hunt had to be organised. Five very good agents from the Agir team volunteered to go back and forth across the countryside, each with a bicycle and map. Michel Hollard split up the terrain and shared out the zones to be explored before returning to Lausanne where instructions from the War Office were waiting for him. The mission he was given corresponded to the initiatives he'd just taken!

The five men wearing worker's clothes each went their separate ways through Normandy, Picardy, and the Pas-de-Calais department, saying they were looking for work. This systematic criss-crossing of the countryside, coordinated by his young assistant, Pierre Carteron, bore fruit. In less than two months, the searchers located sixty or so similar installations, where the building was already well advanced.

The installations taken as a whole described a wide arc centred on London, which extended from the Cotentin Peninsula in Normandy to the Belgian border. The enemy were obviously planning vast destruction using a surprise attack, which was why they were protecting their secrets so fiercely.

Ever since he'd looked round one of the sites under construction, Michel Hollard kept on studying the plan he'd drawn up from memory. He tried in vain to see the logic of the way the strange buildings and concrete paths were set out. On the other hand, in his mind's eye he could clearly see the trajectories extending in a straight line from the ramps and converging on the English capital.

Chapter 22

Infiltration

To replace military personnel, almost all the German technical services tried to employ French civilians, but by doing so, they risked not being able to protect certain confidential details sufficiently. The previous year, an Agir network agent, Robert Rubenach, from Lorraine, had started looking for information on aerodromes. Helped by his good knowledge of German, he had not hesitated to get himself taken on in the administration department of a firm that depended on the famous Organisation Todt.[1] The information he collected led to the destruction of the airbase the enemy had set up at Bernes-sur-Oise, to the north of Paris, on the site of the present-day aerodrome at Persan-Beaumont.

One day, the office which Robert Rubenach worked with started advertising strange job offers, whereby the occupation authorities were offering an attractive package to the best qualified technicians. In exchange for an excellent salary, the chosen candidates had to agree to relocate for a while to 'a simple but healthy countryside setting'. Where they were to live was not specified, but they would be situated in a 'beautiful French provincial site'.

When Robert Rubenach told Michel Hollard about the advert, Hollard cried out, 'You can bet those jobs have something to do with what we're interested in! Somebody like you has to get one of those jobs. Will you do it?'

'They're not recruiting in my speciality. Besides, I can't give up what I'm working on at the moment. But André Comps, a young engineer friend of mine in my outfit, has probably got the required qualifications. He's a very serious technician. He is, however, very timid, excessively so, reserved. As I think I can vouch for his discretion, we should organise a meeting for the three of us.'

Listening to what the other two had to say, the young man was flabbergasted. Up until then, he'd devoted himself entirely to his job, which he liked a lot. However, like a lot of his fellow countrymen, he'd resigned himself to working for the Germans.

The two Resistance workers explained to him that, strangely enough, as luck would have it, he now had the opportunity to do his country a big favour by agreeing to apply for this job. After mulling it over for a long time, the young engineer ended up letting himself be persuaded and went off to ask to be transferred. His brilliant results in the technical tests he was asked to sit earned him an offer for the post almost immediately, and he was assigned to 'an important job as an industrial draughtsman, in an establishment in Picardy'. He was made to sign a contract which, in substance, specified in particular: 'The interested party will be informed of where he's going to be living the day before he starts. He'll be given regular leave and will have to respect the essential rules of discretion.'

The 'countryside setting' and 'beautiful French provincial site' promised in the job offer turned out, in reality, to be rather rudimentary premises in the middle of an industrial area; a rural environment admittedly, but with none of yesteryear's pastoral charm.

The place, called Bois Carré, was not far from the village of Yvrench, near Abbeville in northern France. The engineer had been informed by Robert Rubenach of the recent investigations the Agir network had made in the region and Bois Carré was one of the sites that had been pointed out. Looking at the still unfinished site, the newcomer soon had to give up trying to understand how it all fitted in. His task was to make drawings and models, finishing off the layout of a series of sites in Picardy, under the supervision of a chief engineer.

After a week, the engineer, whose work seemed to satisfy his superiors, asked for and was granted permission to take a weekend off. Without a moment's hesitation, he rushed off to Paris, where Michel Hollard and Robert Rubenach were there waiting for him.

'How you describe the Bois Carré site confirms what we have seen for ourselves,' the boss stated. 'In spite of all the information we've accumulated, we unfortunately still don't understand very much about how this catapult works, nor what it's catapulting. But, right under your nose, important parts of the puzzle seem to be falling into place bit by bit. Are you ready to go the whole hog?'

'What you're asking is quite impossible. I'm not free.'

'It's a race against time we're up against here. If nothing's done to stop them, the Germans will try to impose their rule over the whole world, and spread terror using all sorts of unheard-of weapons. At this moment, what they're building all points towards London and it's almost finished. We must get hold of the exact description of one of the sites. You must know we're counting on you to get this essential piece of information!'

'But they watch every move I make, and anyway, I don't have access to all the files.'

'Listen, I don't know you very well yet. But the fact you're here is proof that you're brave and Robert here has spoken highly of you. Your skills have got you into what is probably a unique position with the enemy. Although it's dangerous, the position will no doubt give you the unhoped-for opportunity to make a mess of their dreadful intentions.'

Until then, Michel Hollard had never had to speak severely to one of his agents, neither had he ever had to resort to giving a direct order. His agents operated as they wished, especially when they had dangerous assignments. Luck had just provided him with the right man who could, without any doubt, obtain extremely important information. But in the face of danger, the man was understandably reluctant.

Michel Hollard, who was himself constantly in danger, put himself in the other man's shoes. He felt the same way, which he'd often experienced, but this time, because the situation was exceptional, for once he had to give a direct order.

'It's absolutely vital for us to get hold of the overall plans of a typical base, with its group of outbuildings and the strange path leading to the ramp. The English have obviously only got a rather vague, partial sketch I drew from memory.'

'At the moment, there's just no way I can see myself copying the documents that cross my desk. Anything like that would be suicidal, because my neighbour is suspicious and hardly ever leaves me by myself. But he's going to be away soon, so I hope to have some peace and quiet then. If there's enough time, I'll try to copy at least part of the plans.'

'Anything you can get will be welcome. Have you any idea of what they need to do to finish off the installations?'

'The main sections of the technical disposition are still unknown. As far as I know, nothing has appeared on any of the sites. My German boss has the plan, of course, but he keeps it to himself. He goes to different areas of the base regularly, unfolds his precious document, aims it carefully at something and writes things down. This paper is most certainly the answer to your last question, but the blighter unfortunately never leaves it behind!... But we must hurry. Nobody in Yvrench knows I'm here and I mustn't miss my train!'

'We'll have to meet again in a fortnight. That should give you enough time to do what you have to do. Let's fix a date!'

'I'm not sure I'll be able to get time off.'

'Well, call in sick! If you pretend to be ill with enough conviction, the doctors can't always tell if you're faking or not. So, it's up to you to put on an act. In a few days' time, start pretending to have persistent stomach pains that are getting worse, until they become unbearable. Then you say that only the specialised medical team at the Hôpital Saint-Louis can get rid of them. I'll warn the head of department, he's one of our friends.'

'I don't think I'm any good at acting.'

'Tell me truthfully, are you frightened?'

'Of course I am!'

'I appreciate your honesty. I too struggle against fear. It oppresses me almost all the time, but we're soldiers serving our country, justice and freedom. The importance of what's at stake means we have to make an exceptional effort! I must add that if you don't go through with it, you'll be considered as a deserter... Will you be back here in a fortnight?'

'I'll try. Goodbye.'

'You have to pull this off. Bon voyage!'

Michel Hollard later recognised that circumstances had made him be hard and inflexible, which went against his own temperament and philosophy. He still had doubts about how bold André Comps could be, since up until then the way he behaved had been rather undecided and submissive. It wasn't long before events showed that Comps had been heartened by his spirited encouragement.

Shortly after returning to Yvrench, the make-believe collaborator was by chance left to his own devices. Indeed, on several occasions, his boss, wearing his *Feldgrau* uniform, was confident enough to leave Comps by himself for several hours.

Their office was a two-roomed wooden hut and the draughtsman had a good clear view of the outside from his table. It was as if he were there lying in ambush, behind the window where he sat all the time. From there, he could spot any undesirable visitor in time to do what was needed to protect himself, so he therefore took advantage of this temporarily favourable situation so he could secretly copy the plans.

But the main document, the layout which described the final item of the set-up, was still inaccessible. This top-secret drawing was carefully folded in the inside pocket of either the German's coat or his raincoat, and the draughtsman's fascination about it became obsessive.

The holder of this 'treasure', an unimaginative but perfectly well-disciplined officer, carried out his every move according to an immutable ritual. The French employee, admiring him in his innermost mind as much as he found him amusing, never ceased to observe this character discreetly. If the latter left the office for any length of time, he would always wear his impeccable coat proudly. When he returned to the office, he would carefully put it on a hanger and hang it on a hook.

Except for food and rest, most of this model soldier's workdays were marked by satisfying his other most vital, more humdrum, need; after a short solitary walk, the man went to the toilet.

The observer took no time noticing that when he went off on one of these calls of nature, the man sometimes neglected his appearance and went there in his shirtsleeves. When there was no rain to put him off, he often left his coat – containing the precious plan – behind in the office, quite unaware of the consequences that lowering his guard might have.

To get to the rustic lavatory, the officer had to walk some 50 or so yards across the site, and from his privileged observation post, the Frenchman could watch him on part of his stroll. Timing each of the man's short visits, he noted that his absences were never less than four minutes. Moreover, these times were not reduced if the man went out without his coat.

As Michel Hollard had predicted, luck gave the young technician a chance to discover the very important secret. The idea of getting hold of the paper and copying at least the broad outline while the man was away started to haunt him and upset his sleep. For three days in a row, he carried on timing his supervisor's walks; there was no variation either in the time they took or in their gravity.

One morning, now almost certain how invariable the routine was, André Comps decided he'd steal the plan at the next opportunity. That day, the weather was warm and dry, prompting the German to take his traditional walk in his shirtsleeves. Watching from behind the window, the observer consulted his watch. Driven on by a sudden impulse, he rushed into the neighbouring room and, hardly trembling, grabbed the document. Back at his post, he checked that the officer was still quietly on his walk. Even before the man had disappeared behind the lavatory door, using a sheet of tracing paper, the engineer managed to draw the outline of something no one except the enemy specialists knew anything about until then. He understood at first glance that the famous ramp pointing towards London was going to be fitted with two metal rails sloping slightly upwards.

The plan confirmed it was a big structure for launching missiles. In less than three minutes, the engineer did his best to copy the drawing, keeping in mind he could always improve his inevitably succinct copy later. He just had time to note down the main points, the exact bearing and the upwards angle of the ramp before the soldier reappeared, but he was still far away enough from the office for the plan to be put back in its hiding place in time.

In the euphoria of what he'd accomplished, the Frenchman strictly followed the directive his network leader had given him and declared he wasn't feeling well. Indeed, he was so convincing that he almost came to feel the pain from which he claimed to suffer! Although the doctor was puzzled, he allowed him to interrupt his work for four days so he could go to Paris to be looked after.

André Comps turned up on time for his meeting that had been arranged in such a haphazard way two weeks earlier. The invaluable documents he brought with him made Hollard very enthusiastic.

'I wasn't expecting so much from you,' he exclaimed. 'I'm happy to note that although you don't say much, you do act forcefully. With most people it's the opposite; they're all talk and no action. Your report reveals a lot, but I don't think I'll really understand it. In its present form, only you can decipher the symbols you've used.

'So that our English friends have plans and information they can understand, we must put together a report which I'll take to my contact in Switzerland. But for the next ten days or so these documents won't be safe at all. First, I have to take them from Paris to Lausanne; on that trip I have to face all the usual dangers. Then they go in the diplomatic bag from Switzerland to England. In wartime, the last part of the journey is particularly fraught with danger and the protection is only relative.

'If the enemy were to get hold of an English letter containing the plans of the Yvrench Bois Carré site, you'll obviously be uncovered! So, before you go back to your job, you'll have to wait for my instructions. I'll make sure your medical leave is extended to sort out your situation.'

Professor Raoul Monod worked as a surgeon not only in the Clinique des Diaconesses but also in the Hôpital Saint-Louis. In order not to arouse the suspicions of the enemy police, and to cover his tracks, he had the administration of the second hospital step in and certify that the engineer was in bad shape. With such guarantees, the would-be patient officially became a person unfit for work.

According to the regulations, the attestation was duly sent to the military authorities at Yvrench. In these rather doubtful legitimate conditions, the Resistance workers sought somewhere peaceful where they could work in relative safety. A friend living in the suburbs gave them the hospitality and the calm they needed.

The documentation the draughtsman had smuggled out from under the very nose of his German employer consisted of various diagrams, all independent from each other. To put them in order, he had to remember and piece together several details that were missing on his sheets, and also make sense of the scribbling he'd done so hurriedly during the soldier's walk to the latrines.

Sorting it out took four days, after which the two Resistance workers were able to get an idea, for the first time, of what the almost-finished site was like. The English specialists obviously already knew of some of the puzzle, but there were gaps which stopped them from putting the pieces together properly. What was missing was a plan of the whole site and this was what their French ally was just about to give them.

During the following night and morning, the Agir network leader travelled from Paris to Lausanne without any problems. With the file in his hands, O.P., his contact and friend, wasted no time sending it to London with absolute priority. The diplomatic bags could only circulate thanks to the goodwill of supposedly neutral messengers, who had to follow complicated routes and cross occupied or belligerent countries, not without risk.

The network leader could have stayed quietly in Switzerland and waited for confirmation that the documents had been put into the right hands, but the idea of twiddling his thumbs during this time didn't even occur to him. Almost instinctively, he slipped back over the border and, to make the most of the days he had to spare, he set up a round trip of southeast France to meet some of his agents and to collect any available intelligence. His life was fraught with unforeseen events which led him often to improvise in this way.

He had just returned to Lausanne when the Intelligence Service contact received a priority coded telegram from London. It was the acknowledgment of receipt they'd been expecting, terse but eloquent: 'Booty arrived safely. Congratulations.'

In the War Office, the plan of the Yvrench Bois Carré site, as well as a list of similar launch sites carefully spotted by the network, were duplicated at once and copies were handed out to the RAF reconnaissance pilots.

A short while later, in November 1943, a plane piloted by a certain Harold Erwin Merlin was shot down during a mission over northwest France. He managed to bail out unhurt and escaped capture. He was also lucky enough to be picked up by Frenchmen, who got him to the British Embassy in Bern. Amongst some of the papers he'd managed to save from the crash, the diplomats came across a diagram of the enemy structures, as well as a list of where they'd been built. These pages in part reproduced the latest files that Michel Hollard had recently sent to the London authorities.

***

However, whilst the Allies now knew what most of the components were and where the new enemy infrastructures were located, what was still missing was the main element. They didn't know with any certainty what sort of machine was going to be catapulted. The plans they had thanks to Michel Hollard and André Comps only included the ramp pointing towards London; the German engineers, the authors of the original drawings, had wisely left out the missile. Moreover, around the sites the Agir network had already reconnoitred, nobody had yet seen any planes arriving or anything that looked as if it was designed to fly.

The experts obviously didn't disregard the brief descriptions of large flying objects that had been sent to them in turn by the eccentric man from Luxembourg and the Danish officer on the island of Bornholm. After flying over the Peenemünde base several times at high altitude, Allied observers were now certain that these casual eyewitness accounts, even though they were a bit vague, were quite serious. Despite the camouflage the German test centre used, photographs revealed a launch site almost identical to the Yvrench Bois Carré site. On one of them, they could clearly make out a pilotless plane ready for flight.

Chapter 23

The Monster in its Lair

Shortly afterwards, suspicious-looking equipment reached Normandy on the quiet. André Bouguet, stationmaster at Rouen-Rive-Droite and agent in the Agir network, kept a close eye on the train movements of military goods either stopping in his station or passing through it. One day, his attention was drawn to a flat wagon with an unusual load. Between the planks of a transport crate, he could see strange, large-size metal objects, cylindrical or tapering.

Noting that the destination of the parcels was Auffay, the stationmaster was quick to inform Michel Hollard. The launch site being built that Hollard had explored at Bonnetot-le-Faubourg was indeed located in the area of the same railway station. He reacted immediately:

'That must be to complete one of the existing platforms in the region.'[1]

The impatience the enemy officers showed because the sites hadn't been finished betrayed the fact they intended to use them shortly.

To risk going alone near equipment that was so well guarded would've been utter madness, but Michel Hollard could rely on the help of Pierre Carteron, one of his clever assistants who had already shown great skill digging up certain German installations scattered throughout several departments. Both men set off for Auffay at once.

The small town's stationmaster, René Bourdon, was also a patriot and was on good terms with his colleague, André Bouguet, in Rouen. Michel Hollard, knowing he was in good company, went up to him confidently:

'A big army shipment very likely passed through here recently. Do you know what's happened to it?'

The stationmaster reacted immediately. He pointed to a little shed not far from the station, along the platform. The shed was separate from the SNCF buildings, but it was linked to the railway network and had been requisitioned by the German Army, which watched it night and day.

Without anyone noticing them, the two men watched the approaches to the little building. A guard walked back and forth for about 20 yards on either side of an opening hidden behind a tarpaulin. When he reached the end of his walk, for a second his field of vision didn't quite take in the entrance to the shed. Counting on this weak point, the two men put together their plan. To give one of them time to sneak inside the building, the other had to divert the guard's attention during that particular moment when he lowered his guard.

Pierre Carteron had just the cunning, presence of mind and playfulness needed for the situation. Calling on his meagre knowledge of German, he played his part cleverly:

'*Guten Tag!*' (Good day!)

The soldier was surprised to hear himself addressed in his own language. Then, no doubt not too upset at finding an opportunity to make his guard duty a little less boring, he slowed down and muttered the same greeting in answer, giving Michel Hollard enough time to slip into the building.

The contrast between the bright light outside and the dark inside prevented him from seeing anything but a dark mass in the middle of the shed. Little by little, his sight grew accustomed to the dark and revealed a flat wagon loaded with big black objects. Several indistinct shapes, all enclosed inside slatted crates, came out in turn from the darkness, with varied contours and volumes, some of them cylindrical, some of them partly truncated cones. When put together, all these elements seemed designed to form some sort of long fuselage.

He leapt onto the wagon floor. As well as the big parts, he discovered others, less apparent but just as impressive: various flat, rectangular crates, no doubt parts of the wings, and strange spheres and long tubing, flared on one side and tapered on the other. All these pieces were no doubt part of an unassembled flying machine. The visitor sketched them in his notepad, then, using a tape from Yvonne Hollard's sewing box, he measured each of the components.

Meanwhile, the other man had managed to carry on talking with the guard in a humorous tone, alternating between the two languages. Once the ice had been broken, the chatterboxes moved on to more saucy subjects.

Their tall stories lasted a full hour, the time limit fixed with Michel Hollard. He could only get out of the shed if his partner managed to distract the guard's attention for a few more moments. As he waited behind the tarpaulin, the talkers passed just in front of him, then their progressively diminishing voices and steps signalled they were moving away. Hollard's accomplice was careful to face the shed so that the guard was forced to look in the opposite direction. Through a gap, Hollard saw that the German was looking the other way and didn't wait for the two men to finish their round to part the tarpaulin and run away.

He hurried back to his Paris headquarters near the Gare de Lyon. There, he copied out his sketches and drew up, before he forgot it all, as detailed and complete a description as possible of the various elements of the unassembled machine. From this shelter, without even resting for a moment, he set off once again for Switzerland, intending to snooze on the train.

The London authorities only knew the shape of the flying machine from the eyewitness accounts of observers who'd come across the prototype's trials by chance, and their information was obviously approximate and conjectural. From the hands of Michel Hollard, the War Office specialists now had the first sketch and the first comments drawn from directly observing a production series machine. After the war, it was noticed that despite the extraordinarily dangerous conditions involved in getting into the shed at Auffay, the Frenchman had taken the measurements with a margin of error of less than 10 per cent.

***

When all the concrete-work for the future launch ramps was finished, the Germans let go of several workers who were no longer allowed on the sites, replacing them with Luftwaffe fitters to carry out the final technical assembly.

Thanks to the complicity André Comps was able to benefit from in the hospitals, he was now coming to the end of his period of so-called convalescence, and the moment came when the French administration could no longer consider him as ill. He therefore had to overcome his feeling of dread and return to his workplace at Yvrench Bois Carré, where he was badly needed.

When he did return to the base, he didn't feel anyone was suspicious. He was reassured to some extent and was unsurprised that he no longer had access to the now secret area of the launch platform, where the military technicians were busy. Despite his freedom being thus restricted, he was able to estimate that the development work, before the first missile was to be launched, would be going on for at least another three or four months.

Michel Hollard received the news of this minimum delay at about the same time he received information on the progress rate at other similar sites. Everywhere things were progressing at about the same rate. The German personnel, however, were showing signs of increasing nervousness. Officers were seen to behave impatiently both with their own subordinates and the public. It was easy to imagine that by trying to speed things up, they were only obeying orders from higher up.

Hitler and his staff were no doubt deluding themselves if they believed all this new equipment would escape their future victims' attention.[2] With the Allies' best agents having devoted themselves for months to finding and examining the mysterious weapons being assembled, the launching of them was no longer likely to catch the British authorities completely off guard. The information from the latest enquiries by Michel Hollard and his agents reached London early enough for the English to take emergency measures.

The British authorities didn't react prematurely and even pretended not to know the new constructions existed. By flying over them at very high altitude, RAF reconnaissance aircraft stealthily carried out photographic sorties, among which were several shots backing up the information supplied by the Agir team.

Near the areas concerned, several members of the network were becoming impatient. Their reports, duly acknowledged by the War Office, included new lists of platform sites with accurate locations, and because they were sure they'd correctly described the targets to be destroyed, the Resistance workers were expecting bomber squadrons to appear at any moment. But the days went by and no friendly planes appeared. The French partisans waited interminably, watching the sword of Damocles hanging over London's head, not immediately understanding the logic of why.

The Allies evidently had no chance of averting the danger unless they attacked before the Germans fired. Choosing the right day for the aerial offensive they set up was, as it was for the Normandy landings five and a half months later, one of the most crucial choices of the whole war. A host of tactical, technical, meteorological and, naturally, human parameters had to be considered. The suspense continued until just before Christmas.

Then, on 22 December 1943, despite the omnipresent and fearsomely effective flak,[3] the RAF bombers finally came in over the targets. The raid had the desired effect. That day, the English bombers flattened a dozen bases that were almost ready to attack, but the Germans pulled themselves together quickly and protected their other sites by bringing into play all the land, air and sea means at their disposal. Merciless fighting raged in the skies of north-western France and over the sea. The Allied air forces, despite heavy losses, continued to pound the new infrastructures, which a week later had been reduced by a third. At the end of January, seventy-nine out of almost 100 first-generation launch sites had been damaged.

The Bonnetot-le-Faubourg base, near Auffay, which Michel Hollard had discovered and explored, was one of the sites that had been hardest hit. At Bois Carré, Yvrench, the only part of the base left standing more or less intact was the little house André Comps used as an office. His German boss ordered Comps to go examine various other neighbouring sites which had been less severely hit so that he could do what was needed to make them operational again quickly. In truth, the programme to destroy the London area with V-1s had been delayed, if not seriously compromised.

After the devastating air raids at Bois Carré, some of the German personnel started looking askance at the Frenchman. In addition to the material damage, the soldiers were very shaken and counted their casualties. The engineer was looked on with suspicion at first and then the attitude became openly hostile. The military police were alerted and sent inspectors to interrogate André Comps. Getting wind of the danger, however, he managed to disappear in time. Hiding in a far-removed corner of the Paris region, he was able to escape the Germans and lived out the last months of the occupation there.

***

It was only because the Anglo-American air forces were considerably reinforced that the operation to rid the regions of these launch sites could be carried out. For the time being, they had to stop assaulting other targets so they could attack the launch pads. Faced with an enemy equipped with state-of-the-art weapons, Sir Winston Churchill, in contrast, called this battle Operation Crossbow, referring to the medieval weapon.

When these special air raids were being prepared, the bomber crews used not only the usual maps and sets of aerial photographs, but also scale models of the launch sites, which had been made using the documentation supplied by Michel Hollard and André Comps.

To further improve the precision of the bombings, the American general, George Marshall, took the initiative to build copies of the sites very quickly, respecting the volumes, the thickness of concrete and the resistance of all the components. They were put up in Florida, in an area where crews were allowed to practice destroying them. These dummy buildings were built using the same materials as those of the enemy.

The similarities between the imitations and the real sites were even taken a step further, with the fake launch pads camouflaged in the same way. To make the training even more realistic, they were equipped with flak batteries firing fireworks to give the illusion of the enemy shooting back.

Faced with the destruction of the sites that the Reich specialists had set up so carefully, the German experts were now forced to change their strategy. Realising that the Anglo-Americans knew about the V-1s, they didn't even try to restore some of the slightly hit buildings that were too easily spotted from the sky. And when they did carry out work on the ruined sites, it was more often to decoy enemy observers as to their real intentions.

On the other hand, they resumed their search in the countryside for better locations. The engineer Helmut Walter designed and had new, much simpler ramps built, made up of prefabricated sections.[4] In order to hide them from aerial reconnaissance, they were carefully incorporated into the natural environment, far better than they had been previously. The maritime and wooded regions of the Pas-de-Calais, Nord, Somme, Seine-Maritime, Eure, Calvados and Manche departments were dotted with these new installations, almost all of them concealed in the undergrowth or camouflaged as farm buildings.[5]

In Lausanne, Michel Hollard was told about the result of the air raids carried out by the Allied air forces on the first V-1 sites. As soon as he learnt of the new, simplified launch ramps, quite apart from the older ones, he told his agents, who were already well qualified in the domain, to start looking for the new ones.[6]

Chapter 24

Betrayal and Arrest

The pace of the network chief's activities had become so hectic that there were long periods of time when he was unable to see his family. There was no security at the house in Saint-Rémy-lès-Chevreuse but this didn't stop him from making a brief appearance to celebrate Christmas 1943 with his loved ones. Towards mid-January, he suddenly reappeared in the house. Yvonne Hollard couldn't help showing how worried she was, more than she'd been before. For an instant, upset by his wife's distress and beset by forebodings, he was tempted to give in, but once the moment had passed, he became his old, determined self again.

'The way we're living at the moment is difficult for you, it's true, I know,' he said. 'But if I were to shirk my responsibilities it wouldn't be worthy of me, especially as my role is perhaps now more important than it's ever been, when we have definite advantages that mean victory will soon be ours! Luck and persistence, together with the help of devoted agents, have permitted me to find the enemy's terrible weapons which, if left unchecked, could draw us further into a world catastrophe.'

After telling his wife and children how he'd explored the shed at Auffay, where one of the horrible flying machines was hidden, he continued:

> As quickly as possible, I naturally transmitted a description of the machine to the Allies, together with diagrams. For several weeks now, our friends have also had the lists I made of the secret building sites intended for launching these machines. They at last decided the moment had come to bomb these sites. Ten or so days after their first air raid, the result was so impressive the Germans had to change their plans!
>
> One of my agents in Picardy kept an eye on the comings and goings of certain officers billeted in the Château de Ribeaucourt in

> the Somme. He noted that every one of these officers went to one of the neighbouring sites every day, and to a disused school where they joined the others. These gentlemen are obviously not going there to play a game of cards! They are getting ready for the next offensive, which is what we are trying to foil.
>
> This information was part of my latest message which left Lausanne for London.[1] In the same message I also told the Allies about the aircraft that had recently landed at Villacoublay, the nearest aerodrome to Paris.[2]

Despite his heavy heart when leaving his family the next day, Michel Hollard tried to overcome his emotions and gently resist any displays of affection that might make him turn away from his mission.

He was on his way to meet Pierre Carteron, his assistant whose clever thinking had enabled him to get right next to the first V-1 to arrive unassembled in Auffay railway station. The man had willingly agreed to take over looking for and keeping an eye on the launch sites. He carried on going back and forth across the countryside, taking on the job of coordinating a small team of investigators spread out in the suspected area. Even to these seasoned researchers, broadening the search zones revealed several installations which, as they'd escaped notice, had been left untouched by the raids.

Michel Hollard reached Lausanne with a new and substantial file whose contents were immediately cabled to London. Ever since the end of the summer, discovering new German war equipment had been taking almost all his time. He'd found himself forced to neglect quite a few agents who were working for him in different regions, and whose information was often essential. It was starting to pile up. So, before going back to the V-1 theatre operational in north-western France, he decided to devote some time to these agents, who were frequently isolated and had been waiting for him in vain and were getting worried.

This tour around the regions of occupied France was to be his last. At the end of January 1944, he secretly crossed over into Switzerland for the forty-ninth time. His English contact and friend, O.P., was alarmed by the fact that he was obviously overworking.

'You've done a tremendous amount of outstanding work which is now starting to bear fruit. Even if your cooperation were to cease today, what you've obtained for us would certainly remain one of the most important parts of what we know about the enemy's new weapons.

'I'm very pleased to announce that as a token of its recognition for all the strategic intelligence you've given us since May 1941, England is preparing to give you an exceptional award. But, just by looking at you, I'm not sure how long you'll be able to continue at the rate you're going. You must rest. Please accept our offer of a two-week stay in the mountains.'

The Frenchman started.

'Thank you. I'm touched and honoured by the personal initiatives you've taken and by those of your country, but I couldn't even imagine interrupting my mission before our struggles are victorious and we've won.

'My face is no doubt a bit drawn, but I am fit enough. My agents are totally devoted and I can't be absent at the moment. Besides, I've already agreed to meet some of them next week. As for my family, I've had to neglect them these last months. They're asking after me insistently and I can't wait to see them again, albeit for a moment.

'I'm very grateful, however, for such signs of appreciation from you and your country. I hope that the day will come when we can look forward to friendly get-togethers more serenely.'

After turning down the tempting offer of a holiday, Michel Hollard also rejected the idea that he needed a rest. However, his toughness, after living as an outlaw for two and a half years, had certainly been weakened. Lack of sleep and irregular, second-rate meals had no doubt taken its toll on him more than the actual physical effort. He'd done a lot of enquiring and researching, covered huge distances not only by train but also by bike and on foot across plains and mountains, in all seasons and in all weathers. His endurance, too, was obviously diminished, but he wouldn't admit any of this and pushed on with his mission regardless, with his usual stubbornness.

In his conscience as the network leader, there was another reason, quite separate from his state of health, which prevented him from halting his activities even for a moment. Every day this man, convinced of the immortality of the soul, devoted a moment to meditation and, in thought, joined his fallen or captive friends. The bad luck that had struck several of his companions-in-arms was a major reason for prompting him to continue the struggle at whatever the cost, as long as he had the strength to do so.

***

On the evening of 4 February 1944, Michel Hollard turned up unexpectedly at the family home, the expression on his face as fervent and determined as ever, but tinged with unusual gravity. As always, his wife Yvonne tried to hide her anxiety, especially in the presence of her children. This time, however, she cried out in anguish in front of them: 'Michel, the devil is after you. I beg you, go into hiding before it's too late!'

She knew her husband had recently met a certain Comte de Kergoat, who'd introduced himself as an aeronautical engineer. He was supposedly the inventor of a landing system for touching down on short strips and said he wanted the Allies to benefit from it.

The impression the so-called count made on Michel Hollard was not very positive, even though the smooth talker had said he was recommended by Simone Boirel, the hotelkeeper and informer at Pierrelatte, herself quite above suspicion. A few weeks earlier, she'd come across an old acquaintance of hers she thought she could trust, but this woman was a dangerous fraud. Once she knew about her friend's patriotic engagement, she hurried off to tell everything to her fiancé, who was none other than this so-called Comte de Kergoat... After they'd succeeded in convincing Simone Boirel they wanted to join the Resistance, the couple cleverly wheedled the Agir boss' professional address out of her.

Early in the morning of 5 February, Michel Hollard had all the trouble in the world tearing himself away from his home. Having had a premonition, his wife tried desperately to hold him back using simple, wise arguments. She even went as far as to grasp his legs, throwing herself onto the ground to prevent him from leaving.

During the previous week, the sham couple had come several times to the *gazogène* company offices in the hope of being able to meet the former manager. Following the usual instructions, Madeleine Boulanger, the secretary, had tried in vain to put off the unwelcome visitors. However, far from being discouraged, they kept hammering away and told an intriguing tale.

'We're sorry to disturb you again, but we just have to,' said the so-called count. 'A friend of ours is being chased by the Nazis and is currently facing arrest and death. As far as we know, the only person who can help prevent such a tragedy is Monsieur Hollard. We just have to speak to him. It's urgent!'

These charlatans, just as persuasive as they were unscrupulous, succeeded in fooling the secretary. Her initial suspicion having given way to worry, she was moved by the news she'd received with such assurance. Like Simone Boirel, she let herself be taken in by grandeur and noble words.

'I can't get in touch with my boss before tonight,' the secretary told them, apologising. 'However, if the case you want to discuss really is so serious and urgent, you can try and consult him briefly at 6.15 pm in the Café des Chasseurs. It's a bistro near the Gare du Nord, 176 Rue du Faubourg Saint-Denis.'[3]

An unlucky sequence of events had obliged Michel Hollard to put off several meetings and, due to lack of time, group them all together. He didn't like doing this because, inevitably, the meeting would be less discreet than usual. When he reached the café at the agreed time, the only members of the network present were Henri Dujarier, Joseph Legendre and Jules Mailly. The latter, without a word, handed over his report to him immediately. Michel Hollard had barely settled down in his seat when he heard a woman's voice calling him. Very surprised, he went to join her, away from everyone else.

'Monsieur Hollard,' she begged in a whisper, 'I must bother you because a man's life is threatened by the Nazis. You're his last hope. Please, help him to get to Switzerland!'

'Listen, Mademoiselle, this isn't the place to talk about this sort of thing. See my secretary and I'll have a look at his case.'

'But, Monsieur Hollard, it's very urgent. They're going to arrest him!'

The charm had worked so well that the Resistance fighter, in turn worried, invited her to go with him to an empty table.

Just as he was going to sit down opposite her, a loud, curt voice was heard from the middle of the café, shocking everyone and stopping all conversation.

'Nobody move! *Polizei!*'

Several plain-clothed inspectors armed with revolvers rushed at Michel Hollard, who barely had time to covertly discard the papers Jules Mailly had just given him. A few moments later, with his hands cuffed behind his back, Michel Hollard was dragged outside. Credit where credit is due. To transfer this distinguished prisoner to their premises, an escort of three men and a private car had been arranged. Such a privilege was not granted to his companions in misfortune. Duly escorted by their guards, they had to squeeze into another vehicle.

Being late for a meeting was not habitual for any of the Agir members, but when Madeleine Boulanger, Lucien François and Robert Rubenach arrived in sight of the bistro, the Gestapo just was finishing off its raid. Being two or three minutes late this time had just saved the three of them! From afar, the secretary recognised the informer in the group of prisoners. To allay any suspicions, the Nazis made her share the fate of her victims...[4]

The convoy of prisoners went across Paris and ended up in Auteuil, in front of a beautiful residence.[5] The Gestapo and the Abwehr, united so they could carry out certain activities, had set up a very special service there and referred to it with the euphemistic title, 'Division of Special Interrogations'.

Chapter 25

The Abyss

As soon as they arrived, the prisoners were seen separately into a vast office where four brutes, apparently not inclined to be kind, were waiting for them. Two of them were playing ostentatiously with bludgeons, whips and cudgels, among other blunt instruments. However, during this brief first contact, they contented themselves with nonchalantly cradling their cruel props.

Without any preamble and peremptorily, one of these characters ordered each of the prisoners to state why he was present at the Café des Chasseurs. Like most agents, the members of the network had already prepared a reason for what they were doing if they were arrested. Joseph Legendre and Henri Dujarier had a fairly good alibi. As they both held cards showing they were *gazogène* sales representatives, they were supposedly meeting the company boss to report on their recent commercial activities. Jules Mailly, a railway worker at Le Bourget station, could just about pass for the man organising SNCF transport for all the equipment made by the Autobloc factory in Dijon.

Michel Hollard was the only one of the four not to have a means of getting out of the situation; the file the Germans had put together on him contained a lot of damning proof. The inspectors were congratulating each other as they looked sadistically at the quarry they'd been chasing for the last year and a half and had only been able to capture because he had been betrayed.

To get his agents off the hook, the leader was ready to take all the blame, hoping their individual accounts would agree both with each other and with his own. The smallest discrepancy, or a few moments of confusion, would no doubt have ruined what his friends had to say in their defence.

As far as he was personally concerned, Michel Hollard had decided to present himself quite simply as a still-active French officer. It seemed to him right and fair to present himself to his enemies as a combatant from both world wars who had to carry out his patriotic duty right up to the very end, given that he considered the Franco-German Armistice of 1940 as an unacceptable agreement.

He was ready to declare bluntly to the interrogators what they already knew; that he was engaged alongside England, an ally of Free France. Trying to deny such a fact would no doubt have aggravated the situation of the other captives, without reducing the danger for himself. Michel Hollard was brought in after his three agents.

'Why were you hiding at the back of the bistro?'

'I wasn't hiding, I was handling routine business with my assistants.'

'What type of business? And why in a café?'

'We are *gazogène* specialists, as you probably know. My assistants live in the northern suburbs of Paris. They can easily join me by train at the bar in front of the station where they arrive. Legendre is head of our sales division. He came to meet Dujarier, who was getting ready to represent the company at trade fairs. As for Mailly, I'd called him in to talk about organising the transport of equipment by train. Due to the lack of fuel, and the increasing scarcity of fuel for the *gazogènes*, we can no longer rely on the lorries…'

While he was talking, a German officer entered, eliciting signs of deference from the four individuals, who were quite clearly his subordinates. The man would probably have appeared affable without the torturers present. He interrupted what the prisoner was saying.

'Monsieur, your explanations are of no interest to us.'

Saying this, he gestured imperatively and disdainfully to his henchmen for them to leave. When they'd left, he approached the prisoner and took his handcuffs off.

'Do you admit to working for the English?'

'I'm a French soldier and am struggling alongside the Allies against you. I would prefer to fight on the battlefield but my country's situation, occupied by your troops, prevents me from doing this.'

'You've been beaten now!'

'Personally, yes, no doubt, but you're losing the war.'

The German, visibly disconcerted, spoke again after a few moments' thought.

'So you were passing on information about the Reich's strategy to British diplomats in Switzerland?'

'Indeed.'

'Who did you give it to?'

'I can answer you, because the person in question even advised me to give you his name, in the event of problems. He is the British military attaché in Bern, Colonel Cartwright. You can check this officer's identity on the list of your opposite numbers your intelligence service no doubt possesses.'

'How did you get hold of the information our enemies are interested in?'

'I went and got it myself on the sites where your units are deployed.'

'Who worked with you?'

'Nobody. I didn't have any help. The people who answered my questions had no idea of what I was doing.'

'Who were these people?'

'People whose names I've forgotten.'

'Are you sure?'

'Quite sure!'

'Your loss of memory might cost you dearly.'

'I'm aware of that.'

'If you refuse to reveal your sources, you're in for some very big trouble. Think again!'

'I have!'

'You've nothing to add?'

Michel Hollard shook his head. After the interrogation, he was thrown into a cell by himself.

'My huge game of hide-and-seek with the enemy could only end in suffering,' he recognised subsequently. 'It was even very surprising that no trap had put an earlier end to my mission. When I was arrested, the network already had three dead and several deported. Other agents had gone through very difficult ordeals. I carried a large part of the responsibility for these tragedies, so I had to consider my share of misfortune as justified.'

Michel Hollard thought about what the consequences of his arrest would be. His family was not safe from being investigated by the police, despite the arrangements he'd made to keep them out of danger in case he was arrested. Rooms were ready and waiting for them in a discreet family boarding house in Paris. In addition, thanks to the generous help from cousins and friends, they had other places to go to that were just as well protected.[1]

What had happened to his three fellow prisoners tormented him, even though the Germans had no proof they were accomplices. He just hoped that none of them would get lost in awkward explanations. If they all justified themselves with a cool head, they might be freed.

***

The suddenness of the raid hadn't left him any time to get rid of his diary containing important annotations, which were scribbled in a form of shorthand or personal code that could only intrigue the interrogators. He was concerned now about the damned notebook that had fallen into their hands. He remembered especially having noted down a meeting for the following morning.

The police chief had warned his prisoner that he'd be in 'very big trouble' if he persisted in refusing to answer him. Instead of frightening Michel Hollard, the threat had sounded like he was challenging him, even goading him on. During the interrogation, he'd had the feeling he'd psychologically destabilised his interrogator, who'd been so sure of himself. Even better, the prisoner thought he'd been able to read not so much hostility as dismay on the German's face, and perhaps even a certain amount of sympathy for him. However, although the officer had shown some signs of humanity, he still acted no less fiercely using the team of brutes under his command who did their dirty job without any apparent problem of conscience.

They'd taken his watch away and without it he quickly lost all notion of time. In the middle of the night, a prison warder interrupted his thoughts and took him through a maze of corridors, galleries and antechambers until they reached a big bathroom, where four roughnecks were sitting on some of the fixtures, in rather ridiculous positions. They seemed to be waiting patiently, sleeves rolled-up, to start a tough maintenance job.

Michel Hollard recognised the four louts who, a few hours earlier, had tested his resistance to panic by brandishing instruments of torture before his eyes.

The bathroom seemed to be fitted out to enable them to carry out a method of interrogation in which they excelled. The leader ordered the prisoner to partly undress but he turned a deaf ear, so the brutes quickly tore off some of his clothes. Two of them bound him hand and foot, with one tying his feet together and another tying his hands behind his back. Then, with the help of a third person, they ducked him headfirst up to his shoulders in a bath three-quarters full of cold water, and held him there.

As he was able to hold his breath for quite some time, the sportsman that he was stood up to this first ducking fairly well. A man who wasn't as fit as he was would probably not have put up with the torture without suffocating. When they allowed him to breathe again, the officer questioned him.

'Your diary contains some scribbling on tomorrow's date, 6 February. You've probably written: 9.20, (then he spelled out) …Aust… and there's no doubt, C.G., certainly somebody's initials. Who is this?'

No answer.

An Agir agent, the Swiss Charles Guillard, lived near the airbase at Étampes-Mondésir, recently done-up by the Luftwaffe. At the Allies' request, having made a detailed map of this base situated between Paris and Orléans, he'd watched the constant stream of enemy aircraft landing and taking off, and made regular written reports. A meeting had indeed been arranged between this Resistance worker and his leader at the Paris-Austerlitz railway station on the following day when one of the Orléans-Étampes-Paris trains got in.

Furious at the prisoner's insolent silence, the torturers' boss nodded to his henchmen. Once again, three men pushed Michel Hollard's head under the water. He was beginning to drown, taking in a lot of water, when the torturers allowed him to get his breath back.

'What does the abbreviation "Aust. C.G." mean in your notebook?'

The only sounds the victim made were irrepressible sputtering and gasping noises.

One of the thugs spoke French without an accent. Although he was more than likely a fellow Frenchman, he was just as cruel as the other brutes, if not more so. These 'special interrogation' experts were used to their victims' reactions and knew very well what the limits of ordinary mortals were when they were being tortured. They knew from experience that in most cases the human body did not stand up to the water torture very long and that most of them cried for mercy fairly rapidly. This method of coercion consisted of a succession of carefully timed duckings. The henchmen worked in such a way that the victim's anguish and suffering always increased. They watched him almost scientifically and constantly checked how his general state changed. The different phases of the torture were deliberately interrupted just before the victim passed out or fell into a potentially irreversible coma.

Michel Hollard was one of those combatants who was able to choose death rather than risk giving in under torture. After the battle he'd just fought by keeping silent, he started to doubt whether he could hold out much longer against such methods.

Hollard knew Charles Guillard would no doubt show up for the meeting the next day, so he had to do his utmost to ensure the safety of his friend who was now unwittingly exposed to danger. If the policemen picked him up, not only would they have captured a fifth member of the Agir network, but the situation for the other members could also be worsened.

To be sure he'd keep quiet, Hollard decided to allow his head to be dunked without resisting. But the torturers wouldn't allow him to go over into the next world. As soon as they put him under, they noticed he'd changed his behaviour, so they hit him furiously. The beating made him react abruptly and he breathed in a whole lot of water. As he was drowning, they pulled his head out of the water to give him time to get his breath back.

As soon as he appeared to have recovered enough again, the eternal question was put to him, but differently.

'What do the abbreviated notes in your notebook mean, dated 6 February, that is, tomorrow, at 9.20?'

Instead of answering, he turned his gaze ostensibly towards the opposite wall. This show of scornful stubbornness earned him another thrashing, more brutal than the previous one, followed straight away by a fourth ducking.

Obeying orders from their superiors, the torturers had to keep him alive, for the time being at least. Although he felt his strength ebbing away, his instinct for self-preservation acted independently of his will. Deliverance by drowning being obviously impossible, he had no other choice but to carry on struggling relentlessly. The series of duckings, questionings and beatings lasted well into the night. After a few hours of this unchanging rhythm, Michel Hollard felt he'd been transformed into some sort of lifeless puppet that the bullies were tossing about everywhere, in and around the tub.

Although he was dazed, it didn't prevent him from hearing the unsubtle names he was being called, like 'pig', 'dirty bastard' or 'scum'… Suddenly, he saw the brutes gathering around their boss. They all walked away together trying to decipher a page from the confiscated diary.

Worn out, covered in bruises, his face swollen, he was lying on the floor shivering when an old woman entered. She was an employee whose task was to take him some bread. She also gave him a smile; an unexpected show of kindness which helped him pull himself together.

A jailer ordered him to get dressed and then follow him. He dragged himself painfully along the corridors to his cell, where he collapsed on the small bed. But his rest was short-lived. Day was breaking when somebody woke him with a start, shouting harshly:

'Come on, off we go to Austerlitz station! Don't forget, your friend C.G. is hoping to meet you there this morning. It wouldn't be very polite of you not to be there to welcome him!'

The prisoner was put in the back of a car, his hands handcuffed behind his back, as on the previous day. Three inspectors, including the driver, went with him. A few minutes before the 9.20 train arrived, the car drew up in front of the passengers' way out. Held at gunpoint, the prisoner was ordered to identify his comrade as soon as he saw him. The warning was clear: if he disobeyed, he'd be shot after the last passengers had gone past. In reality, the policemen were only trying to intimidate the prisoner.

Instructions had been given to bring him back alive, because the officers in charge of looking into his case were still hoping to get information from him.

Charles Guillard was among the first people off the train. Because the police car was civilian, he walked right past the trap without even seeing it. His boss, who was always on time, was not at the meeting point and this worried him. Following instructions, he continued calmly on his way and vanished into the crowd. The passengers at first flowed past as a pack, then this gradually thinned out and stopped altogether. A few latecomers brought up the rear.[2]

As soon as they realised the operation had failed, the henchmen, as furious as they were crestfallen, gave free rein to their frustration and anger, and lashed out at the unfortunate prisoner who was already weakened by the previous night's tortures. These professionals took turns beating him and were only satisfied when he was writhing in pain, his head all bloodied.

Back at the Division of Special Interrogations, Michel Hollard was brought up in front of two other individuals who were there to complete his file. In contrast to the previous brutes, they were strangely friendly. Hollard's surprise gave way to indignation when one of the Germans, introducing himself as a judge, offered him freedom in exchange for 'loyal cooperation'. That was what the man of law called treason! The judge was not offended by the disdainful gesture with which the prisoner silently answered his offer.

Michel Hollard was then taken to a former living room converted into an office. An officer greeted him with surprising courtesy. He was a magistrate-instructor who was already well acquainted with his case and knew that the defendant faced the death penalty. He still didn't know what discoveries Michel Hollard and the Agir network had made about the V-1 set-up, the description of the weapon, the plans and where the launch ramps were located.

The magistrate had been warned of the accused's exceptional obstinacy and his ability to resist torture, even at the risk of his life. The interrogation quickly changed into a surprising conversation. The exchange was frank, and even cordial.

***

The most recent interrogators had not been able to ignore the fact that the prisoner's face showed signs of violence. They'd also certainly noticed his suffering, despite his efforts to show nothing of it. In the damp and dark cell, the pain nagged with increased intensity. It perturbed the rest his battered and sleep-deprived body was crying out for.

His dire situation didn't break his spirit. Like any prisoner, he was waiting for the opportunity to escape. While he was being driven in the police car, he'd already had to stop himself from being tempted to lash out suddenly at the thugs and make a desperate dash for freedom. Despite his diminished physical condition, he felt he was ready for any new ordeal if there was a small chance to break free.

The lavatory, situated at the far end of the corridor, had a small window from which it was probably possible to jump into a little neighbouring garden. This opening, although it was high up, was not out of reach for a determined acrobat. To use this room, you had to be accompanied by the guards and put up with one of them being present all the time. However, the irksome individual waited discreetly, the time that was needed, behind the toilet door, which was left necessarily ajar.

After visiting the place in question two or three times to prepare, Michel Hollard put together an escape plan. In the middle of the night, with the guards slumbering, he managed the first part of the climb. Crawling painfully through the narrow opening, he poked his head outside. Alas, this foretaste of freedom suddenly turned bitter. While a final lurch and a few leaps into the night would have been enough perhaps to save him, the prisoner suddenly felt his feet being held. The guard, pretending to be asleep, had watched everything he was doing without being seen. He threw him to the ground and made him pay for his boldness with a hail of blows.

The day after his escape attempt, Michel Hollard was expecting some form of retaliation from his torturers, but they were so furious at having wasted so much time trying in vain to get such a headstrong person to talk that they turned away wearily.[3]

***

The Agir boss was worried about the fate of the other prisoners. During each interrogation, he protested vehemently against their being kept in prison, repeating that they were only business associates and had nothing to do with his underground activities. While awaiting the German court's decisions, the Gestapo decided to take the prisoners into custody in Fresnes Prison.

Since being imprisoned, the men had been deprived of any way of keeping in touch. Luckily, only one Black Maria, split into little individual cells, was used to transport the four prisoners simultaneously, and they were at last able to communicate with each other through the opaque partitions inside the vehicle. Despite the guards' presence, the three agents managed to reassure their leader using ambiguous and pre-arranged words and sentences to describe what they'd said to the enemy. They told him that, although they'd claimed they were innocent, they'd been severely ill-treated, but hadn't been subjected to the bathtub torture.

Chapter 26

'In Defeat: Defiance'!

In May 1941, the first time he'd visited the British Embassy in Switzerland, Michel Hollard had etched the four sayings by Winston Churchill written on the wall of the waiting room in his memory. In captivity, his stubbornness and his sense of honour commanded him to apply the second precept energetically: 'In Defeat: Defiance'!

The enemy judges had too much evidence against him for him to harbour any illusions about the pending verdict. According to his last interrogator, the sentence would be given within three and five weeks. Still refusing to admit the inevitable reality, he clung to the idea that he'd be able to find an opportunity to escape during this time. He carried on observing all the new places they took him to and where he stayed, with the fanciful hope that he could plan an escape. But when he arrived at Fresnes Prison, he had to admit the security was such that it was almost impossible.

The prison's health regulations stipulated that new arrivals pass through the disinfection service. While their clothes were put through the first treatment, the men had to take a shower in a neighbouring room. To get there, the four comrades had to join the long line of newcomers being led by not enough guards to prevent them from having private conversations. The Agir agents were therefore able to agree on what each of them was going to say in his own particular situation. Despite the gravity of his case, Michel Hollard was facing up to the situation better than his friends, so he tried to comfort them.

As they went along, the column of men followed a long corridor in which there were openings that gave them a glimpse of the prison walls beyond a walkway. Seeing a little building against this surrounding wall, Michel Hollard remarked to his companions that, with a bit of imagination, one could envisage climbing to freedom from there. He knew this plan wasn't exactly realistic because first they'd have to slip past the guards' watchfulness. Although none of them harboured any illusions as to such a crazy plan working out, the idea had the merit of stimulating their imagination and giving them moral support.

After being disinfected, the prisoners waited for a long time, shut up separately in cupboard-like cubicles, to be taken to their cells. Michel Hollard was placed in N° 394, located on the third floor of Division III.[1] It had been designed for one man, but the Germans had arrested a lot of Resistance fighters, meaning the number of those unfortunate men, added to the common law prisoners, far outdid the prison's capacity.

Three men were already there, patriots accused or suspected of scheming with Resistance organisations. Michel Hollard had the impression they weren't very happy about his arrival. Their attitude was understandable; their space was reduced by each newcomer.

His companions of misfortune noticed immediately that his face showed he'd recently been beaten. He was asked a lot of questions and tried to satisfy their curiosity, evoking the torture sessions he'd been through but without going into too much detail as he didn't like to complain. At nightfall, the rudimentary sleeping material, piled up on the only bed during the day, had to be laid down. The floor was then completely covered by the mattresses.

The morale of the inmates in cell 394 was low and they couldn't sleep very much. One of them, going through a moment of distress during the night, didn't hesitate to wake the newcomer up. Muttering some vague excuse, he said the anguish was oppressing him. His whisperings drew the attention of the other two, also depressed and whose sleep was perturbed. All three of them needed to talk for a while to reassure themselves. Michel Hollard's fellow inmates, who were already thankful for his pertinent opinions, sought comfort from him.

'Our presence here,' he said, 'is the logical and almost inevitable consequence of the sacrifices we have made to serve France and freedom after an unacceptable capitulation. According to reliable information, the enemy is now showing signs of weakening. This reversal in their situation has been greatly helped along by the Resistance organisations you belong to. You can therefore consider that your contribution to France's resurrection has already borne fruit.

'Obviously, our individual prospects are not particularly encouraging and my own case, as you know, isn't looking good. However, what you've told me about your different situations tells me that each of you has fairly good arguments for your defence.

'Only recently, in the heat of the action, you were brave. You are therefore strong enough to face other tests. We're all in good health. As long as there's life, there's hope!'

Michel Hollard felt that those listening to him were gradually getting more peaceful. He went on.

'Here are a few lines about sleep. Maybe they'll help you to drop off':

A calm without equal has taken hold of things; *Man has stopped his frenzy and the birds their singing;* *All the voices in the world fell silent at once* *And everything seems to have fled, like the setting sun…*	*Un calme sans pareil s'est emparé des choses ;* *L'homme a cessé sa fièvre et les oiseaux leur chant ;* *Toutes les voix du monde à la fois se sont closes* *Et tout semble avoir fui, comme a fui le couchant…*
But no! It is sleep that frees men. *It's the precious moment of our enchantment* *That makes us forget who we are for a while* *Like a warm covering laid over our torments.*	*Mais non ! C'est le sommeil qui délivre les hommes.* *C'est l'instant précieux de nos enchantements* *Qui nous fait oublier un peu ce que nous sommes* *Comme un manteau douillet posé sur nos torments.*[2]

Discreet, regular snoring interrupted the silence that followed…the others fell asleep in turn. Michel Hollard, worn out but still calm and in control, also fell asleep.

***

Most of the prisoners held in Division III were waiting helplessly for a decision from the German courts. By talking to each other, they were trying not to become downhearted. The little group in cell 394 was in the habit of listening carefully to what Michel Hollard had to say, his natural authority asserting itself on its own.

His cellmates asked him how the war was going; his own very serious personal situation didn't stop him from painting a fairly optimistic picture that he concluded more or less as follows:

> The United States and the USSR are certainly determined to throw all their weight behind the fight alongside England. Quite a few Frenchmen have been able to join General de Gaulle in London. This means our country is present on all the fronts: land, air and sea.
>
> The Germans imagined they'd succeed in enslaving France. To put an end to their greed, we've chosen, you and I, to fight an extremely dangerous battle on French soil, which the enemy occupies.
>
> I can assure you the Allies already know all about the new weapons the Germans are threatening them with. There's going to be a huge confrontation, which we hope will have happy outcome.

Subsequently, his three companions often asked him to make up little speeches. He made these men aware of a wide range of scientific, artistic, theological and literary matters throughout history. His memory enabled him to recite extracts from the works of Hugo, Vigny, Verlaine, Valéry, etc… and a few fragments of his own writings.

***

On the morning of 6 February 1944, his secretary, Madeleine Boulanger, who had only just managed to avoid being caught in the raid on the Café des Chasseurs, arranged for Yvonne Hollard to be immediately informed of the disaster. My mother had been expecting to receive bad news but after a moment of despondency, she got hold of herself and, ignoring the danger, rushed to the Gestapo headquarters to ask the personnel there if they knew anything about what had happened to her husband.

The 'grey mice' in this administration advised her to contact their main chaplaincy. A meeting was arranged with a pastor of the German community in Paris, Hans Helmut Peters, who was also chaplain to the prisons in the Paris region and held an officer rank in the Wehrmacht. Before being received by this man of the cloth, she said to herself, 'I must be wary of a military clergyman who works closely with the enemy police. His state of mind will obviously be hostile to the Reich's enemies.'

The pastor hadn't met Michel Hollard yet, but he received his wife quite politely and with a certain solemnity. Saying what she needed to hear, he did his best to placate her: 'My duty consists in lessening the prisoners' suffering, in particular those whose cases are the most serious. Please believe that I'll do all I can to help your husband. He's being held at Fresnes and I'm going there to see him soon.'

Yvonne Hollard wanted to see the chaplain again after he'd visited her husband, so a second meeting was arranged for the following week. In the meantime, the German visited the French Resistance fighter that he knew was under threat of death. 'You are a fighter who is struggling, but you are still fervent and keen,' he said to him. 'I salute you as a man of conviction who is still hopeful and dignified, in spite of everything.'

Following this encounter, the second meeting his wife had asked for took place in a much warmer atmosphere than the first. The chaplain renewed the promise of his good offices. He often met the prisoners' families, all of whom were distressed and confronted with a host of problems. He was concerned about being of help to them and made communication among the families easier.

Through his intercession, the family of one of the occupants of cell 394 wrote to Yvonne Hollard. 'We know,' they wrote, 'that there's a marvellous cake, exactly what the prison population needs; they never get enough to eat.'

There was indeed a wonderful cake, which was quite readily available. Its creators presented it at private meetings and was quite simply a type of large brioche. Some resourceful bakers offered it for sale discreetly,[3] but it was very expensive because flour was very rare. Its size and consistency were such that a skilful hand with a thin knife could dig out a deep cavity in which a little letter could be inserted, folded in four. Using a paste made from the inner part of the brioche, clever camouflaging made this surprise food look quite untouched. Mixed in with other plain cakes, it was almost impossible to tell that it contained any correspondence.

My sister Francine showed such consummate skill in the art of making doctored brioches that the trick was never discovered, despite systematic searches.

Luck gave the prisoners the opportunity to be crafty as well. As he was clearing out their cell, Michel Hollard noticed that on the ground, in a corner, was a little crevice containing some bits of wood. Having managed to get them out, he discovered the remains of a crushed pencil. After carefully sifting through these fragments, he found two or three pieces of pencil lead concealed there! A treasure for such a man cut off from his family and deprived of means of communicating.

The scarcity of basic raw materials like cardboard meant that food boxes had to be used again. The prison authorities therefore allowed cake boxes and other packaging to be sent back and forth between the senders and recipients of parcels. The four men managed to give a jam jar a virtually invisible double bottom. The carefully tampered-with object slipped by the checkers without arousing any suspicions and enabled messages to be sent several times without any problems.

***

Cell 394 gave right onto a vast green space accessible to the public. Although its window was almost opaque, they were able to look out at the neighbourhood through a hole concealed by a removable bung. From this observation post, while the guards were elsewhere, the inmates took it in turns hoping to see one of their loved ones. Indeed, in the secret messages, the unfortunate men had told their family that at certain times of the day they could see a part of the outside world. They also said where exactly their window was.

With his eye glued to the tiny opening, Michel Hollard suddenly felt his heart beating frantically when two graceful young ladies came into sight. He thought he recognised his wife and daughter, and his doubts vanished when they waved affectionately in his direction.[4]

The pastor, Peters, visited him several times. One evening, in answer to a wish he'd made, he offered him a Bible and a hymnal. After humming in front of his fellow inmates several songs of praise, the prisoner drew their attention to one of them, deeming it particularly relevant to their situation. It was the hymn the people aboard the *Titanic* sang in 1912 at the moment the vessel started to go under, 'Nearer, My God, to Thee'.

Right away, four voices sang in unison, shyly and approximately, but fervently. They repeated all the words so they could memorise them. The next day, at the same time, the singers improved their interpretation, inspiring others to join them, through the walls, in the neighbouring cells. This spiritual singing was repeated as more and more people joined in, spreading evening after evening. In less than a week, when the call came from the invisible choir leader, all the men in the building got into the habit of becoming a huge choir at dusk.

***

Occasionally the prisoners were led outside from their cells to stretch their legs a little. Agir's boss was happily surprised when he came across his assistant, Joseph Legendre. Under the guards' watchful gaze, their reunion was risky; they had just enough time to exchange three or four sentences. Speaking low, they managed to give each other their cell number and realised they were on the same corridor. His assistant confirmed he was still not accused of anything and therefore hoped to be freed shortly. If that was the case, Michel Hollard wanted to hand over control of the network to him so that he would ensure the pending missions were continued.

Joseph Legendre no doubt had the required ability for such a job but, to be able to act, he needed some written information. When he was back inside, the leader began drawing up a note for his second-in-command. His abundance of stationery – namely laughable bits of pencil lead and pieces of wrapping paper – enabled him to do so. However, the message still had to reach its recipient.

Taking advantage of the presence of a cordial NCO with whom he'd already talked several times in German, Michel Hollard approached him.

'Sir, don't you think this building's cleanliness leaves a lot to be desired? I've noticed you've already given certain household chores to some of the prisoners. If you need anybody for the cleaning, *Ich bin Bewerber!* (I'm a candidate!)'

The soldier nodded and left without saying anything. However, shortly afterwards, the guard came to get the volunteer cleaner who, once equipped with what was needed, was told to sweep and scrub his floor's corridors.

He scoured everywhere, looking for dust in every nook and cranny. The care he took with the task was such that the soldier instructed to watch over him complimented him: '*Gut, gut!* That's an impeccable job. The rest of the prison should be just as clean!'

The volunteer cleaner reached the cell of his friend who, attracted by all the fuss, had started listening. The little note folded in four was pushed discreetly under the door and picked up by its recipient.

***

The German secret services no doubt thought the Hollard case would go no further. The military tribunal reached a verdict in the absence of the accused and a judge summoned him later. In a serious tone, the magistrate announced the sentence:

'Mr Hollard, I regret to tell you that the court has reached its decision. Because of your intelligence activities with the enemy, and in spite of the plea made on your behalf by your German barrister, you have been sentenced to death...'

The Resistance leader had been preparing himself for death for a long time. During the torture sessions, he'd even tried to hasten his end. Nonetheless, the announcement horrified him, but his mysticism saved him from becoming demoralised. His thoughts went out to his family, and then to his comrades-in-arms.

Our family only learnt the news a week later. Meanwhile, my mother found the packet of documents at the network's HQ[5] that my father was going to hand over to his English correspondent, O.P. Certain sheets accurately showed the location of several new V-1 launch sites.

My mother at once realised the importance and urgency of these reports. Just like her husband, she didn't hesitate to go to Lausanne and back. Pressed for time, and not knowing enough about the routes or the traps along the way, the young woman had to use a smuggler's services. Moreover, when she arrived at the Swiss customs office she was received very curtly and had to wait a long time for the incredulous civil servant to respond. The intercession of her brother-in-law, Dr Charles Guisan, enabled her to get to Lausanne and deliver her captive husband's last crop to the right people.

Meanwhile, the condemned man, thinking his end was near, considered each new day as another stay of execution.[6] Thinking about the exemplary behaviour of his assistant Olivier Giran, shot a year earlier, he was able to resist becoming distressed. He even intensified his enthusiasm in carrying out his cleaning job that the guards continued to give him, just as he'd wished.

He continued to observe the premises, in the vain hope he could find a flaw in some locking device, or an easing up of the surveillance. But Fresnes proved to be too well designed a prison and the personnel too hard to fool. One or more guards continually kept an eye on the prisoner while he worked.

However, the group washing session, in the shower room on the building's lower level, gave Michel Hollard the opportunity to think up another escape plan. Near the kitchens, an area gave access to a dumbwaiter distributing the food to all the floors. The lowest level of this lift was next to a corridor which led out to the perimeter path. If a fugitive managed to get to this path, he could enter the little building with a roof, leaning against the boundary wall, which he'd already spotted with his network friends. But to get there, the last but one stage, he'd have to get over several other obstacles first.

When the first prisoners, lined up in single file, reached the bottom of the stairs, Michel Hollard, who'd placed himself at the rear, slipped out of sight of the guards. Rushing up the stairs four at a time, he went back to the third floor in a few seconds. He approached the dumbwaiter, which luckily was there. It was just big enough for a slim person to crouch inside it. One press on the electric button, within reach of the user on the outside mounting, and he'd have been off down to the ground floor, an area where there were fewer people around at that time.

He tiptoed towards the lift, risking everything once again. It seemed he was just about to pull it off when a door opened abruptly. A German prison wardress assigned to the women's quarters burst in. Panicking, she alerted a guard on duty nearby. The prisoner had enough presence of mind to pretend he was lost:

'I was late going to the shower with the others and I went the wrong way!' he claimed.

After this rather unconvincing explanation, the supposedly disoriented prisoner considered himself lucky just to be booted back to his cell without more ado.

***

Three months after the four men had been arrested in the Café des Chasseurs, luck smiled upon two of them: Joseph Legendre and Henri Dujarier. With as much skill as stubbornness, they had succeeded in dispelling the suspicions the Germans had about them and they were released.

Unfortunately, the same was not true for Jules Mailly, whom the German inspectors had found in possession of suspicious documents. Sentenced to deportation, he disappeared in Mauthausen concentration camp.

Joseph Legendre carefully held on to the directives his boss had given him, written furtively on a piece of paper in the prison. These instructions indicated the enquiries that had to be made urgently, and the assistant conscientiously did his best to carry them out to revive the paralysed network. With the agents from Normandy and Picardy, he continued searching for the modified V-1 sites, now increasingly better camouflaged. Thanks to the help of the *montagnards*, his boss' friends, he was able to cross the border several times and get to Lausanne to hand over the precious information.

***

Michel Hollard's stay in Fresnes lasted three and a half months; 105 days and as many nights waiting for punishment which, for the moment, was long in coming. His ability to keep his morale almost intact for so long under such circumstances shows the man's strength of character.

One day a guard came to take him to see a German doctor. In a few moments and without saying a word, the doctor had evaluated Hollard's general state of health.

'Why does the health of a man sentenced to death interest them?' he wondered, baffled at first, and then having a vague premonition. He soon had the answer from the NCO who'd allowed him to become a cleaner in the prison.

'Your name,' said the soldier, 'is on the list of prisoners being deported to a concentration camp in Germany!'

Upon hearing the incredible news, Hollard praised Providence. 'The Heavenly Spirit,' he thought, 'has decided to watch over me, because what I'm doing is right.'

Believing he'd been saved by a miracle, he remained calm and clear-headed, remembering that on the other side of the Rhine the regime put its opponents down fiercely. But since he'd recently overcome vile acts of torture, he was unafraid of having to endure further suffering. He was, however, quite incapable of imagining the savagery of the treatment meted out to the horde of deportees he was soon to be part of.

To satisfy the Reich's insatiable appetite for new material to be used by its armies, German industry exploited the free labour it drew from the concentration camps. Considered as sub-humans, the deportees were reduced to slavery and obliged to work to the limits of their strength on the most exhausting jobs.

In view of Germany's final victory, which would've meant the surviving prisoners being completely exterminated, the country's military authorities considered, with full knowledge of the facts, that sending somebody to a concentration camp was tantamount to sentencing them to death.

Chapter 27

Down into Hell

One of the departure points for French prisoners sentenced to deportation to Germany was located at the Royallieu camp, near Compiègne. During the second fortnight of May 1944, more than 2,000 prisoners were temporarily held in this simplified prison made up of modest buildings on a large plot of land, surrounded by three fences of barbed wire.

The guards didn't prevent the prisoners from wandering around inside the enclosure, and a lot of inmates saw this apparent act of kindness as a good sign for the future. They'd been told how captured French soldiers had been treated relatively well in 1940 and some of them believed they'd be treated likewise. They had no clue about the horrors they'd be facing at the end of a terrible journey.

In the middle of a crowd of strangers, the Agir network founder suddenly recognised Jean-Henri Daudemard, the SNCF engineer who'd revealed to him the presence of secret German building sites in Normandy. He too had been denounced and arrested, and was suffering the same fate as him. The two men found solace in each other through their chance meeting.

The illusion of semi-liberty didn't stop Michel Hollard from looking for a way of getting out. Near the sleeping quarters where he'd been given a straw mattress, he noticed there was a weak point in the surrounding wire netting. With a bit of skill and luck, it seemed he could escape, as long as he'd noted beforehand how often the guards made their rounds. He used his assistant Joseph Brocard and his exploit as an example.

As soon as all the others seemed to have dropped off, he got up noiselessly. Feeling his way along in the darkness, he reached the fence. The almost total lack of visibility didn't prevent him from bending several defective metal strands out of place. He had a real opportunity of forcing a passage through the first fence, a way through just big enough for his slender body. After that he'd have to climb the other, more rudimentary barrier, which he thought he could get over even though it was covered with spikes.

He carried on breaking through the fence, encouraged by the progress he was making. As soon as the breach was half open, he jumped. Jean-Henri Daudemard, who'd just tapped him on the shoulder with a firm hand, whispered:

'I think you're risking your life needlessly.'

'Please don't disturb me, I'm in a hurry.'

'But you're going to get yourself killed when victory is in sight! You've contributed a lot to that. What further help can you give the Allies now? What's more, our living conditions are already improving, even here.'

'The end of the war is still a long way off. As for the life the Germans are reserving for us, I'm not at all optimistic.'[1]

Although they were talking quietly, several other prisoners had heard them and joined them. When they found out what was being discussed, they in turn became agitated, and others who were curious also joined them. All this animation risked drawing the guards' attention.

So those who'd started the disturbance wisely decided to put the twisted strands back more or less as they'd been before and go back to bed at the same time as the others. Even though he was annoyed, Agir's leader couldn't blame Jean-Henri Daudemard. In his opinion, the engineer had been too cautious, but he'd acted in good faith.[2]

***

A long, peculiar train was waiting for them in Compiègne station. At first glance, it seemed to be intended for transporting cattle, but the line of livestock wagons was interspersed with passenger carriages at regular intervals. However, these were for the military escort, not the prisoners. What was more, on the last wagon there was an observation platform equipped with a machine gun.

On foot, lined up in rows of five, the prisoners heading for Germany were led to the platform and then made to stand in front of the convoy. Whips in hand, the SS[3] forced the prisoners in the first row to get into the leading wagon, outside of which could be read the following: 'Number of places: 8 horses or 40 men.'

From afar, Michel Hollard, who was not in the first group, verified how true this estimation was. After the fortieth passenger had climbed aboard, the wagon's normal capacity had obviously been reached. The SS, apparently proud of what they were there to do, cracked their whips. Under the threat of swirling leather straps, the victims crowded together even further into the back of the wagon. Quite indifferent to the lack of space for each man, the brutes savagely whipped the last men in. The whipping and the shouting only increased the jostling. The first wagon, thus extremely overcrowded, as the others were also soon to be, was only locked up after the hundredth man was forced in.

On several occasions already, Agir's leader had observed the behaviour of terrified crowds in circumstances that posed a threat to the group. He knew that danger could incite a man to protect himself by a primary selfish reflex, much to the detriment of others.

Watching his comrades huddled near the door of the wagon in fear of being whipped, an altruistic idea came to him. If he managed to intercept or at least cushion some of the lashings with his hand, his fellow passengers would be spared somewhat. Agile enough to divert some of the swirling whips, he bravely rendered this service to his companions, suffering some painful welts himself. Considering it a minor sacrifice, he refused all thanks. However, no one else, at least on that particular day, chose to suffer to prevent others suffering.

Michel Hollard was among the last to enter the wagon, which was suddenly darkened by the SS closing the door, and found himself wedged between his neighbours and the wall. Little by little, the space organised itself. To get to the vile container that served as a latrine, you had to work your way through the crowd and wait your turn patiently, forgetting any sense of modesty you might have had. Certain forms of propriety now belonged to another world.

The appalling conditions of the trip, which lasted three days, were made worse by the torrid heat at the beginning of June 1944. Before leaving Royallieu, each deportee had been given a modest snack. They had to save this precious food as much as possible in order to hold out until the end of the journey…and hope to be given a little water along the way.

Twenty-four hours after they'd left, the deportees started wasting away. Several of them, overwhelmed and dehydrated, only remained standing because the closeness of their neighbours held them up in place.

The SNCF employees in Compiègne had contacted their colleagues in some of the stations along the route the train was going to take. Thanks to this chain of solidarity, the railwaymen managed to get containers of drink into the wagons. The lack of water brought out the selfishness in certain men. A boor who was still in good health managed to get hold of a bottle and started shamelessly quenching his thirst, ignoring a man next to him who was about to pass out. Michel Hollard didn't hum and haw. By surprise and force, he snatched the bottle from him and gave it to the ill man to drink. But the infuriated lout fought back, waving his arms furiously, and managed to take the bottle back, forcing the people around him to intervene.

***

At the end of his stay at Royallieu, Agir's founder still hoped to find a way of escaping during the trip. Before leaving the camp, he'd noticed two groups who separately seemed to be plotting something. One of them consisted of forty-odd Boy Scout-looking young men, led by a priest called Le Meur. 'A very nice group but, honestly, far too large to pull something off,' Michel Hollard had thought. He consequently contacted the other group, made up of only three men.

'It's true, we're getting ready to try and escape,' one of them confirmed. 'We're going to make an opening in the floorboards. At night we'll jump onto the ballast. If all goes well, you could follow us.'

These words were unfortunately not followed by any action. The three men, prostrate right from the outset, didn't attempt to rip up any floorboards and in spite of their inaction, refused to lend anybody the pieces of scrap metal – the makeshift tools they'd managed to steal. Disappointed by the would-be escapees, the man who'd joined them to try to escape realised too late that he'd backed the wrong horse. Father

Le Meur and his group of young people, whom Michel Hollard could've joined, managed the tour de force of escaping from the neighbouring wagon at night before the train had even left French soil.

The group of youths having bowed out, the convoy went slowly across a large part of Germany, as a scorching sun continued to torment the prisoners huddled together, perhaps even more so than cattle on their way to the slaughterhouse.

Supposing that all the available space was shared out fairly, everybody would have had just enough space to stretch their arms and legs, but there wasn't enough room to sit. Some of the men around Michel Hollard tried to figure out how the wagon's 100 occupants could be accommodated as well as possible, but the operation was only partially successful because some of the people had no qualms about stretching out to the detriment of the others.

In the end, the majority decided to squeeze further to one side so that everybody could take turns benefiting from a short period of rest. Everyone was able to lie down, some even slept a little, while the others patiently waited their turn, packed in tightly standing up. Fortunately, a storm broke out and, because the wagons' waterproofing left a lot to be desired, precious streams of water flowed in, making the temperature drop momentarily.

During a long halt in Cologne station, the unfortunate prisoners experienced an additional heartbreak, hearing on the loudspeakers that a fast train with sleeping cars was bound for Paris.

***

Chugging along on its advance northwards, the convoy made several other halts before stopping once and for all in a little station near Hamburg. The opening of the doors startled and blinded the dazed passengers. Plunged into darkness for three days, starved and thirsty and deprived of sleep, it took them a long time to recover some of their faculties. They first needed a while to get used to the light so they could see the out-and-out rolling hovel they were in, of which they only knew a small part. Most of the space was occupied by people with haggard faces, slumped on the floor or in a heap, all on top of each other; some seemed to have fainted. No one was surprised to learn that the convoy was counting its dead.

Guards, even more brutal than their Compiègne colleagues, were waiting for this delivery of humans and they treated them like everyday goods. With a series of whiplashes and the help of dogs reared to bite the calves of any laggards, they wasted no time urging the men on, forcing the sick to use up what little energy they had left. Using their feet, they scornfully rolled the bodies of the weak men who'd collapsed over to the side.

Columns of five abreast were formed, just like those that had left Royallieu three days ago. The SS was responsible for managing and operating the concentration camps. Its staff had acquired a lot of experience in exploiting this reserve of slaves.

German industry was afflicted by the fact that there were a lot of people leaving the workforce; more often than not being called up to serve in the army. Since the military situation required production to be intensified, the Nazi leaders had simply decided to use slave labour to make up the numbers.

Building these huge industrialised prisons was speeded up, guarded and watched over like citadels. Innumerable political detainees of all nationalities were mixed with German common law criminals. The objective was to kill two birds with one stone: use the energy of people hostile to Germany until they dropped dead. The military tribunals in Germany and in the occupied countries had received instructions accordingly. These courts were called upon to take into account the professional background of the accused whose sentences they passed.

Under the guidance of Heinrich Himmler, the SS officers had meticulously established and calculated the conditions of selection, transport, imprisonment, work and even the time the captives would probably survive. *Vernichtung durch Arbeit* – extermination through work – was the principle laid down by Minister Fritz Sauckel, the organiser of forced labour.

The time the convicts worked – until their strength wore out – rarely lasted more than a few months, and they quickly became skeletons due to being extremely malnourished, overwhelmed, sick and harassed by the pitiless guards. It wasn't long before they collapsed.[4]

Chapter 28

Neuengamme Concentration Camp

The authorities of Neuengamme camp, near Hamburg, prided themselves on having made it one of the most feared camps in the world. Michel Hollard, who was thrown into this hell in the first week of June 1944, was given the registration number F 33948. Like any newcomer, he had to put up with all sorts of degradation, which turned him into a real convict.

Equipped with hair clippers, a *Kapo*[1] cut a regulation strip lengthwise down the middle of his hair. This ugly gash was called an *Autostrade* (motorway) and was intended to single out the prisoner in the eyes of the outside population in case he tried to escape (an idea which was almost impossible to imagine).

Next, Hollard was forced to get rid of his clothes. In their place, he slipped into one of the outfits handed out by a second *Kapo*, in charge of clothing. The warehouse contained a bric-a-brac of uniforms from all the armies in the world, and also no less bizarre civilian getups.[2] It didn't matter if the prisoner's shoes were of good or bad quality. He was ordered to exchange them for a pair of simple sandals, which were ordinary little planks with simple straps to hold the feet in place.

The change the prisoners underwent in the camp gave them a collective appearance that was both grotesque and tragic. Each day, at the time of the general roll call, the deportees formed up in four columns, making a big square around the central quadrangle. They were regularly obliged to watch one or several executions; hanging was the price to be paid by anyone caught sabotaging military materiel, or even stealing food.

Michel Hollard was shocked by the first tragedy of this type that took place before his eyes and wasn't long in sketching an account mentally. Since he had no means of writing it down, and in order to remember it accurately, he gave it the form of a poem whose different stanzas he gradually learnt by heart.

CARNIVAL

The treeless square is all grey.
Despite the summer, the bitter North wind
Rips through the torn clothes.
They are ten thousand, in tight rows,
A humble and shivering multitude,
Frozen in a dreary wait,
Lifeless eyes, sullen masks,
Indifferent and resigned,
Lost in their grotesque rags,
They form picturesque ranks
Made of astonished ghosts
Half alive, half damned...

All around the pale square
Lies, without a sound, the haggard troop.
Breaking its obsessive silence,
Music, without sweetness
Now comes to fill the area.
Twenty loud brass instruments, in the square
Blare out a triumphant air
That sounds like a carnival.

At this moment, we can see
First of all, without recognizing it,
A strange dark wood frame
Which, slowly, is brought forward...
Then, like a fairground game,
To the sound of music, is raised
In the air a disturbing trestle
Where swings a noose.

The music has ceased its celebration.
A child of twenty, bareheaded,
His forehead high, his complexion sepulchral,
Mounted on a platform
Stands under the structure.
His clear gaze looking out over us
Seems to seek the distant sky
And his hand, with a childish gesture
Closes on the white sling
That covers a whole sleeve
To support a bruised arm.
From behind, to the emaciated body
Is tied the other, still agile.
Nearby, with a quiet movement,
A fat, leonine-necked creature,
Stopping with his broad hand
The light loop that was dangling,
Puts it round the pallid throat,
Which receives it without a tremble.

CARNAVAL

La cour sans arbre est toute grise.
Malgré l'été, l'amère bise
Fouille les habits déchirés.
Ils sont dix mille, en rangs serrés,
Multitude humble et grelottante,
Figée en une morne attente,
Yeux éteints, masques renfrognés,
Indifférents et résignés,
Perdus dans leurs haillons grotesques,
Ils forment des rangs pittoresques
Faits de fantômes étonnés
Moitié vivants, moitié damnés...

Tout autour de la cour blafarde
Gît, sans bruit, la troupe hagarde.
Rompant son silence obsesseur,
Une musique, sans douceur
Vient, maintenant, remplir l'espace.
Vingt cuivres bruyants, sur la place
Font jaillir un air triomphal
Qui sonne comme un carnaval.

À ce moment, on voit paraître
Tout d'abord, sans le reconnaître,
Un cadre étrange au bois foncé
Qui, lentement, est avancé...
Puis, ainsi qu'un jeu de kermesse,
Au son de la musique, on dresse
En l'air le chevalet troublant
Où se balance un nœud coulant.

La musique a cessé sa fête.
Un enfant de vingt ans, nu-tête,
Le front haut, le teint sépulcral,
Installé sur un piédestal
Se tient debout sous la machine.
Son clair regard qui nous domine
Semble chercher le ciel lointain
Et sa main, d'un geste enfantin
Se ferme sur l'écharpe blanche
Qui recouvre toute une manche
Pour soutenir un bras meurtri.
Par derrière, au corps amaigri
Est lié l'autre, encore agile.
Tout près, d'un mouvement tranquille,
Un gros être au cou léonin,
Arrêtant de sa large main
La boucle qui voguait, légère,
La pose sur la gorge claire,
Qui la reçoit sans un frisson.

So left alone, the boy
Full of mystery and silence
Seems to have a huge body,
Thus standing on his platform.
Around his neck, like a dark collar,
The loop makes an adornment.
From below they shout an insult at him,
But his silent mask
Is now only turned towards the heavens.

The platform has dropped.
At the same time, in the icy air,
We see a body fall, spinning
At the end of the rope, and bending
Above the wet cement.
For a long time, the bent young body
Turns at the end of the dark rope
Describing endless circles
And when this carousel stops
His eyes stare at the sky...

The huge square that nothing adorns
Becomes still and gloomy again.
Near the unused portico,
A moment ago, they untied
A body which is now only an obstacle.
Someone, next to the show
That he watched with indifferent eyes,
Waits, in the expiring day.
The wooden base is put back.
With a deft and straightforward stride,
He climbs onto the platform
As one boards a boat;
And it's like opening a way,
At a speed where nothing wavers
But the haughty sailor
Facing his new fate.

The floor drops again.
In its place a being falls
With, at the neck, a short tie
Which, without us hearing anything,
Stops him in the middle of his fall.
Then comes a grim struggle
Between a being with a sacrificed body
And death, too close, too soon.
He struggles furiously,
With an ardour that has not run dry,
Crouches and jumps twenty times
For mysterious contests
Which are played out in silence
Under the cold night ahead.

Alors, laissé seul, le garçon
Plein de mystère et de silence
Paraît avoir un corps immense,
Ainsi dressé sur son palier.
Au cou, tel un sombre collier,
La boucle fait une parure.
D'en bas on lui crie une injure,
Mais son masque silencieux
N'est plus tourné que vers les cieux.

Le piédestal s'est effacé.
Au même instant, dans l'air glacé,
On voit choir un corps qui tournoie
Au bout de la corde, et se ploie
Au-dessus du ciment mouillé.
Longtemps, le jeune corps plié
Tourne au bout de la corde sombre
Décrivant des cercles sans nombre
Et quand cesse son carrousel
Il a les yeux fixés au ciel...

La place immense et que rien n'orne
Redevient immobile et morne.
Près du portique inemployé,
Tout à l'heure, on a délié
Un corps qui n'est plus qu'un obstacle.
Quelqu'un, à côté du spectacle
Qu'il a vu, l'œil indifférent,
Attend, dans le jour expirant.
On remet le socle de planche.
D'une enjambée habile et franche,
Il escalade le plateau
Comme on monte à bord d'un bateau ;
Et c'est comme on ouvre une voie,
D'une allure où rien ne louvoie
Que le navigateur hautain
Fait face à son nouveau destin.

Le plancher à nouveau s'abaisse.
À sa place un être s'affaisse
Avec, au col, un court lien
Qui, sans que l'on n'entende rien,
L'arrête au milieu de sa chute.
Après, c'est une sombre lutte
Entre un être au corps immolé
Et le trépas, trop tôt frôlé.
Il se débat avec furie,
D'une ardeur qui n'est point tarie,
Se ramasse et bondit vingt fois
Pour de mystérieux tournois
Qui se livrent dans le silence
Sous la froide nuit qui s'avance.

A noise rises from the blackened ground. The procession leaves, numb To the rhythm of its shuffling footsteps. It brushes past the arena Where broods the dark duel With its long, unreal gaze. Under the rope that devours him, Where the wrestler still persists In fighting his fate, Now, a final assault, Which shakes the whole gallows, Ends in a weak dance Which lasts into the night Under the eye of the laughing moon.	*Un bruit monte du sol noirci. Le cortège s'en va, transi Au rythme de son pas qui traîne. Il effleure, en passant, l'arène Où couve le sombre duel De son long regard irréel. Sous la corde qui le dévore, Où le lutteur s'obstine encore À combattre son sort fatal, À présent, un assaut final, Dont tremble toute la potence, S'achève en une faible danse Qui se prolonge dans la nuit Sous l'œil de la lune qui rit.*
The main square, now deserted Is all shadow covered. The heavy sound of cadenced steps Decreased, then faded away. All that can be heard, in the soulless air Where no flame flickers, Is the slight twitching Of a rope that can be felt moving.	*La grand'place, à présent déserte Est toute d'ombre recouverte. Le bruit lourd du pas cadencé A décru, puis s'est effacé. On n'entend plus, dans l'air sans âme Où ne palpite aucune flamme, Que le tressaillement léger D'une corde qu'on sent bouger.*
The movement, so gentle and frail That it feels like the beating of a wing, When the moon is waning, Becomes even more tender. It's no more than a humble caress Coming out of the thick darkness And which slowly fades away Far from everyone, facing the firmament...	*Le mouvement, si doux et frêle Qu'on dirait un battement d'aile, Quand la lune est sur son déclin, Se fait encore plus câlin. Ce n'est plus qu'une humble caresse Qui sort de la ténèbre épaisse Et qui s'épuise lentement Loin de tous, face au firmament...*

Neuengamme, June 1944

The two unfortunate men had been executed for stealing some bread, and when the horrible ceremony was over, an older prisoner, seeing the anguish on Michel Hollard's face, said to him, almost nonchalantly:

'What you've just seen horrified you. But soon you'll be forced to watch so many of these executions that you'll get used to it. You'll be less upset.'

'Maybe, but I'm sure you're only making out that you're fatalistic and indifferent.'

'You have understood by now that for the SS we're sub-humans, good enough only to be exploited until we drop. Even if hunger doesn't drive us to steal bread, we won't be leaving this camp alive.'

'I'd like to believe that what you're predicting is far too ominous!'

A short while after they'd arrived at Neuengamme, the newcomers were sorted out by a team of *Vorarbeiter*,[3] who were responsible for directing each of them to where they'd be the most useful.

Questioned by one of these people about his earlier professional activity, Michel Hollard made the mistake of revealing his knowledge of *gazogènes*.

'I've just made a wrong move,' he immediately thought. 'Just as much as in the past, I have no moral right to let the Germans benefit from my experience in a field they know little about. I have to find a way out of this.'

The hoped-for opportunity to get out of being recruited into something too beneficial for the enemy came almost at once. An annex of the camp, the Metallwerke factory, a general mechanics service, said it was looking for people with basic technical know-how. He was enrolled at once.

The factory did indeed carry out work for the Wehrmacht, but the French prisoner had promised himself that as soon as he could, he'd continue to be a nuisance for the forces of the Reich, and he kept his word.

From then on, the deportee's daily timetable was invariably the same throughout his confinement. At 5 am, the *Blockführer*[4] woke everybody up noisily.

'I didn't wait for his signal to go to the water fountain,' my father once told me. 'Before dawn, I'd go to get ahead of the general commotion. Firstly, to do my daily exercises, which I felt I needed more than ever, even though I was undernourished. Secondly, so that I could have access to the water tap to wash quietly and miss the rush.'

'Did you get any food before you went to work?'

'Two deportees in charge of handing out food lugged around a big wheel-mounted drum. They dished out a strange liquid. It was indefinable, dark grey and quite tasteless. We used old rusted bowls for plates. The starving crowd voraciously gulped down this unappetising broth. At the same time, we were all given a piece of black bread. That was our morning menu, which was the bulk of our daily ration.'

'So that paltry food was considered as a real meal?'

'Indeed, it was our only more or less substantial meal of the day! In the morning we were given a slice of bread, smaller than the previous one, and later another plateful of the usual greyish liquid. After that, nothing, we had to go without food until the next day.'

'Were you ever given, even as an exception, a portion of vegetables or a bite of meat?'

'No! Our diet was never improved. And we had just enough time to swallow this meagre meal, without even being able to sit down, before the morning bell rang and everybody had to get to the *Appelplatz* as quickly as possible. Everybody went to their assigned *Kommando* (work unit) which lined up in columns of five behind its *Kapo*.'

As soon as the brass band's notes sounded, all the *Kommandos* moved off. The one Michel Hollard was in crossed the camp boundary closely supervised. The group, wearing only those derisory sandals, made its way painfully towards the factory, located 1.25 miles away. Any latecomers were savagely beaten. Everybody hobbled along in step, to the sound of the trumpets.

'What was the band for?'

'It was said the SS attached great importance to it. By playing marching tunes, they were trying to stimulate the prisoners' ardour during their walk, on the way to and from the workplace. In addition, the brass ensemble carried out a loathsome chore: it accompanied the condemned men to the gallows before they were hanged.'

'Did the musicians play properly?'

'I must admit they often impressed me. They were all detainees, top level musicians, mostly professional. The *Musikdirektor*, toadying to the SS, was tyrannical with the musicians and arrogant with the other inmates.'

When Michel Hollard entered the factory, an engineer greeted him. Seeing he was faced with another engineer, the German behaved relatively well. But the Frenchman's attitude was fiercely reserved. He carefully abstained from revealing all his skills since he intended to exercise only minor functions.

He did, however, benefit from a certain degree of independence, which soon turned out to be invaluable. He was in charge of checking how well several machines were working and had to carry out some finishing operations on machine gun breeches. It was an unbearable torment for him to have to take part in producing the enemy's armament. The enemy who'd managed to capture him now wanted to associate him to its wartime industry! At all costs, he had to do something to offset this vile job, even if only symbolically, or else he wouldn't be able to live with his conscience.

On his first day at work, he noticed the parts coming through his workshop didn't bear a serial number. At the end of the day, he seized the opportunity which a moment of solitude gave him and grabbed four breeches being machined, slipping them into his pockets. Clearly, the perpetrator of such a crime risked the gallows.

On the way back, the long procession – 200 prisoners in rows of five – ran into an SS patrol. A few men were searched. Some way off, Michel Hollard clutched his trophies tightly at the bottom of his pockets. During the walk, he gripped them firmly to prevent them from knocking around, as he had to act discreetly, since some of the prisoners were suspected of squealing. The first thing he did when he reached the camp was to go and throw the bulky objects into the latrines.

Encouraged by this initial success, Michel Hollard organised himself so he could do it again. Although he invariably left the factory with his pockets full, he was lucky, cool-headed and skilled enough to always slip through the SS net.

But the cumbersome parts soon raised the problem of how to get rid of them. The Neuengamme camp complex consisted of a veritable town built on former marshes on the banks of the Elbe. Its very rudimentary latrines comprised a series of huts, rows of planks with a number of holes over deep ditches. At the beginning, despite the almost endless stream of momentary visitors, the undesirable objects could be dropped without much difficulty. But after weeks of continuous dumping, there was a lot of invisible metal in the ditches. When a part was dropped, it more often than not hit one already there with a suspicious clang. However, for Michel Hollard, there was no question of giving up the only way he had of resisting.

But another danger was lurking. Regularly checking the surface level of the ditches into which he was throwing his booty, he saw that, while the metal objects were indeed heavy enough to sink into the viscous pit, the overall level was creeping higher all the time. The day of the big clean-out or drainage was perhaps drawing closer, with the threat of discovery followed by enquiries that might confound the saboteur.

Suddenly, an extraordinary rumour momentarily dispelled this threat when news that the Normandy landings had taken place on 6 June reached the camp. No one knew how the rumour started, but it spread like wildfire. At first people couldn't believe it was true, then the news was confirmed, enhanced with geographical and strategic details.

The deportees of the Compiègne-Neuengamme convoy, including Michel Hollard, realised their descent into hell had more or less coincided with the arrival of the liberation troops on French soil. An immense ray of hope illuminated the entire concentration camp population. In the general euphoria, many people thought the hour of freedom would soon be upon them. This made their disillusionment all the more bitter.

The SS became even more arrogant and aggressive than before. They had always been forbidden to chat with the inmates or to get to know them in any way. However, as soon as they learnt that certain *Vergeltungswaffen* (vengeance weapons) were beginning to be used, some of them, without even knowing what they were, couldn't help boasting about the 'revolutionary new weapons with which Germany was going to punish the enemy'.

All these assertions, despite their inaccuracies, overwhelmed Michel Hollard. But after he'd thought about it a bit, he regained confidence. He calculated that no less than nine months had passed since he'd discovered the various components of the flying machine, and before his arrest,

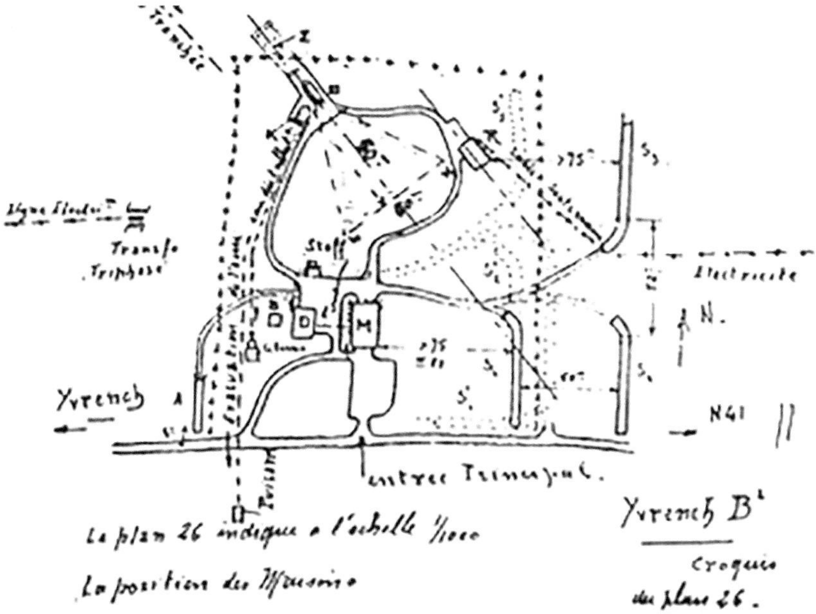

The drawing of the V-1 base at Bois Carré, Yvrench, communicated to the Secret Intelligence Service by Michel Hollard and André Comps in October 1943.

The same site photographed by the Royal Air Force on 3 November 1943.

Remains of the non-magnetic building where the V-1's automatic pilot was to be set. Bonnetot-le-Faubourg, in the commune of Tôtes (Seine-Maritime).

The marble plaque at the former site of the Café des Chasseurs where the four men were arrested on 5 February 1944. *Clockwise from top left:* Michel Hollard, Joseph Legendre, Jules Mailly and Henri Dujarier.

Stela at 207 Rue de Bercy, Paris 12[e], commemorating the members of the Agir network who died fighting for freedom.

Until the end of his life, Michel Hollard honoured the memory of his departed comrades.

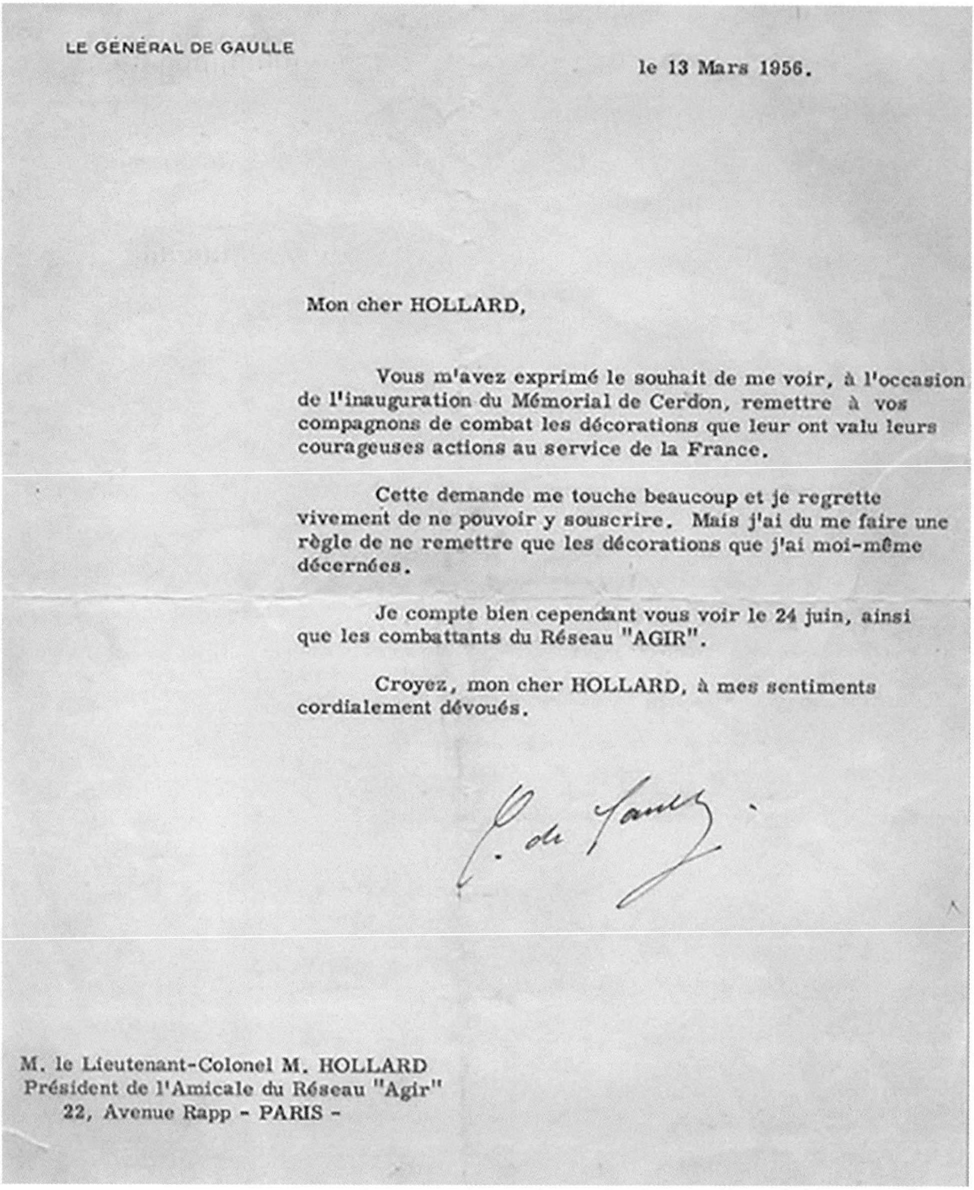

LE GÉNÉRAL DE GAULLE

le 13 Mars 1956.

Mon cher HOLLARD,

Vous m'avez exprimé le souhait de me voir, à l'occasion de l'inauguration du Mémorial de Cerdon, remettre à vos compagnons de combat les décorations que leur ont valu leurs courageuses actions au service de la France.

Cette demande me touche beaucoup et je regrette vivement de ne pouvoir y souscrire. Mais j'ai du me faire une règle de ne remettre que les décorations que j'ai moi-même décernées.

Je compte bien cependant vous voir le 24 juin, ainsi que les combattants du Réseau "AGIR".

Croyez, mon cher HOLLARD, à mes sentiments cordialement dévoués.

C. de Gaulle

M. le Lieutenant-Colonel M. HOLLARD
Président de l'Amicale du Réseau "Agir"
22, Avenue Rapp - PARIS -

General de Gaulle's response to Michel Hollard's request to honour his comrades-in-arms.

13 March 1956

My Dear Hollard,

On the occasion of the coming inauguration of the Mémorial de Cerdon, you have expressed a wish for me to present your comrades-in-arms with the decorations which their courageous actions in the service of France have earned them.
I am greatly touched by your request and sincerely regret that I cannot subscribe to it. I have had to make it a rule to bestow only those decorations that I myself have awarded.
I look forward, however, to seeing you and the combatants of the AGIR network on 24 June.

Yours sincerely,
(C. de Gaulle)

Michel and Yvonne Hollard circa 1950.

Michel Hollard, the rebel with a big heart.

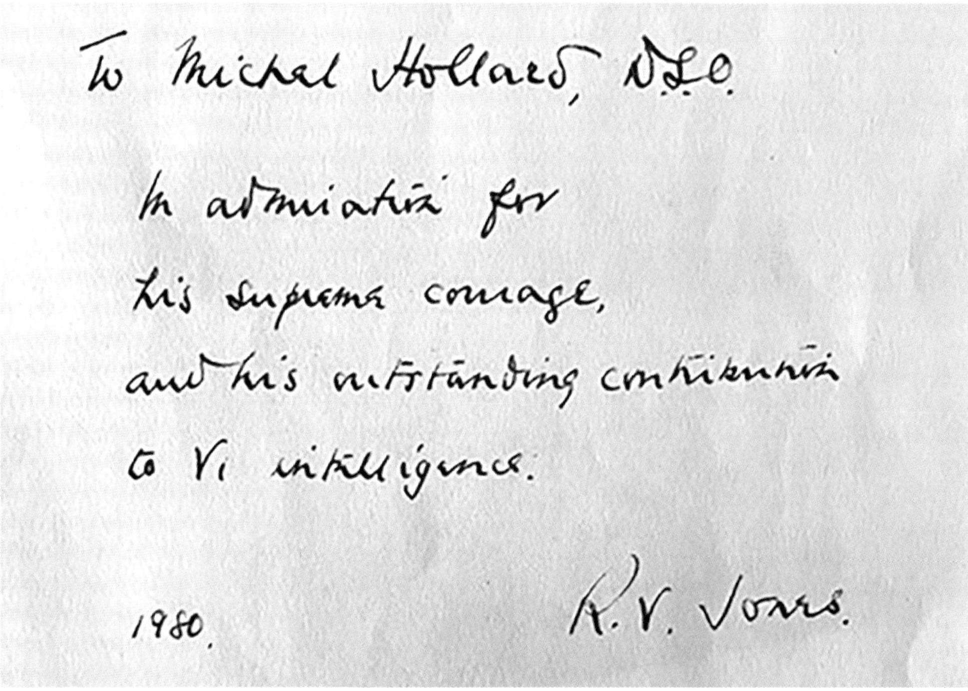

To Michel Hollard, D.S.O.

In admiration for
his supreme courage,
and his outstanding contribution
to V1 intelligence.

1980. R.V. Jones.

R.V. Jones' inscription in the US edition of his book *The Wizard War: British Scientific Intelligence 1939-1945*, which he presented to Michel Hollard. The book was published in the UK as *Most Secret War: British Scientific Intelligence 1939-1945*.

Ernst von Bressensdorf, Michel Hollard's German cousin, who bravely contributed to saving Paris.

Final resting place of Michel and Yvonne Hollard at Gorniès (Hérault).

Inauguration of the Paris–London Eurostar locomotive named after Michel Hollard on 27 April 2004. Waterloo International Station, London.

Michel Hollard's children (Florian, Francine and Vincent) at the London inauguration of the Eurostar locomotive bearing their father's name.

Florian Hollard, son of Michel Hollard, orchestra conductor and author of this book.

Michel Hollard in 1988 with his grand-nephew Philip Sandt, co-translator of this book.

Allied aircraft had already bombed many of the launch sites, most of them thanks to his information. He knew that unless the Agir network went through another crisis, it would continue investigating. At any rate, the attacks on London by unmanned aircraft could only have started after considerable delays.

As well as the far-fetched news that often went round the camp, some of the deportees assigned to the Metallwerke factory were sometimes able to read a local newspaper brough in by an engineer. Ironically, it was in this German newspaper that Michel Hollard found confirmation of the Normandy landings. The information was perfunctory and distorted, and presented the most fantastic landing in history as a simple strike, of no importance whatsoever!

When the first V-1 explosions shook London on 14 June 1944, the Allied units, which had landed in France on 6 June, had already been there for a week and were continuing to progress.[5] Nazi propaganda tried to demoralise them by dropping leaflets saying:

> You're trapped. Why has Germany waited a whole week after you landed before using its secret V-1 weapon? It was to encircle you. You're now roaming around a small area chosen by the Germans, while the flying bombs destroy the ports that are supposed to be supplying you. Your fleet is blocked. You're going to run out of materiel. Look for a way out of this mess. Think about it!

The Neuengamme deportees knew nothing of the dates or the order of the events which they had learnt about from the rumours. They had rejoiced too soon about the good news bringing hope, whilst the SS guards bragged about 'unbeatable German forces, now equipped with unstoppable weapons'.

***

When autumn came, a thick, cold fog covered the marshy region on the banks of the Elbe, making the atmosphere in Neuengamme prison even unhealthier. When the temperature dropped severely, only the toughest resisted the cold. All the seriously ill people were relegated to the huts wrongly called the *Krankenrevier* (infirmary). As there was no care there, they almost all died quickly.

In the dead of winter, Michel Hollard decided to help a fellow Frenchman abandoned there and cruelly deprived of food. He succeeded in getting into the kitchen without being seen and got hold of a piece of cabbage, which he took to the man. This extremely risky undertaking went off without a hitch, but it did make Hollard late at the departure point for the factory.

As he was unable to explain away his lateness to the SS henchmen, he had to atone for what he'd done at once. In this case the penalty was twenty-five strokes of the *Schlague* (steel-ribbed rubber truncheon). Losing his balance during the flogging, he rolled onto the ground, but the guard didn't stop the punishment. On the contrary, taking advantage of the prisoner's greater vulnerability, he savagely kicked him all over his body. Thanks to the closeness of a wall against which the prisoner managed to brace himself, he picked himself up just as the brute was counting out the final blows of the sentence.

This punishment left a permanent mark on Hollard: as he was lying on the ground, the brute had kicked his head and left ear with his heel. His eardrum was ruptured and he permanently lost some of his hearing. The severest trials never altered this mystical man's morale permanently; his energetic and meditative nature saved him from despair.

Despite the agitation in the workshop, he'd learnt to dissociate his actions from his thoughts. While doing the bare minimum of forced labour, he was able to find his favourite refuge in poetic meditation.

Still deprived of writing materials, he continued the remarkable mental effort by which he had conceived and memorised his harrowing poem, 'Carnival'. Thus the hero, poet and prisoner, went on to write several more texts, one of which was to become 'Redemption' (see Appendix 7) and another, the following poem, 'Offering':

OFFERING

My homeland was enslaved, and She was the most beautiful.
Her smile and Her voice had been stifled.
A flood of oafish soldiers had seized Her
To enslave Her soul and dictate Her laws.

Bruised in my flesh by so much servitude,
I came to offer myself for France, one fine day.
Many a night I have walked in the harshest weather
Crossing snow and water, in turn.
I've known ambush and dogs hot on my heels
And many other rigours that seemed very gentle to me.
For Her, I emptied their cup with love.

With joy in my heart, I was able, for more than a year
To work tirelessly against our oppressors.
I deflected the throwing of a poisoned weapon
Whose horrors they secretly reserved for us...
To foil their plans, I put in all my effort
And reaped, through them, more than a full harvest
On thorny ground, of liberating grains!

One evening, the enemies surprised my work
And quickly threw me into a dark dungeon,
Then they took revenge, and I knew their rage,
But I only had the prison on a distant shore
And my heart, despite everything, was able to keep hope!

Misery of the convict, stripped of his being;
Abduction of the most humble object and the last garment,
Defeat of the one who feels himself disappearing
In a sordid nothingness where his whole self perishes...
Distress of falling into full decline
Under a torrent of abuse heard in helplessness
Of a fate nourished by hope, which today everything bruises...

Atone, in exile, for the misfortunes of France;
Receive the *Schlague* and the knout there, every day,
No, this cannot be a suffering for us
Since we were able to serve Her, in our turn!
If we pay for Her, in fervent silence,
All our ills today serve Her deliverance:
Let's offer them to Her cheerfully, as a pledge of love!

OFFRANDE

Ma patrie était serve, et c'était la plus belle.
On avait étouffé son sourire et sa voix.
Un flot de lourds soldats s'était emparé d'elle
Pour asservir son âme et lui dicter ses lois.

Meurtri jusqu'en ma chair par tant de servitude,
Je suis venu m'offrir pour la France, un beau jour.
Maintes nuits j'ai marché par le temps le plus rude
En franchissant la neige et les eaux, tour à tour.
J'ai connu l'embuscade et les chiens à mes trousses
Et bien d'autres rigueurs qui m'ont paru très douces.
Pour Elle, j'ai vidé leur coupe avec amour.

J'ai pu, la joie au cœur, pendant plus d'une année
Travailler sans répit contre nos oppresseurs.
J'ai détourné le jet d'une arme empoisonnée
Dont ils nous réservaient, en secret, les horreurs...
À déjouer leurs plans, j'ai mis toute ma peine
Et fait, à travers eux, plus d'une moisson pleine
Sur un sol épineux, de grains libérateurs !

Un soir, les ennemis ont surpris mon ouvrage
Et m'ont jeté bien vite au fond d'un cachot noir,
Puis, ils se sont vengés, et j'ai connu leur rage,
Mais je n'eus que le bagne en un lointain rivage
Et mon cœur, malgré tout, a pu garder l'espoir !

Misère du forçat, dépouillement de l'être ;
Rapt du plus humble objet et du dernier habit,
Défaite de celui qui se sent disparaître
Dans un néant sordide où tout son moi périt...
Détresse de tomber en pleine déchéance
Sous un torrent d'injures ouï dans l'impuissance
D'un sort nourri d'espoir, qu'aujourd'hui tout meurtrit...

Expier, dans l'exil, les malheurs de la France ;
Y recevoir la schlague et le knout, chaque jour,
Non, cela ne saurait nous être une souffrance
Puisque nous l'avons pu servir, à notre tour !
Si nous payons pour Elle, en un fervent silence,
Tous nos maux d'aujourd'hui servent sa délivrance :
Offrons-les-lui gaîment, comme un gage d'amour !

Let us give Her, without regret, our pains and our sorrows	*Donnons-lui, sans regret, nos douleurs et nos peines*
And a certain heavy burden, of all, the cruellest...	*Et certain lourd fardeau, de tous, le plus cruel...*
From our harshest torments let us hold out the cups full	*De nos plus durs tourments tendons les coupes pleines*
Of pure incense rising from the prison to the sky!	*D'un pur encens montant du bagne vers le ciel !*
Our homeland, then, enriched by a free gift	*Notre patrie, alors, d'un don libre enrichie*
Will feel new life growing within Her	*Sentira croître en elle une nouvelle vie*
And will see Her eternal triumph blossom anew!	*Et verra refleurir son triomphe éternel !*

Neuengamme, summer 1944[6]

To obtain the solitude he needed, Michel Hollard regularly didn't hesitate to break the rules the SS had made. At night, while a lot of men were still chattering, he would sneak out of the sleeping quarters. Still wearing his rags, he went to the sink, the only oasis of solitude accessible to him. One evening, around 10 pm, the door opened abruptly. It was the *Lagerältester*.[7]

'When I saw who it was, I thought I was finished. Dressed and still up after the curfew, I was going to be guilty of trying to escape.'

'*Was machst du da?*' (What are you doing here?) he asked.

'*Ich bete*' (I'm praying).

The man had the power of life and death over any detainee he suspected of insubordination. Without saying a word, he left the premises to return soon after, carrying a metal stool.

'I was expecting to be hit on the head with that stool, but with a sign of his hand he invited me to sit and then withdrew quietly! From then onwards, he refrained from coming so as not to disturb my moments of introspection.'

Michel Hollard was not just content with being able to observe a daily moment of solitary contemplation. Several of his companions, who were impressed by his energy, turned to him seeking words of hope. Although meetings of more than two people were forbidden, each week he comforted a number of people eager to join in his meditations.

The masters of the Reich had long since realised that near uninterrupted labour, seven days a week, quickly wore out even the strongest convicts. The lack of a labour force for industry, however, was becoming increasingly serious. To make better use of their slaves' energy before death took them away prematurely, certain dignitaries, including some of those who held sway at Neuengamme, were resigned to instituting a break on Sundays.

I asked my father about this:

'What did the deportees do on Sundays with suddenly nothing to do?'

'They first had to clean the sleeping quarters. Then they wandered around the main square, talking noisily. The SS stood guard, constantly yelling at someone, bludgeon in hand. Within the immense enclosure swarming with people, it was impossible to find a remote, quiet place.'

Nonetheless, every week in the middle of the crowd, a circle of seven or eight men formed up around Michel Hollard, violating the SS regulations.

'It was only an attempt at contemplation, continually disturbed by the overall noise, and also impaired by lack of comprehension from most of the deportees. Our group, it's true, could only make sense to those who had enough notions of French.'

'What was the meditation about?'

'There was no question of outlining a real sermon. Each time, in a loud voice, I quoted a very short verse from the Bible. For example, "God is Love", or "Faith Can Move Mountains", or even "The Lord is My Shepherd". I would then add a few sentences of commentary. I was asked to pray. So, in the middle of all the shouting from the people wandering around, I tried to out-shout them with: "We ask the Lord to help François' mother to get better, to help Jeannot's family who is without resources…"'

'The guards never noticed anything?'

'No, this means of communication, lost as it was in the hubbub, didn't attract too much attention.'

There were more and more alerts as the SS continued to worry that Allied bombs would breach the camp's outside fence. In the case of paratroopers landing, such openings would have encouraged a large number of prisoners to escape. Each time an air raid was announced, the guards hurried to lock the prisoners up in the shelters as best they could.

Their checking and surveillance system was weakened by all this. During one air raid, several deportees going down to an underground passage were surprised to find a group of children whose presence there was being kept secret. Little faces of boys and girls, aged 5 to 12, looked on with terror at the strange-looking newcomers who, as attentive observers, were convinced these children had been subjected to medical experiments. After he'd heard the news, Michel Hollard took a big risk by announcing to his weekly congregation in the middle of the chattering crowd, for all to hear:

'Our thoughts go out to the youngsters in this prison; we fear they're shamefully being used as guinea pigs!'

Later, these fears were to be tragically confirmed. After several months of tests carried out secretly, the young Jewish victims suffered from increasing and irreversible disorders. In the spring of 1945, with the Allied armies fast approaching, the group of children was hurriedly evacuated. Under the bombs, and in the confusion of a series of orders and counter-orders, the young martyrs were transferred to Hamburg where the SS forced them down into the basement of a disused school where they were then anaesthetised before being finished off as they slept.

The SS wanted to eliminate all witnesses of their crimes. They hanged the four members of the medical surveillance team (two French doctors and two Dutch nurses, all deportees) who'd been assigned to accompany the children. But British justice caught up with the murderers and, having been made to account for their crimes, they were sentenced to death.

Chapter 29

Floating Tomb

At the Nuremberg Trials, certain camp commandants tried to exonerate themselves by claiming they'd received a confidential telegram from their minister, Reichsführer-SS Heinrich Himmler. The message, they said, contained the following directive: 'According to a formal order issued by the Führer, no prisoner must be allowed to fall into the hands of the enemy alive.'

Towards mid-April 1945, the Neuengamme detainees heard the first echoes of gunfire. These sounds were of course a great source of hope but, on the other hand, the Allied soldiers' advances caused most of the camp guards to panic and it increased their aggressiveness. For the huge majority of the inmates, this renewal of confidence proved to be misleading. The SS were unable to control their exasperation and became even more savage than before. Their first initiative was to force the weakest inmates to pile into goods wagons ready to leave for other camps.

Several convoys got under way and travelled for days, slowly. They followed winding, disorderly routes, with a lot of stops along the way. More than half the passengers died during the journey from thirst, hunger and exhaustion. Among the survivors, many were carried off by typhus at Bergen-Belsen. Others, whose wanderings had stopped at Gardelegen, suffered the same fate as the martyrs of Oradour-sur-Glane; they were locked up in a barn full of hay, which was then set on fire by the SS.

There was one notable exception, however. After roaming by train, then on foot and by sea, a group of deportees, cooped up in the hold of a ship called *Rheinfeld*, reached the port of Flensburg, near the Danish border. Two doctors, officers in the Kriegsmarine who were inspecting the ship, discovered the unfortunate people. Indignant at the pitiful condition the prisoners were in, they decided to help them.

Thanks to the intervention of these German Good Samaritans, the sailors took the deportees' defence against the fanatical and pig-headed SS. A scuffle broke out between the two German groups, which the sailors won. The deportees were handed over to a Danish diplomatic mission that managed to get them across into neutral Sweden, where they were cared for before being returned home.

The history of the Second World War has thus recorded many amazing rescues, among which should be included the freeing of Michel Hollard.

After fifteen months' detention, three-quarters of which took place in a concentration camp on a starvation diet, he was only skin and bones. His alarming thinness made him unrecognisable, but had in no way diminished either his courage or his tenacity. The physical exercise, which in spite of everything he kept up every morning, and his constant cerebral activity kept him in a condition which drew the admiration of his companions. Several of those who were liberated recognised the decisive influence of his exemplary conduct and his comforting words. They declared that in the absence of his formidable demonstration of energy, they wouldn't have held out until they were freed.

Another advance by the Allied armies hastened the complete evacuation of Neuengamme, demanded by SS headquarters. Before leaving the area, each prisoner was surprised to receive one of the many American Red Cross food parcels that had been sent to the camp. As these were high-quality food preserves, the SS had at first helped themselves. Then, in all the hurry, they were quite incapable of taking this godsend with them, so they had suddenly hit on what seemed to be a more generous attitude.

***

Between 20 and 28 April 1945, the 10,000 or so inmates still present on the site were hustled into cattle wagons. Long convoys set off without anybody anywhere knowing anything about where they were going. After half a day's travelling, the train carrying Michel Hollard reached a big town. A signpost told them they were entering Lübeck station. The trip went on to the edge of the Baltic Sea, in front of a quay in the outer harbour of Travemünde, where there were several ships docked in pairs, next to each other. For a few moments, several prisoners deluded themselves into thinking they would soon be sailing to Sweden, but the SS's unchanged behaviour soon dispelled any illusions they might have had.

'*Schnell, schnell! Los, los!*' (Quick, quick! Get out, get out!) the henchmen shouted, handing out blows with their bludgeons, hitting the most vulnerable people in particular. The group had to climb over the deck of the first ship, an old boat seemingly unusable which was used as a pontoon. From there, shaky gangplanks led to the *Thielbek*, a big and almost as dilapidated merchantman. The prisoners, all jostled along a winding succession of passageways and abrupt stairs, followed each other in single file, going deeper and deeper into the bowels of this second ship.

'There were almost 2,000 of us,' Michel Hollard was to say later, 'going down into the hold of the ship. We had to get used to the dark since even in broad daylight there was barely any light down there.

'Several men succumbed, both from exhaustion, starvation, and from ill-treatment by the prison warders. Their corpses lay in a corner, piled up for lack of space, waiting for the SS's discretion to throw them overboard.[1]

'A big metal vat was used as the latrines. It was already overflowing when we arrived. Shortly afterwards, it was hoisted up to the ceiling. To empty it, it had to be lifted to the upper deck through a hatch, but this refused to open and the vat then overturned, spilling its contents all over the poor people on the wrong side. As for me, I was hanging onto a nearby ladder, so I was able to escape the filthy downpour!'

Michel Hollard was unable to say how much time he spent in this floating prison. A reconstruction of the events based on the former belligerents' archives shows it lasted ten days. The few survivors from this period didn't talk about it very willingly. My father ended up answering my questions:

'At the bottom of the floating prison, what did you do? What did you talk about? I suppose the prisoners weren't inert, they must have done something…'

'But they were, they didn't! Most of the time, they were completely stultified. At the beginning, we did talk a bit. After the vat flipped over, we had to coordinate our efforts to remove the excrements as best we could to avoid wading endlessly in this quagmire. It was obviously intolerable.

And the SS – they found the incident hugely funny – were in no hurry to hand over any buckets or cleaning things that we needed.'

'How were you fed?'

'The American rations we got before the camp was closed allowed us to hold out longer. The group of friends that we formed had organised itself so that for each of us, we limited our daily intake of the precious food we'd pooled. But the moment came when our reserves ran out and we had to go back to our ordinary daily ration of undefined leftovers the SS deigned to bring us, and that occurred less and less frequently. Our strength quickly diminished.'

'Those extreme conditions probably forced you to interrupt your physical exercises.'

'Not at all! Being among the last to reach the bottom of the hold, I wound up next to the foot of a ladder, which went through a hatch to the upper decks of the ship. Certain crew members, and the SS guarding us, used it regularly. Their trips down among us lasted several minutes, during which time the exit was left open. I took advantage of opportunities like these to go and do my exercises on the upper levels.'

'Did your comrades follow you?'

'I asked them to, but no one did. Climbing the vertical ladder with widely spaced rungs needed a lot of effort and most of the men were exhausted. More often than not I paid for my escapades by getting beaten, but at that price, I was able to keep up my regular physical training and could give myself invaluable gulps of fresh air.'[2]

The ship's hull would echo with the lapping of waves and the engine noises of the vessels manoeuvring in the harbour. Thus, on 22 or 23 April, the captives heard another big ship docked nearby getting under way. It was discovered later that this was the freighter *Athen*, also converted into a prison.

Although the German rout was getting worse, the *Thielbek* lingered in the harbour for no apparent reason. But then, one morning, the crew was unusually agitated. From all sides came the screeching of pulleys, cables and chains, while the engines were rumbling outside. The mystery was later cleared up: the freighter's engines had given up the ghost and two tugs had been called in to help prepare for a hauling operation.[3]

The sound of guns announced the approaching Allied troops. Why didn't the Germans, inexorably condemned to flee, just leave and abandon the unfortunate people where they were? This over-simple solution would have freed thousands of witnesses to a shocking prison organisation, so they had to be silenced forever.

Some of the prisoners analysed the situation very well and were careful not to think of this rush to leave as a promising opportunity for emigration; on the contrary, they saw it as a bad omen.

***

On 30 April 1945, in the darkness of the hold, in the middle of the prostrate and silent crowd, Michel Hollard overcame his own distress and decided to break the silence. The group assembled around him consisted mainly of people he knew and even numbered some of his most faithful friends. Knowing that most of them spoke or understood French, he said something like this:

> My companions and brothers, we're off again to somewhere we don't know. The Germans are indeed losing the war, but we're still at their mercy. Their failures, to which we've all contributed, make them even more aggressive and redoubtable than ever before. In these circumstances, even more than during the happy earlier periods, we have to show energy and generosity of spirit. You don't necessarily share my Christian convictions, but the obvious reason for your presence in the middle of this hell is because you once served an ideal. To all who feel they're concerned by these words, I suggest we form a chain.

Holding out his hands to the left and right, he set the example, and with his neighbours began a line that grew rapidly, forming a curve on both sides. When the two ends joined up, he continued:

'Those of you who've had some religious instruction know that Jesus said, "For where two or three are gathered together in My name, I am there in the midst of them."[4] In our distress, let us pray to the Lord to watch over our families, to accompany the captives cooped up like us in a ship and, more generally, protect those who are victims of injustice and barbarity…'

To finish, Hollard invited his fellow prisoners to honour, in silence, the memory of their brothers and sisters who'd fallen as martyrs.

The men had listened with fervent attention, or at least respect, to their friend's message. With that, a strange silence settled upon them.[5] It was at that moment that, without much surprise, a series of events, up until then quite inconceivable, took place.

A creaking sound was suddenly heard coming from the upper deck. The hatch opened unexpectedly, flooding the inside with blinding light. Then there was a strange order, spoken awkwardly in two languages:

'Those who speak French are ordered up onto the deck!'

Although it was the voice of the SS duty guard, it had lost something of its usual arrogance and authority. Caught on the hop and overwhelmed, the prisoners concerned didn't react immediately. The SS, decidedly less surly than usual, repeated his call. At that moment, Michel Hollard's intuition told him that this was *the* moment.

'Come on, lads!' he exclaimed. 'The order we've just received is for all the French speakers amongst us. Such a move can't be by chance. Hurry up and let's get out of here!'

Realising that climbing the ladders would be too much of an effort for some of the men, Hollard spared no effort and lent a helping hand to those who needed it. He took it upon himself to shake some of them rather violently, otherwise they wouldn't have budged. Held up by the ones he was helping to climb out, he slipped out of the hold just before the hatch closed back down once and for all. It fell onto his foot, but luckily not too heavily.

Without really knowing why they'd been grouped together, about 140 men were now outside on the deck, all vibrant with crazy expectations. These haggard-faced French, Swiss, Belgians and Dutchmen only started to believe in a miracle when they noticed how the SS guards were behaving. As if by a miracle, the guards had become as gentle as lambs. They were now looking meekly at their erstwhile victims.

The police contingents included the 'grey mice'. Sitting behind desks, they questioned the prisoners individually, noting the identity of each of them. For these prisoners whom the SS referred to only by their numbers, these formalities were like a resurrection. Not believing what they were going through, the former slaves had the impression they were reacquiring a bit of human dignity, as well as their real names.

'After living for ages in the most indescribable filth,' said Michel Hollard, 'deprived of all sanitary supplies and all basic toiletries, we were repugnant. Without waiting for water to be available to us, we took advantage of the puddles left by the rain on the deck to wash ourselves, at least summarily.'

Outside the hold, the ex-convicts seemed to have acquired a sort of prestige with the SS guards, who'd become almost polite and now guided the procession towards a gangway down to the quayside. The idea of a departure, although still somewhat vague, lifted the men, and even those most unsteady on their feet tried to follow the movement enthusiastically.

A cattle wagon from Neuengamme had halted not far from the cargo ship. Its floor was completely covered with ill or wounded deportees. The unfortunate men benefited from the dedication of one of their own who was able to look after them, the American doctor Sumner Waldron Jackson. The physician's own son, Phillip, was among the patients.

In the past, Dr Jackson had had a top job at the American Hospital of Paris in Neuilly-sur-Seine. In the camp, he'd met Michel Hollard several times. Both men had drawn similar conclusions from the way the war was going and they respected and liked each other.

The doctor, on the threshold of the infirmary wagon watching over his charges, saw the group of French speakers approaching. Michel Hollard spotted him and left his companions to run and tell him of the still unexplained circumstances of their exit from the boat, without worrying about how the SS guards would react; they were now curiously indifferent watchdogs.

'You lived in Paris,' he argued. 'You speak excellent French. Your place is unquestionably with us!'

Without commenting, the doctor turned his head towards his patients. Some of them were dying. He looked sadly at the wagonload of men, deprived of everything, even pallets, and for whom he felt responsible, morally as much as medically.

The gesture he made meant 'Goodbye' or 'Farewell' and invited Hollard to leave and catch up with his group, already a long way off, while there was still time.

***

The deportees, led by their now cautious SS guards, approached a magnificent white cargo ship. None of them could have ever imagined that their tattered horde would've been worthy of such luxury. They thought they were dreaming when one of their escorts started to climb the gangway and made them follow him.

The ship, named *Magdalena*, flew Swedish colours. The whole crew, beginning with Captain Lindberg, did all they could to comfort, care for and pamper their guests as soon as they came aboard. They were spread out in various dining rooms and given only a very light snack.

'Please excuse how meagre your first meals are,' the cooks announced, 'but be patient! We know your stomachs have been starved for so long that medically they would be unable to stand you eating anything substantial at the moment. So, because Sweden wants you to get better in the best possible conditions, you'll just have to make do with not very appealing menus and small portions for some time yet!'

In spite of the touching kindness the Swedish sailors showed them, the travellers still remained in doubt as to the reality of their release. This scepticism was due to the continued presence of an SS NCO who still accompanied them. Although he said nothing, he still caused anxiety. Moreover, once the *Magdalena* had got under way, a small German ship followed her out to the open sea.

Suddenly, the Swedish ship stopped. The ex-prisoners saw their last guard use the outside ladder to jump aboard the boat that had escorted them and was now alongside. Both ships immediately set off again, but this time in opposite directions.

***

For a short moment, seeing the German ship disappearing, the passengers looked at each other questioningly. When it became obvious that the boat was vanishing forever, everybody became delirious with euphoria. There were joyful hurrahs, soon followed by *La Marseillaise*. The national anthem was sung not only by those who'd escaped hell, be they French, Swiss, Belgian or Dutch, but by most of the ship's complement.

The former deportees learnt from the sailors that they probably owed their salvation to Count Bernadotte, the Vice-Chairman of the Swedish Red Cross and the representative of a famous family of French ancestry. This well-known figure had been working all out to save as many detainees as possible of all origins, defying the SS. The veil surrounding these difficult negotiations has never really been completely lifted but, most likely, the liberation of the French speakers aboard the *Thielbek* was part of a bargain. A group of women from Ravensbrück boarded another Swedish ship, the *Lillie Matthiessen*. These deportees had probably benefited from the same barter.

Overcrowded with the sick and the wounded, German hospitals had run out of medicine. The Swedish Red Cross had most likely agreed to supply them on condition that, after unloading their precious merchandise, its ships could go back to sea with as many prisoners as possible aboard.

***

While the *Magdalena* was on her way to Sweden looking after her still-stunned passengers, a tragedy was taking place in the Bay of Lübeck.

Before the *Thielbek* left Travemünde's outer harbour, the SS forced a new group of captives to climb aboard, among whom were Dr Jackson and his remaining patients, the other occupants of the infirmary wagon having almost all perished. Helped by two tugs, the ship, with damaged engines, only sailed a couple of miles along the coast towards the port of Neustadt. It dropped anchor near three other ships, all turned into prisons, all outstations of the Neuengamme camp.

Two of these ships, the impressive liners *Cap Arcona* and *Deutschland*, could hardly move because there was no longer enough fuel. The third, the cargo ship *Athen*, the only one that was able to sail, had been used to deliver the prisoners to the bigger floating prisons.

On 3 May 1945, towards midday, as the *Athen* headed for Neustadt, an RAF reconnaissance plane flew over the four ships at low altitude. The plane was shot at by several of the on-board machine guns without being damaged. On the outside, the ships obviously showed no signs of having been converted into prisons. After it had finished its reconnaissance flight, the observer logically concluded the ships were carrying retreating German troops as they tried to escape from the Allies who were about to appear at any moment. Back at base, the pilot alerted a squadron of fighter-bombers, which took off immediately and rushed to the bay. The *Cap Arcona*, *Deutschland* and *Thielbek* were quickly sunk, while the *Athen*, less severely hit, was returning to port.

The death toll was certainly close to and probably higher than 7,000 prisoners drowned or burned, to which must be added several hundred German victims serving in the Kriegsmarine or the SS brigades.

***

Some prisoners, however, still fit enough and smart enough, had managed to escape the ships in distress in time. To make up for the lack of life jackets, which the Germans had all swiped, the captives threw overboard any large unsinkable items – tables, doors, wood panels, etc. – they'd managed to free before jumping into the sea after them. The water was very cold and, although many tried to cling to lifeboats, all full of soldiers, blows from the oars and boathooks caused a large number to drown.

Others disappeared in even crueller circumstances. Various witnesses saw fast motorboats deliberately sailing over the swimmers, many of whom perished after being crushed or cut up by the propellers. Some of them, just as they were about to reach the shore, were mowed down by machine gunners or riflemen.

There were nonetheless some 350 survivors from the huge *Cap Arcona* and fifty or so from the *Thielbek*. As the *Deutschland* had sunk further away from the shore, there were no survivors. The *Athen*, only lightly hit, was in Neustadt harbour with 1,998 prisoners in the hold.[6] Up until then the ex-prisoners had been prostrate, but they now noticed there was an unusual calm hanging over the deck, and one of them was emboldened to push up the flap of the hatch after finding it unlocked.

'*Sie sind alle weg! Es lebe die Freiheit!*' (They've all gone! Long live freedom!) he shouted to everyone's amazement.

Indeed, the SS and the crew, taken by surprise at the sudden appearance of the first British tank, had taken off. In an indescribable unleashing of enthusiasm, there was a massive rush for the exits, which were unfortunately too narrow.

The English soldiers couldn't hide their dismay when they found these emaciated, ragged deportees, many of whom were staggering. The liberators immediately did what they could to ensure these ghost-like men were given emergency care and decent temporary shelter. On the same day, the miraculous survivors from the other ships received similar attention. Phillip Jackson managed to escape from the wreck that was fatal for his father. Despite his fragile health, he kept calm and survived the ordeal of having to swim. Several flak boats (anti-aircraft defence) crossed the zone where he was swimming with others. In their hurry, the pilots of these boats picked up a good number of men they saw were in dire straits before realising they were prisoners; they decided to get rid of them by dropping them off on the nearest shore.

Along the coast there were still strongholds of overexcited SS fanatics who, with their machine guns, cut swathes through the groups of men who'd just landed. Luckily for some, the English vanguard arrived almost immediately to put a definitive end to their nightmare.

Phillip Jackson was among a group that escaped the machine gun fire. Taken in hand by the British, he joined other survivors picked up at various points on the shore.

An English officer wanted to speak to the little group of French-speaking Neuengamme survivors. Phillip Jackson, who spoke perfect

French, was one of them, as was a Paris engineer, Maurice Gacheny, who'd escaped from the *Athen*.

'We're looking for a Frenchman called Michel Hollard. He was held for a long time in the same camp as you. Did you ever meet him?'

'Michel Hollard!' said Maurice Gacheny, startled. 'Of course I know him! He's even an excellent friend. But I'm very worried for him. We last saw each other in the camp. Afterwards, I think the SS threw him into the *Thielbek* almost two weeks ago now. If you hear anything about him, please tell me. Unfortunately, the chances of seeing him again seem very slim, since the ship has been sunk...'

Phillip Jackson broke in at that moment saying he'd just lived through that tragedy when he escaped from the cargo ship:

'I was aboard the *Thielbek* myself. I managed to get out onto the deck when the ship started to capsize. My father remained in the hold. When I tried to save him, there were 1,500 people all trying to get out. Now they're almost all dead and how I survived is a miracle. As far as Michel Hollard is concerned, I think there's still a chance of finding him again. Towards the end of April, I was lying ill, half-conscious on the floor of the infirmary wagon. I remember hearing somebody talking to my father, it was probably Michel Hollard. He said that we perhaps had an opportunity to get away to freedom, but we were in no state to follow him. The next day the SS forced us out of the wagon and locked us in the depths of the ship.'

'Your being here and what you say are both invaluable and moving. As for Michel Hollard, it's rather encouraging,' declared the Englishman. 'Until we know what's happened to this man, we'll continue looking for him. He played a very important part in the Allied war effort. He was one of the architects of victory that is now virtually assured.'

***

On 8 May 1945, when peace was officially proclaimed, the Hollard family had no idea whether Michel was still alive. We obviously knew nothing about what he'd been through, and while the streets of Paris vibrated with the dancing and parties of the wild crowd, we were thinking only of our missing father and husband and were not in the mood to take part in the celebrations.

On 25 August the year before, the German invaders, formerly boasting arrogantly, had been marched through the streets with their hands up, officers first, in front of screaming crowds. The media commented on the interminable agony of the Third Reich, that superpower which, according to Hitler, was supposed to rule the world for a thousand years.

***

When a repatriation centre for returning deportees was created, Yvonne and Francine Hollard – mother and daughter – volunteered to work with the reception committees.[7] At the meeting point set up in the Hôtel Lutetia, Boulevard Raspail in Paris, they met many returning ex-prisoners. Most of these former slaves bore the obvious traces of suffering, both physical and mental; all were atrociously thin and some of them staggered. A year earlier, when the sentences were commuted for certain prisoners, nobody in our entourage really knew what the SS concentration camp regime was like.

'Your husband is receiving preferential treatment,' a 'grey mouse' of the German prison administration had told my mother, not without cynicism. So, she imagined that her husband was being detained in decent conditions, as the soldiers captured in 1940 had been.

When Yvonne and Francine Hollard met ex-prisoners returning from the various German camps for the first time, they got a real shock. Trying not to let it show, while their own searches remained in vain, they provided the newcomers with warm-hearted assistance. The statistics we received about the liberation of the camps showed an appalling number of deaths, and we came to believe that our wait was without hope.

However, none of the repatriated men that passed through the Hôtel Lutetia came from Neuengamme; this was explained suddenly by the providential arrival of a man who declared to the welcoming committee:

'I'm Maurice Gacheny. I left northern Germany the day before yesterday. On 3 May, I managed to escape from the naval disaster in the Bay of Lübeck. The SS had shut up thousands of deportees in the holds of four ships, three of which sank. Most of my comrades didn't survive. I was in the only boat that wasn't sunk.

'I've come here with an urgent message for the family of one of Neuengamme's inmates. I'm afraid I don't have his address. Perhaps you can help me. His name is Michel Hollard.'

My mother, quite dumbfounded, cried out trembling:

'Michel Hollard is my husband. I'm extremely worried and I dread what you're about to say. However, even if the news is bad, I want to know at once!'

'Please don't worry, Madame, he's safe and sound, after many close calls with death. Just recently he almost drowned, but now he's safe. You won't be seeing him right now, though. At the moment he's with other survivors somewhere in Sweden – the country that saved them. They'll be looked after there until they're fit again. Those lucky devils will be back looking much better than me!'

'If what you say is true,' she said deeply moved, 'You're a messenger from Heaven!'

Gacheny finished his rundown of recent events, telling them of his meeting with the English officer on the Baltic coast who, true to his promise, had told him that Michel Hollard and his French-speaking companions had embarked aboard the Swedish cargo ship the *Magdalena*.

Yvonne Hollard impatiently wanted to listen longer to this bringer of marvellous news and had suddenly become as radiant as she'd been before.

'Would you like to join me and my three children tomorrow for a family dinner?' she asked him.

Maurice Gacheny didn't need much persuasion to come and sit at our table. Although he was still a bit pale and thin, he spoke vividly, and even succeeded in introducing a touch of humour into what he said about his worst memories. He started by completely reassuring us that his friend Michel Hollard would be coming back soon; he had as much admiration for him as he did affection. Then he made us all shudder when he told us about some of the daily barbaric acts the SS had been guilty of for years.

Maurice Gacheny's visit was followed the next day by that of a British diplomat, whose twofold task was first to inform my mother that her husband had just landed at Trelleborg, in the south of Sweden, without any problems. He then informed her that His Majesty the King had decided to present the French hero with the Distinguished Service Order; the highest decoration Great Britain could award to a foreigner.

***

The journey aboard the *Magdalena*, which covered about 125 miles, had lasted not less than three days. As the sea was strewn with mines, the ship travelled slowly, dropping anchor each evening. On the way, the passengers saw German ships sailing past, flying their flags at half-mast. This sign of mourning was explained to them after they reached Sweden; the Führer, Adolf Hitler, had committed suicide on 30 April.

A delegation of the Swedish Red Cross was waiting for the cargo ship on the quayside at Trelleborg. Two deportees had died of typhus during the crossing, so the doctors took emergency measures to contain the outbreak and several patients had to be taken to the hospital.

Female volunteers protected by special masks and suits looked after the rest of the group. They started by inviting all the men to have a long shower, using powerful disinfectants, and then gave them a set of underclothes and a new suit to replace their rags, which were then burnt.

As there was still a risk of contagion, the medical authorities deemed it necessary to have their guests watched and to prevent anybody going near them for the next twenty days. The newcomers spent this quarantine period in an isolated area. As well as a message of welcome, the French Embassy sent them writing materials, saying it would send the letters to their families.

Michel Hollard had his doubts, though, about the efficiency of the diplomatic route. Having written and sealed a second letter, he weighted it down with a stone and threw it into the street. It landed at the feet of a passer-by, who picked it up and looked upwards. He spotted the thrower behind a window, holding up a piece of cardboard with 'POST' written on it. With his hands, he imitated a plane flying. Both letters reached their destination but the first, the one sent through official French channels, arrived ten days later.

When the doctors were certain their patients were no longer contagious, they settled them in a convalescent home tucked away in the countryside, in a village called Stenjöholm. Treated like royalty, the ex-detainees let themselves be cared for and spoilt until they had recovered their health.

For the rest of his life, Michel Hollard always showed his gratitude towards Sweden, and in particular to the Swedish Red Cross, to whom he owed his salvation. From the initial cruise aboard the *Magdalena* from Travemünde to Trelleborg until the return flight to France, he often praised the fabulous holiday 'offered by a generous nation to a cohort of disease-ridden survivors'.

The return flight from Stockholm to Paris was made in groups of about ten passengers. Hollard had not asked for any particular favour, but was designated by his companions to be on the first flight back home to France.

A French figure generally regarded as important, wanting to mark this great day solemnly, went to Stockholm airport. He made a speech in honour of the patriots lined up in front of him. Agir's founder, however, knew this man had distinguished himself during the war by his indulgent and opportunistic attitude towards the enemy.

Once he'd finished his speech, the prominent man went up to each of the deportees with a self-important and patronising air to complement them individually. When he came face to face with Michel Hollard, the latter showed he was quite clearly indifferent to what the man was saying to him. At the end of his hypocritical words, which he found repulsive, Hollard looked skywards and, keeping his arms rigidly alongside his body, refused to shake the collaborator's hand.

The English authorities, now knowing that their revered French associate was alive and benefiting from Swedish hospitality, had decided to look after him once he was better. They wanted to give him a warm welcome in London before accompanying him to Paris. However, because of a coordination mistake between the British and Swedish administrative services, the man chosen to accompany Hollard to London arrived to find out that he'd just taken off for France.

On the day he was repatriated, there was a traffic jam at all the large airports in the Paris region, so the plane was diverted to the base at Villacoublay. As soon as the plane touched down, the euphoric ex-convicts couldn't wait any longer. Without listening to the captain, they got up all together and rushed to the exit. The stewardess, quite understandingly, opened the door for them as soon as the plane stopped.

Unfortunately, the authorities were overwhelmed and badly informed and had therefore not been able to tell the families in good time when and where the plane was going to land. The ex-prisoners had been dreaming of hugging their loved ones for so long, but they weren't there to meet them at their arrival.

Once they landed in France, the new arrivals were faced with another problem. It was all very well getting out of a luxurious (for the period) means of transport, but they didn't have a penny to their name. The aerodrome authorities put a telephone at their disposal but, to cap it all, after an absence of eighteen months, Michel Hollard couldn't even remember his phone number!

At the time, he hadn't wanted to be listed in the directory so he was now ex-directory and the switchboard operator at directory enquiries wasn't allowed to reveal his personal number, even to him. Nevertheless, she was touched by the incredible situation in which he found himself. Unable to provide any proof of his good faith, he did get her to promise to pass on a message to the Hollard family.

He asked the operator to tell his family that he'd be arriving at the end of the afternoon in Ivry-sur-Seine. An aerodrome service personnel bus would drop him off at the home of his friend Alphonse Bottin, who was the director of the chocolate makers Jacquin and a member of the Agir network. The telephone operator kept her word. As soon as she called, we rushed off – our mother, Francine, Vincent and myself – to the meeting point. Husband and father had arrived just before us.

'That moment of our reunion was exceptionally intense. The beauty and the richness of such moments made up for all the years of suffering,' he was to say later.

Chapter 30

Renewal

The deportees arriving back from Germany, like Maurice Gacheny, were all emaciated, with sunken faces. We were therefore expecting our father to be very thin too. To our great surprise, however, he seemed to be a bit more filled out than before! But this unexpected extra weight was only temporary. Despite the wise advice the Swedish doctors had given them, their patients weren't careful enough with how much or how badly they ate. The ex-prisoners soon had digestive problems, then put on weight because of a physiological reaction. As soon as he realised this, Michel Hollard imposed the appropriate dietary regime upon himself. Having intensified his daily exercises, he returned to his former athletic figure in record time.

On the other hand, he never really shook off some of the physical and moral after-effects, but he put up with them without complaining. So as not to miss anything of what was being said, he always had to make sure that the person speaking to him was on his right, his left ear having been kicked by the SS guard who'd beaten him and kept going at him when he was down. His teeth had been damaged in other violent incidents, so he kept his lips tightly closed until a dentist was able to give him his smile back.

On the evening of his homecoming, barely restraining his impatience, he called some of his brothers-in-arms. He was thus able to talk to Robert Rubenach, Joseph Legendre, Madeleine Boulanger and Henri Dujarier. His four assistants had learnt the good news through Yvonne Hollard three weeks earlier. When they recognised the voice of Agir's boss, they each expressed their joy in their own individual way.

It was decided to have a meeting – for the first time without any danger of being interrupted by the enemy! The homecomer, listening to the unanimous advice of his entourage, took a few days' rest at Saint-Rémy-lès-Chevreuse while his former teammates rallied the other group members.

The meeting took place at the very site of the raid, in the memorable Café des Chasseurs, near the Gare du Nord. Only three of the four victims of the tragedy were present; Jules Mailly hadn't survived the hell of deportation.

The network also numbered other martyrs. Robert Rubenach and Madeleine Boulanger, who'd searched in the hope of finding traces of all network members who'd been deported, had just learnt that several of them were no longer alive. And other bad news was to be feared. Michel Hollard read out the provisional list of the deceased and then asked those present to rise for a minute's silence in tribute to their memory.

Since the network hadn't had a name during the war, it was fitting to give it a name, a posteriori. For the leader, the simple verb 'agir' (meaning 'to act') came naturally to mind.[1]

It was unanimously decided that similar meetings should be held at least twice a year, preferably on 5 February, the anniversary of the four arrests, and on 8 May, the anniversary of VE Day.

The former English contacts in Switzerland, O.P. (James Kruger) and Victor Farrell, had returned to England and wasted no time getting the War Office to welcome and honour their French friend in London. Their guest had not been expecting the enthusiastic response he received, and he was even more surprised to learn that the British War Office had decided to show its gratitude by offering a sizeable sum to the man who'd discovered the V-1 weapon. However, he didn't want to keep any of it for himself, not a single shilling. Despite his own precarious financial situation after the end of his involvement with the Intelligence Service, he decided to hand out this unexpected windfall to the widows of the agents who'd died because of their loyalty to Agir's ideals.

'You must believe me,' he said, 'when I say that I'm aware of the overwhelming responsibility weighing on my shoulders today and of the terrible obligations that it creates for me morally. What must the widows of those who never came back think? Never will we be able to acquit ourselves of the debt we owe them!'

When he returned from London by plane, as he was boarding, he dared ask the navigator, 'When we fly over Normandy, I'd like to see the remains of the V-1 launch site at Bonnetot-le-Faubourg. Would that be possible? It's not far from Auffay, between Dieppe and Rouen,' he added, showing the spot on the map.

'It might not be so easy to find!' answered the flight captain. 'But they've announced good visibility for today. We'll do all that we can!'

The air controllers authorised the plane to change its course slightly, and for a few precious moments, the traveller was able to see the buildings whose destruction he'd caused. There was nothing left now but rubble.

On 5 February 1946, exactly two years to the day after the raid at the Café des Chasseurs, the members of Agir gathered together there once again, at 176 Rue du Faubourg Saint-Denis. The network was now organised into an association with a steering committee, namely Michel Hollard, President; Victor Guerreau and Charles Jeanrenaud, Vice-Presidents; Robert Rubenach, General Secretary; and Joseph Legendre, Henri Dujarier, and Madeleine Boulanger.

Before a gathering of former agents, mixed with a host of admirers, the President reminded them once again of how the team was broken up:

> Today we commemorate the anniversary of a disaster. I was about to join three friends in this café to pick up their reports when an unscrupulous seductress approached me. I was trying to get rid of her when a bunch of Abwehr inspectors, for whom she was just a snitch, rushed at us brandishing revolvers and handcuffs.
>
> Earlier, several among us had experienced similar catastrophes. Bad luck subsequently hit others. Our losses were heavy. In all, our organisation mourns the loss of twenty Resistance workers. I invite you to honour the memory of these valiant soldiers out of uniform whose names follow:
>
> - Olivier Giran, Gaston Brogniart and Paul Moreau: executed by firing squad.
> - Jacques Bouroche: killed during the Normandy landings when guiding the liberators.
> - Jules Mailly, Hilaire Racine, Alexandre Roman, Roger Cuénot, Étienne Giran, Alexandre Baumstein, Henri Chan, Robert

Desnos,[2] Jean Maiffret, Louis Maiffret, André Mandar, Étienne Mauchaussé and Louis Hénon: died in deportation.

- André Bouguet and René Ragondet: died after their return from deportation.
- Pierre Pamard: killed in an ambush during the Liberation.

The members of the association were now bonded by almost family-like ties.[3] On the following 8 May, everyone gathered again in front of Michel Hollard's other strategic building in Paris, the little Hôtel d'Annecy, 207 Rue de Bercy, only a few steps away from the Gare de Lyon. It was his hideout, the springboard from which he'd dashed off so many times across France to Switzerland so as to inform the Allies.

Henri Dujarier, Michel Hollard's faithful lieutenant, had brought a big sign listing the names of the twenty fallen.[4] Upon arrival, those present were surprised to be welcomed with music by a band from the Garde Républicaine. Accompanied discreetly by brass and muffled drums, the assembly paid tribute to the dead.

***

Soon after it was created, the Fédération des Amicales de Réseaux de la France Combattante noted that a certain number of suspicious individuals had got into the ranks of the Resistance. In addition to some thugs and villains, who were trying to pass off their heinous crimes as Maquis mishaps, true patriots had compromised themselves in serious acts which were matters for common law. Faced with so many contentious cases, the tribunals declared themselves incompetent. They asked that a special committee of former Resistance workers, obviously irreproachable, be convened who would agree to look into the more controversial dossiers. The Jury d'Honneur de la France Combattante was thus created.

Called upon by his peers, Michel Hollard joined this commission, whose work was carried out on a voluntary basis, at a time when he was still unemployed and drawing on his last savings. The spectre of destitution didn't prevent him from acting selflessly once again. The Jury d'Honneur elected him successively to the posts of Vice-Chairman and Chairman.

These positions required him to study a succession of cases that were complex, enigmatic and often tragic. With his usual ardour, he put his all into this new task.

His cooperation with the War Office in London had come to an end and he now urgently had to find himself an industrial job. He had no hope of resuscitating his once flourishing *gazogène* company, as the truck drivers wanted nothing more to do with those ugly machines whose whims and dirt they'd had to put up with when there was no petrol.

Unemployed at the age of 47 and physically weakened, the survivor of Neuengamme went through a new troubled period. He came out of it thanks to a chance encounter while he was a member of the Jury d'Honneur. After a working session, a lawyer, who was there in a consultative capacity, spoke to him about the difficulties paralysing a Paris radio and electricity company. As this was a field he knew about, Michel Hollard examined the case. His opinion was deemed convincing and he was asked to look after the business temporarily.

His enthusiasm attracted the attention of Westinghouse, the automobile equipment firm, whose Paris branch was looking to recruit an experienced engineer. The post interested him but he refrained from telling anyone about his earlier service record. He wanted to be chosen solely on the basis of his professional qualifications. When the recruitment office picked him, he found himself on the threshold of a new, belated career.

He distinguished himself in the job until he retired, despite his physical and mental troubles. His sleep was often restless, troubled by nightmares that he generally couldn't or wouldn't talk about. He occasionally made laconic allusions to them. Alternating scenes of torture and hangings popped up from his subconscious. These were followed by images of unfortunate people dying, crammed into cattle wagons or in the holds of ships going to be sunk.

Yet these dreamlike appearances, as hideous as they were, did nothing to alter his spirituality or his morale for long. Still able, as he approached his ninetieth birthday, to mix humour and gravity, he said to me: 'A sacred cause is never lost for eternity. As for me, I'd so often seen my last hour come that I finally thought that I was on a permanent reprieve!'

As soon as they heard he'd been freed, the Société des Poètes Français paid him a warm tribute. Following a unanimous vote by the committee, the poet-Resistance leader, who was already a member of that illustrious society, was made a fellow.

***

Michel Hollard received a great number of expressions of respect and admiration. However, in certain circles of former Resistance fighters and of the army, the independence and originality of the path he'd chosen weren't always understood very well. Within the military reserve hierarchy, his promotion was assured. From captain, he immediately reached the rank of lieutenant colonel. However, it didn't take him long to realise he was being cast as a maverick who'd deliberately chosen to serve under British colours, and he had to make a great effort to explain why he'd been engaged with the War Office:

> In 1941, against my will, circumstances made me an independent Resistance fighter, deprived of any contact with the structures created in London by General de Gaulle.
>
> However, a bit later, I decided to speak frankly about this incongruity with my correspondent in Switzerland, the officer O.P. of the Secret Intelligence Service. I begged him to try and understand my position and my reasons. I told him that it seemed natural and legitimate for me to try and hand over my future reports to a representative of the French Resistance who was in touch with the French authorities in London. 'If you definitely want to use this channel, which I can understand you doing,' the Englishman had answered courteously, 'I'll willingly give you all the necessary addresses and details. But I must warn you that before reaching the Allied General HQ, the documents thus forwarded will have to travel long and hazardous routes. Our diplomatic bag moves much quicker. It also offers most certainly better guarantees.'
>
> This sensible reasoning made me less reticent. There's no need to hesitate any more, I said to myself, all that matters is the speed and reliability of the means of transmission. So, I continued to cross

> plains and mountains regularly, as quickly as possible, to inform the Intelligence Service's office in Switzerland directly.

This part of the story leads me back to an earlier event: a famous appeal made on 18 June 1940 by General de Gaulle on the BBC, which was occasionally French-speaking. Even though those who actually listened to the historic broadcast were fewer than claimed, the news caused a sensation and spread like wildfire. Well beyond Europe, we learnt that a French voice had spoken out on the English radio. Denouncing his government's defeatism, a military leader was bold enough to urge those of his fellow countrymen who could get to London to disobey the French authorities and continue the struggle under his command.

On 28 June, ten days after the radio broadcast by the providential General, the English officially recognised him as the leader of the Free French. A month later, the total strength of those enrolled under his flag with the Croix de Lorraine numbered some 7,000 men.[5]

After the June 1940 Armistice, most French people didn't believe the Allies could ever win. But this disenchantment didn't prevent a good number of citizens from expressing outright their admiration and even attachment to the leader in voluntary exile, sometimes even in front of the occupier.

Because they were unable to confront the domineering enemy that was everywhere, many people imagined how they could be a nuisance. Like Michel Hollard, leaders set up various strategies to resist underground. Some succeeded in getting in touch with the Bureau Central de Renseignements et d'Action (Central Bureau of Intelligence and Operations), abbreviated BCRA,[6] in London, which worked to coordinate, in an overall structure as coherent as possible, the various Resistance groups they were able to get in touch with. Thus was born the Conseil National de la Résistance (National Resistance Council), with Jean Moulin as its first leader.

Michel Hollard and his team never had the opportunity to liaise with this group. The division thus created among the underground groups, as regrettable as it was, perhaps prevented the Agir network from suffering a disaster like the one which cost Jean Moulin his life. But after the Liberation, the independent mavericks, like the members of the Agir network, had trouble getting themselves recognised and treated as equals by their brothers-in-arms belonging to organisations affiliated with the BCRA.

While General de Gaulle was in London, there was inevitable tension between his staff and the British administration. At the time these difficulties arose, the Agir network was already supplying strategic information of capital importance directly to the Intelligence Service.

Was the Free French leader upset when he learnt that the above-mentioned information, of French origin, had reached his English hosts without ever transiting through his headquarters? He never said a word about it after the war. But his attitude towards the founder of the Agir network always remained somewhat aloof. I questioned my father about this.

'You were overlooked by the Ordre de la Libération. What do you make of that?'

'My underground activities developed independently, unrelated to the BCRA and probably without the general's knowledge. I would've liked to carry out my missions under his authority, but strategic considerations prevented me from doing so. When I came back from deportation, I devoted my time to the Jury d'Honneur and to looking for a job because I was penniless! I didn't go to most of the meetings and the official veterans' gatherings. I was absent so I was neglected.'

'Didn't you ask the General to honour your agents?'

'Yes, I did, because they were unfairly kept in the background. I'd managed to get the higher decorations awarded to the most deserving of them. The right sort of ceremony was to have taken place under the auspices of General de Gaulle. In a letter, I expressed my wish that he include my brave companions in the group of recipients. But he refused, saying he only decorates the recipients of distinctions he'd personally awarded.'[7]

'Your teammates nonetheless had nice celebrations. As for you, you were recognised by the United Kingdom and the French authorities – precious tokens of recognition…'

'Even before I was arrested, the British Embassy in Switzerland had told me I'd be receiving such an honour.'

'After the war, King George VI indeed awarded you the DSO[8] and you have an impressive array of French decorations.'[9]

'Indeed, and these distinctions do please me. But I do hope I'll avoid the conceit awaiting medal bearers.'

'You deserved your medals a thousand times over.'

'Nobody is ever made any greater through ostentation!'

Chapter 31

Agent Extraordinary

During the war, one of the British civil servants living in Switzerland only worked, apparently, in the passport office. But this activity was a front for something else. In the tangled diplomatic nest of vipers that was Bern, where the delegates of all the belligerent powers rubbed shoulders, Captain Victor Farrell above all occupied the position of secret correspondent for the Intelligence Service.

This function made him one of Michel Hollard's privileged contacts, along with his colleague James Kruger. He learnt very quickly about the huge launch ramp at Bonnetot-le-Faubourg aimed at London, and also looked at the first sketches made of the V-1 components seen in the Auffay hangar.

Back in Great Britain, when peace returned, Victor Farrell enthusiastically told his family about the Frenchman's many different exploits. As luck would have it, the diplomat's brother-in-law was George Martelli, a respected journalist and historian from London. The writer immediately saw how important the hitherto unknown events were, particularly as he knew about them from a first-hand source. As a reporter, his reaction was to start enquiring. Indeed, in order to go back over the facts faithfully, a lot of extra, often confidential, information was needed.

First of all, he had to meet Michel Hollard in person, even though the latter, despite his apparent robustness, was still suffering from the physical and moral after-effects caused by his deportation. The memory of countless brothers-in-arms who'd tragically disappeared obsessed him and he was tormented by the resurgence of all sorts of memories.

The English writer came to see him in Paris in the hope of obtaining a series of interviews.

'I'm not in a state to meet you, at least not for the moment,' declared the Neuengamme survivor.

Various French reporters and biographers, on hearing of his miraculous rescue by the Swedish Red Cross, had already come to interview him, but he'd politely turned them away. Others, looking for anecdotes, still pestered him. His answer being invariably negative, albeit courteous, they went on their way disappointed.

Given Michel's penchant for writing, his family didn't understand why he didn't just pick up his pen and write down an account of own story. When asked, he always said: 'Perhaps I'll consider writing my autobiography when decrepitude has finally forced me to remain immobile!'[1]

George Martelli proved to be a fine psychologist and showed great patience. For years, he came to visit him without ever alluding to the book he still hoped to write. His constancy was not in vain. To everybody's surprise, Michel Hollard ended up giving in to the Englishman's unexpected request.

George Martelli's research and writing started well after the end of the war and spanned nearly a decade. The Englishman obtained permission to consult certain military archives belonging to the former belligerent nations. He also managed to gain access to certain RAF files and even to some from the Intelligence Service. He met Michel Hollard regularly and also others involved in the underground war.

The English edition of George Martelli's book was initially called *Agent Extraordinary* and was published in 1960, with a preface by Lieutenant General Sir Brian Horrocks.[2] BBC executives had asked Field Marshal Montgomery's former colleague to select several examples of heroic acts carried out during the Second World War. The senior officer's preface contains the following assessment: 'I have been privileged to read many stories of incredible courage. This, however, is the most remarkable story of them all, for Michel Hollard was the man who literally saved London.'

Sir Brian Horrocks was without doubt one of the best-informed people, and therefore the most qualified, to make such a judgement. George Martelli had no hesitation in changing the title of the book, which from the second edition onwards became *The Man Who Saved London*. Soon translated into French (*L'Homme Qui a Sauvé Londres*)[3] and other languages, the book triggered a flurry of press articles in Europe and around the world. In serial form, *Die Weltwoche*, the German-language weekly in Zurich, revealed Michel Hollard's exploits not only to its readers in German-speaking Switzerland, but also to its German and Austrian readership, who were undoubtedly disconcerted, but no less admiring. The American magazine *Reader's Digest* published a condensed version of the story, which made it widely known all over the world and, naturally, in France. Colonel Rémy devoted a major part of his *Missions Secrètes*, published in Geneva, to the founder of the Agir network.

***

In 1972, *L'Homme Qui a Sauvé Londres* was adapted for the small screen by the film-maker Jean L'Hôte and broadcast on France's Second TV Channel. This film consists of both the reconstruction of an extraordinary wartime epic and the testimonies of people who lived through it. A group of actors re-enacts the main episodes, more often than not in the places where the events took place. Marcel Cuvelier plays the underground leader caught up in the struggle. Thirty years after the events, Michel Hollard himself, his former British contact in Switzerland O.P. (James Kruger) and a former German Army chaplain, as well as several members of the Agir network, gave the TV film its authenticity with their unique memories and commentaries.[4]

***

Many pages of the Resistance story couldn't have been written without the personal accounts provided by the Resistance fighters. It is therefore easy to understand why some of them, too often, gave in to the temptation of exaggerating their own performance.

Michel Hollard, on the other hand, tended to moderate his own accounts. His instinctive reserve even made him play down his achievements. During certain veterans' reunions, he was called upon to talk in public with people who'd been very much less committed in fighting the enemy. Such speakers were skilled in repartee and didn't embarrass themselves with anything like scruples; they thus took advantage of his excessive discretion and, diminishing his merits, managed to make themselves seem more important than he was. This even took place in front of media microphones and cameras, which naturally thrilled the attention-seeking smooth talkers.

During these regrettable scenes, Michel Hollard, at a loss for words, never knew how to defend himself. Worse still, by reacting abruptly in a disordered and chaotic manner, he aggravated the confusion which was precisely what the arrogant debaters were trying to propagate.

Formerly, in the face of deadly danger, this leader of men had exercised an irresistible ascendancy over a host of others, both by his exemplary courage and his natural powers of persuasion. It is therefore surprising that once the war was over, such a convincing leader could be so awkward during run-of-the-mill verbal confrontations.

Unfortunately, he was incapable of fending off verbal trickery other than by mumbling explanations which, though certainly true, were made clumsily. Regrettably, he was entirely lacking in the most elementary sense of debate. This weakness was no doubt compensated by the unique skills that had enabled him to carry out his exploits.

***

Although Michel Hollard had lost interest in taking part in some official events because of these disappointing experiences, the Agir reunions, over which he presided regularly for more than forty years, soothed his heart. An organising committee consisting of Victor Guerreau (now manager of the Paris Heliport), Robert Rubenach, Henri Dujarier and Charles Jeanrenaud prepared these meetings.

Many a network survivor considered these periodic reunions as events they'd not miss for anything in the world. To take part, some would cross the whole of France. Moreover, an influx of admirers gradually made the audience larger.[5] These reunions always began with a tribute paid to their departed comrades, and Michel Hollard would then present a topic of his choice. Here, for example, are the main ideas of a talk he gave on the theme of faith.

This notion was the driving force behind our action and will no doubt reflect our path into the future. The *Larousse* dictionary defines the main nuances of the term: 'faithfulness in fulfilling one's engagements, loyalty; confidence in somebody or something; belief in the teachings of a religion; the religion itself; fervent belief: *patriotic faith*.'

The last of these definitions cannot be better illustrated than by the formidable energy our team showed. We had set ourselves a distant, almost insane, but dazzling objective. For us to get near it, it was worth our facing dreadful obstacles and taking all sorts of risks.

History has shown that faith can generate unsuspected strengths, enabling people to reach seemingly unattainable goals, like Joan of Arc, Christopher Columbus, Louis Pasteur, Sir Winston Churchill, General de Gaulle…

Our initiative was not the result of a pragmatic decision. It burst forth like a swollen mountain stream that nothing could stop. It was a sacrifice instinctively offered to a higher cause.

A lot of Resistance fighters rejected any references to religion. But most of them accepted the idea that faith could move mountains, especially in the struggle for the ideals of justice, liberty, and honour. The other patriots we encountered on our way almost never refused to help us. By far, the larger part of the population behaved with dignity, regardless of their political opinions or spiritual convictions. Despite the misleading propaganda the Germans and their Vichy accomplices put around through posters, radio and newspapers, people never stopped hoping that a landing would take place that would free them all, however implausible it seemed, given the presence of gigantic fortifications along the coast.

Of course, some of the population heard General de Gaulle's passionate words and the encouraging news from the BBC. But it was faith which helped the French to survive during those dark years.

The official inauguration of the permanent memorial to the fallen members of the Agir network took place on Saturday, 24 June 1961. The ceremony was attended by General André Bouchardon, commanding the Garde

Républicaine, and Canon Noël Carlotti, President of the Fédération des Amicales de Réseaux de la France Combattante, both former Neuengamme deportees, and a number of other prominent figures. An ensemble from the Garde Républicaine provided music for the occasion.

A marble plaque replaced the modest wooden board that Henri Dujarier had made in 1946. It was unveiled by the widows of five of the twenty martyrs whose names were engraved on the stone. Addressing the crowd gathered around him, Michel Hollard summarised the tragedy like this:

> While France and much of Europe were occupied and oppressed by the fascists, we refused defeat and chose to continue the struggle here on French soil. Our way of fighting was to keep tabs on the enemy, to note what they did and to tell the Allies about it.
>
> A few steps from here, a little hotel room served as our headquarters and letter box. The mail which piled up there was intended for the English military correspondent we'd managed to get into contact with in Switzerland, despite the borders being closed.
>
> The secret services in London examined our information with ever-increasing interest. One day we learned the occupying army had started building a large number of very alarming constructions in north-western France.
>
> A long series of enquiries enabled us to unravel the mystery: the enemy was getting ready to launch a multitude of flying bombs at London. We warned the Allies, who bombed the launching installations which were already almost operational. But the occupier then hurried to hide others in the forests. Our team found several dozen. In the end, after being delayed by at least six months, Hitler's strategists were only able to launch a very considerably weakened attack.
>
> The Allied armies, meanwhile, liberated France and Europe. At the moment of victory, however, none of Agir's companions-in-arms could take part in the general rejoicing with a light heart. There was too much heartbreak around them. The team had been cruelly stricken – every step of the way, a lot of its members, among the best, had disappeared.

> The present marble plaque has been placed here to perpetuate the memory of our comrades.

Upon these words, the drums sounded the muffled roll of 'Attention'. My father then named the twenty Agir agents, soldiers without uniform who'd died for France. Then he carried on:

'In their memory, out of respect for their self-sacrifice, and also in tribute to other comrades who have fallen elsewhere, I propose we observe a minute's silence.'

After that, the band played the 'La Sonnerie Aux Morts' (equivalent of 'The Last Post' or 'Taps'). My father said in conclusion:

> Yes, our fallen companions, we remain close to you in spirit, quite aware of the inestimable price that your sacrifice represents. Your names will be engraved in stone for a long time to come, but they shine forever in our hearts in letters of fire. To the passers-by who read them, they will recall the privilege we had of fighting alongside you, contributing to the restoration of justice and the rebirth of a country and a world admirable enough for you to have sacrificed everything for them![6]

In October 1953, an initiative by former French deportees, supported by the French Embassy, led to a first deportation memorial being created at Neuengamme camp. Twelve years later, on 7 November 1965, at the same site, German and international institutions erected a tall commemorative stela bearing the following inscription:

EUER LEIDEN, EUER KAMPF UND EUER TOD SOLLEN NICHT VERGEBENS SEIN

(Your suffering, your struggle and your death shall not have been in vain)

Michel Hollard, already present at the 1953 inauguration, was among the French delegation that took part in the second event. The day before, they'd been received lavishly in Hamburg, the nearest big city. The future

Chancellor of West Germany, Senator Helmut Schmidt, was amongst the officials who welcomed them.

Ever since the survivors had been repatriated twenty years earlier, many of them had never returned to the place where they'd suffered to the point of exhaustion. They were not only surprised to discover a modern city, almost completely rid of scars of the war; their biggest surprise came from the friendliness of the people who welcomed them. It seemed to them that society here was suddenly similar to French society.

The guests naturally wanted to return to the places where they'd been detained so long ago, but they were very disappointed to find these areas changed by the appearance of recent buildings.[7] Nonetheless, they appreciated the trouble the German organisers of the event had gone to. Wanting to give full meaning to the inauguration of the memorial, the organisers did not hesitate to take on an ensemble with soloists and choir. On approaching the new monument, various extracts from Beethoven's opera *Fidelio* could be heard. The unexpected, fine quality of the musical performance impressed Michel Hollard. Some parts of the work appeared to him to be symbolic of the ideals of the Resistance.[8]

The deportation survivors then continued their pilgrimage to the Baltic Sea. On the shore of Neustadt Bay, they commemorated the three wrecks that happened nearby on 3 May 1945. In a few simple sentences, Michel Hollard paid tribute to the 7,000 companions engulfed inside the prison ships, just as the war was coming to an end. Then, with the help of a sailor who'd spontaneously invited some of the men to climb aboard his small boat, wreaths of flowers were tossed into the waves.

Chapter 32

The Providential German Cousin

Michel Hollard never knew his paternal grandmother, who was born Jenny Bernus and died in 1877 at the age of 35. She was German by birth, originally from Frankfurt. Jenny had been able to gain the affection and respect of her new family and, in the aftermath of the Franco-Prussian War, to maintain good relations within a large family divided by the hostilities.[1]

My father knew his ancestry on the Monod side – his maternal lineage – included international branches, but time and distance seemed to have erased most of these family ties, or made people forget about them.

However, in 1988 I received a surprising letter from Starnberg am See, a small town in Bavaria. The sender, Ernst von Bressensdorf, introduced himself as a distant cousin and a keen genealogist of our common family history. His discoveries, with supporting evidence, demonstrated that he descended, as did the Hollards and the Monods, from the eminent French historian Paul de Rapin de Thoyras, born at Castres (Tarn department) in 1661 and who'd died at Wesel (Rhineland) in 1725.[2]

Because he was a Calvinist, Rapin de Thoyras had been forced to flee from France at the time of the revocation of the Edict of Nantes. He was an officer, teacher, scholar and a polyglot, speaking seven languages, including Latin (no mean feat at the time), who lived in Holland, then in England. His long exodus ended in Germany, where he settled once and for all with his large family.

The work of the family genealogist revealed that Michel Hollard's parents, Auguste Hollard and his wife Pauline (née Monod), were among the descendants of Paul de Rapin de Thoyras, but they had no idea this cousin existed! They also had no idea that some prominent people were relatives of theirs. Among these, to mention but one famous name, was Count Ferdinand von Zeppelin, who'd fascinated the world with his airships.

Cousin Ernst von Bressensdorf, born in Leipzig in 1917, studied literature, engineering and art in his native town. In particular, he took singing lessons in the legendary St Thomas Gymnasium, steeped in the memory of Johann Sebastian Bach, its eighteenth-century Kapellmeister. In his letter, the German relative made no secret of his military past. Mobilised in 1939 and assigned to a Wehrmacht engineer regiment, the young man became a lieutenant instructor in the intelligence service. As a telecommunications specialist, and also because of his fairly good knowledge of French, he was put in charge of the military telephone and telegraph installations in the Paris region in January 1944.

'I've heard of and admire your father's heroic story,' he wrote to me. 'Sadly, because of the suffering he endured, I wouldn't think he has much sympathy for Germany and the Germans! But since 1945, the mentality of most of my compatriots has changed…'

In my reply, I told him that despite the torture and physical abuse my father had suffered in deportation, he felt no hatred towards the German people. Shortly afterwards, this distant cousin came to France and we had the opportunity to become acquainted. It was then that I learnt about the surprising final episode of his military activity:

'During the period just before the Liberation of Paris, I was in charge of signals in the headquarters of General Dietrich von Choltitz, the Governor of Gross Paris (Greater Paris). My office was in the Hôtel Meurice on Rue de Rivoli. On the evening of 22 August 1944, we only had one operational line left because the rest of the network had been destroyed or cut. Suddenly, through this one intact channel, came a coded message from Berlin.

'When I'd finished deciphering it, I was very worried. In my hand was the document by which, on the Führer's orders, the most beautiful city in the world was to be destroyed! My duty was to pass it on at once to the General. The teams ordered to blow up the bridges and the stations, to destroy the main industrial centres, to demolish the Eiffel Tower and a certain number of famous monuments, were just waiting for the final order to get started.

'I realised how monstrous this would be. Feeling personally responsible, I was torn. The war, unleashed by a tyrant who'd gone mad, was taking an increasingly catastrophic turn every day. I loved France, to which I was attached through family ties. It seemed evident to me that obeying such a heinous order would've prevented the reconciliation of our two countries for centuries.

'My watch said 8 pm. The streets were congested with a bustling crowd. I knew enemy tanks were approaching the capital. After hesitating for thirty minutes, I decided to keep the dispatch with me overnight. General von Choltitz[3] received it the following morning and, well, you know that nothing was done…'

'When you had the deciphered text in front of you,' I asked, 'were the Wehrmacht's technical teams really in a position to commit the irreparable?'

'What is certain is that the German occupying units could no longer move around freely because the French Resistance was watching them and fought them openly. The morale of some of our troops suffered from this, even if some of them were still extremists. By not handing over the telegram at once, I was hoping that it'd then be too late to do the job. But I can't say what leeway the artificers had.'

'You put off delivering the last message from Hitler's HQ to your superior by about thirteen hours. My father will certainly be interested to learn of this initiative taken by a relative he had no idea existed. Although he was detained and ill-treated in a concentration camp, you're mistaken if you believe that he still harbours any resentment or bad feelings in his heart towards Germany and the German people. In spite of the pain he still suffers, feelings like those are almost completely foreign to him. Moreover, he's always loved German culture. No doubt he inherited some traits from his German grandmother, who died before he was born. He would certainly be receptive to a letter, or even a visit from you.'

He was very keen to establish contact with my father but he hadn't dared take the initiative. My acting as go-between fulfilled this wish. An exchange of letters prepared them for their first meeting, which took place in Michel and Yvonne Hollard's home.

Perhaps they'd once crossed paths in this busy area, the gaze of the franc-tireur avoiding that of the man in uniform. Forty-five years after that hell, the two ex-belligerents got along well with each other at their first meeting. From the outset, they avoided bringing up what were clearly bitter memories, and began by discovering they had the same literary and artistic tastes.

I'd previously told my parents about the episode of the telegram from Berlin our cousin had kept in his pocket. Michel Hollard, obviously captivated by this story, told him:

'If it's true that you wilfully delayed handing over that terrible order, your conduct in the end was akin to ours!'

'In my awkward position as one of the occupying enemy,' said Ernst von Bressensdorf, 'I felt responsible for protecting Paris, a capital threatened with destruction by a doomed Führer. My dear Michel Hollard, you carried out certain major acts of international resistance. How can we not admire your supreme courage? Because your exploits, in protecting the London metropolis, made a vital contribution to the Allies' victory on 8 May 1945.'

Chapter 33

Final Act

At the end of the 1980s, a delegation from the Association des Français Libres was received by Queen Elizabeth II at Lancaster House, and Michel and Yvonne Hollard were among the guests. Here is what my father had to say upon his return to France after his meeting the Queen.

'We'd placed ourselves to one side of the path the Queen was to take, to satisfy my wife. If only briefly, she longed to see up close the famous embroidered hat that Her Majesty would likely be wearing.

'Her wish was granted beyond all her expectations. When the Queen went past us, she immediately spotted the DSO (Distinguished Service Order), which the Protocol Secretary had asked me to pin onto my suit. As the Queen had stopped in front of me, I said:

'"Your Majesty, I owe this rare distinction to King George VI."

'In perfect French, she answered:

'"*Vous êtes donc le Colonel Hollard !* (So you must be Colonel Hollard!)"

'I was very impressed. General Jean Simon, who was leading our group, hadn't missed anything of the scene. Intrigued, he approached us and asked the Queen:

'"Your Majesty, did you know that it was Colonel Hollard who saved your country from the V-2s?"

'The truth obliged me to rectify his assertion.

'"Excuse me, General, but I don't even know exactly what the V-2s were! I was just happy to inform our English friends about the V-1s, six months before they were ready to be used!"

'The Queen, nodding in approval of what I'd said, added:

'"Besides, it wasn't the V-2 which worried us most because that came later. It was the V-1 that caused the most victims. If we hadn't been told of the threat early enough, we wouldn't have been able to take the necessary steps and probably not a single building in London would have been left standing!'"

***

The big V-1 attack on London started in June 1944. People were terrorised, already alerted by the buzzing sound of each machine until it fell to earth followed by a devastating explosion.

Every morning, Londoners were in the habit of scanning the small bit of sky these devilish machines flew across. But never did the Britons' anxiety turn into panic. According to official estimates, a total of 2,340 V-1s fell on London causing about 5,500 killed, 16,000 seriously wounded and untold collapsed buildings. These figures include the tragedy that occurred in Central London on the morning of Sunday, 18 June 1944. A V-1 ended up hitting the roof of The Guards' Chapel during a religious service, killing 121 faithful and seriously wounding 141 others.

Belgium also suffered terrible V-1 attacks, especially on Antwerp and Liège.

***

Michel Hollard never ceased to marvel about the way he'd been saved by the Swedes, and often paid tribute to his benefactors. He declared publicly, in substance: 'It is thanks to the Vikings that I can still admire, at dawn, one of my favourite sights: the rising sun.'

Despite the worsening after-effects of his deportation, the former Resistance fighter quietly overcame various troubles and handicaps through sheer force of will. But no suffering ever distracted him from his work, and he was deeply affected when the age limit brought his career to an abrupt end.

Apart from the disarray caused by the forced retirement of this hyperactive man, the financial consequences hit him hard. Trusting and idealistic to a fault, and also lacking foresight, my father had worked for several companies intermittently because of the wars. At the request of the social services, Yvonne Hollard tried to piece together her husband's entire professional career, but he'd lost most of the supporting documents.

Clearly, he had an unparalleled war record. However, because he showed a complete lack of interest in himself once again, he didn't even think of finding out whether the legal social security benefits applied to him.

Without his knowledge, it was my brother Vincent who took the necessary steps. A while later, Lieutenant Colonel Hollard was surprised to learn by official letter that his army retirement file (which he'd no idea existed) had just been regularised! Furthermore, Vincent even found a way to provide our parents with a comfortable apartment.

Michel Hollard's temperament was still brimming over with energy, but compulsory retirement forced him to rest now whether he liked it or not. Without such restrictions, he'd no doubt have continued working without looking after his health. Even though he did his utmost to appear in good health, some of his faculties, diminished by the torture and the physical abuse he'd suffered as a deportee, let him down more and more frequently.

This sudden, unwanted free time enabled him, more than in the past, to follow the activities of his children and grandchildren. His love of music thus turned him into a keen listener to, and commentator of, my concerts.

One of the last musical evenings in which I had the pleasure of having my parents present in the audience took place in the Madeleine Church in Paris on 13 March 1990. For this event, the two ensembles of which I was the resident conductor (the Tours Symphony Orchestra and the choir of the Oratoire du Louvre) had been exceptionally brought together to perform Beethoven's Ninth Symphony.

The following day, when concluding his comments, my father said to me: 'I observed a number of people leaving the building. They seemed transformed by hearing the masterpiece. Their radiant and peaceful-looking faces appeared still lit up by the music! It therefore augurs well for the future of the world that "Ode to Joy"[1] has become the anthem of the European Union.'

***

Shortly afterwards, he underwent a hip operation. To get about, he now had to use crutches. His sight and hearing were also greatly impaired; he wore enormous glasses and for a short while tried using a hearing aid, but he lost it and stubbornly refused to replace it. But the ills from which he suffered didn't impair his still lively and optimistic character. At the age of 94, after his morning session of physical exercise followed by a wash, he still escaped from the apartment to go out alone, every day no matter what the weather, and confront the vagaries of the public thoroughfare. The neighbours used to shudder when they saw the old man crossing the avenue, propped up on his sticks. Half an hour later, he would reappear going the other way, carrying croissants for his Yvonnette's breakfast. Often, he would also bring her a little bunch of flowers, or some other small surprise.

When anyone asked him how he was, the former adventurer would elude the question with this type of answer: 'Thank you for your concern. I don't feel either ill or old. There's nothing to report regarding my health!' An inner flame inspired these confident words while he silently put up with his various ailments. His eyesight, in particular, was constantly diminishing.

In the spring of 1993, Michel and Yvonne Hollard left Paris intending to spend the summer in Gorniès, their little corner of paradise in the Cévennes. My sister Francine had gone on ahead to get things ready so that their old country home was ready for them. The whole hamlet was expecting the famous guests, each villager being ready to help them if needs be. Their stay looked as though it was going to go smoothly.

All was going well until the end of June. At almost 95, the lieutenant colonel still showed how spirited and almost youthful he was. At daybreak, he always did his physical exercises. However, in spite of the considerable effort he made, he could no longer hide his ills. His extraordinary impetuosity, which he no longer fully controlled, caused growing concern around him.

The accident that everyone feared, except of course the man himself, happened at the beginning of July. Early one morning, Francine was busy getting breakfast ready for everybody when she discovered the head of the family lying on the floor of the dining room. He'd not passed out and seemed almost normal; he explained that in the dark he'd probably caught his foot in the carpet! With his usual stoicism, he put up with the obvious pain without moaning or complaining. He just said that his legs, badly hurt after falling, just wouldn't allow him to get up.

The doctors in the nearby town of Ganges diagnosed a broken femur near where he'd been operated on earlier. To repair the damage, a metal frame was needed to hold the broken bones in place. In the Saint Louis Clinic where he was admitted, the patient was liked by everyone. Affable, cheerful, he came up with jokes to amuse both the doctors and the nurses. The operation took place in apparently favourable conditions. The patient was back to normal shortly after waking up and seemed to be on his way to recovery.

The consolidation of the bones that had been reset required a fairly long stay in hospital, so his 95th birthday, on 10 July, was celebrated in the clinic. All the staff joined the family to celebrate his birthday and the successful operation. A cake with candles was brought in and the patient shared it with his guests.

This overall optimism was unfortunately short-lived. A few days later, the patient suddenly suffered from severe circulatory problems and the unexpected complication progressed rapidly. On 16 July 1993, Michel Hollard passed away holding the hands of his wife and daughter. He bowed out in just the same way he had accomplished his most daring feats, discreetly.

***

The funeral service and burial, in Gorniès' little cemetery, was attended by a close circle of family and friends. The neighbouring population, among whom the deceased had only friends, swelled the funeral procession.[2]

The echoes of the Bastille Day celebrations on 14 July and the traditional summer holiday exodus partly eclipsed the news. The press waited a bit before paying tribute to the hero. It was logically in England that the most important articles appeared about the man many called 'The Man Who Saved London'.

For a long time, a London Education Department civil servant and her husband, Pamela and Albert Edwards, had been telling the English about the Frenchman's courageous behaviour during the war.

As soon as the Hollard family had told them of the death, Mrs Edwards contacted George Martelli immediately. The writer was more qualified than anybody else in Britain to write the deceased's obituary, which was published by *The Times* on 23 July 1993. It ended as follows:

> It was 15 years after the war before the details of his courage and heroisms were made public in a biography *Agent Extraordinary* written by George Martelli. Asked, on its publication in 1960, why he had waited so long to tell his story, Hollard said that 20 of his men had been caught, tortured and killed by the Germans while another 15 had been caught and managed to survive the torture. He did not want to feel that he was taking any kind of glory, he said.

'The creations of the human spirit which move me most are those of the great musical geniuses,' he once told me. After he passed away, the memory of this statement stayed with me as I drew up my concert schedule for the coming season, a task I did at the same time every year.

If I was given the wherewithal, I decided I would prepare a series of important concerts as a tribute to the hero. I managed to do this thanks to the help of Sir Christopher Mallaby, the British Ambassador to France, and of my brother Vincent. Below are the main programmes I had the honour of conducting to celebrate the memory of my father, the guardian angel, the man who saved London and defended our freedom.

- Paris – Oratoire du Louvre, 25 October 1994: Mozart's Symphony N° 40 and *Requiem.*
- Tours – Grand Théâtre, 30 October 1994: Mozart's Symphony N° 40 and *Requiem.*
- New York – Carnegie Hall, 11 May 1995: Fauré's *Requiem.*
- London – Saint John's Smith Square, 27 June 1995: Beethoven's Symphony N° 3 '*Eroica*' and Mozart's *Requiem.*

Chapter 34

Tributes

Michel Hollard's merits sparked off unanimous praise from the companions he knew from that terrible period. When peace returned, I had the opportunity to note down some of their memories and impressions.

***

I have often mentioned James Kruger, his correspondent in the Intelligence Service, aka O.P. He told me the following:

> From the very first time we met, your father inspired total confidence by his frank and determined attitude. I quickly felt liking and respect for him. The importance of the intelligence he brought me improved steadily, culminating in the discovery of the infernal V-1. This feat soon had a major impact on the rest of the conflict, while he was holed up in a camp!

The officers in the Swiss Army Intelligence mentioned earlier also expressed their interest in the traveller from the other side of the Jura Mountains. André Gagnaux recalled in more or less these terms:

> He made a very strong impression on my colleagues and me. Our General Staff lacked information about the movements of German troops in occupied France. I began to question him on the subject. 'Listen,' he said, 'as long as the Allies have no objections, I'm quite happy to hand over the information that I've got. But please understand that when I come to Switzerland illegally, my main mission is to inform the English, who are keeping up the struggle that the puppet Vichy regime has given up!'

> Unofficially, I did my best to facilitate the contacts he made with the British Embassy in Bern. From then on, we consulted him regularly. The information he brought us from France was indeed intended for the British secret services, but it also interested our own strategists a lot. So, I was the first person in Switzerland to hear about a secret weapon being installed near the Channel coast. Having seen Michel Hollard in action, I consider him to be the bravest, and perhaps the most extraordinary man that I've ever met!

I also mentioned Jean-Pierre Grandy, the other Swiss officer, a veteran of that chaotic period who supported the French Resistance fighter in June 1941.[1] Almost sixty years after the events, he welcomed me to his home in Neuchâtel. This alert veteran remembered the appearance of his remarkable visitor perfectly well:

> Michel Hollard's energy and evident uprightness earned him the general esteem of those around me. My colleagues and I had no hesitation in helping this courageous man to accomplish the dangerous mission he had set himself.

At the end of January 1944, under the pseudonym Thévenaz, the officer Pierre Huser was the last Swiss person to speak to the Frenchman before he was trapped by the Gestapo a week later. Several years later, Pierre Huser found kind words to tell me how much he valued his associate during those troubled times:

> The qualities of foresight, resourcefulness and perseverance, as much as his devotion and warmth, coexisted in this man in a very rare combination. The exploits he carried out wouldn't have been possible without such a combination of aptitudes. He was a unique figure.

Ernst von Bressensdorf was very ill when he learnt of the death of Michel Hollard, his distant relative and former adversary who'd become a friend. Despite the seriousness of his condition, the German cousin found the strength to write me a long message of condolences. Here are the essential points:

> The news of your revered father's decease reached me today. [...] I hasten to express the sincere distress I feel at the passing of this man who was so worthy of admiration and respect. [...] The day I met him was a high point, if not *the* high point of my work on our family tree. I hope that the news will receive the publicity it deserves in France and England.
>
> When I discovered the family ties which linked me to the Hollard family, I must admit that at first I lacked the courage to enter into a personal relationship at once with your father – the man who saved London and indeed England and, by taking great risks, had greatly influenced the course of the war. [...]
>
> Even in heaven, I will not forget the words he pronounced during our family reunion.[2]

Readers of this account already know about the acts of bravery accomplished by Joseph Brocard (who escaped from his jailers by jumping from a small upper window of his prison). Still dashing and mischievous at the age of 84, despite the after-effects of his injuries, the survivor of the Agir network paid tribute to his chief:

> For me, Michel Hollard had become a god. So, I was inspired by his example. That lasted until the day he found me seriously wounded with nothing to show for my trouble. Nonetheless, if I'm alive today, it's thanks to him, and to the Swiss who cared for me like one of their own.

For all its monstrosities, the concentration camp world did show up its most glowing characters more than any other communal organisation. Michel Hollard triggered the admiration of his companions in misery. The future generals André Bouchardon and Pierre Brunet were among the survivors from Neuengamme. During public veterans' meetings, they paid tribute to their co-detainee with eyewitness accounts whose salient points I have recorded below.

> Michel Hollard didn't talk, even though he'd been tortured by SS butchers using their favourite bestial ill-treatment. Then he was deported to Neuengamme, where I was honoured to know him. His conduct in this hell was always exemplary in its courage and dignity. (General Bouchardon)

> Michel Hollard is the distinguished example of what had to be done so that liberty could triumph in the end. (General Brunet)

Epilogue

The series of ordeals Michel Hollard went through in no way altered his character, although nightmares haunted his nights for the rest of his life. By turns serious and cheerful, including in his public speeches, he never lost the spontaneity he had as a youngster. Poetry from his own pen bears witness to this and makes up the epilogue to the present account of a story which is unimaginable, yet true from beginning to end.

To their great joy, Michel and Yvonne Hollard had nine energetic grandchildren, and this little band of cousins would often gather in their presence to enjoy their company. On one of these occasions, the head of the family, visibly enchanted by all his descendants being present, asked for silence and spoke.

'I have written a little poem,' he said simply. 'Each of its four verses features a character who discovers a providential treasure. Please give me a moment's extra attention so that I can read this unassuming piece to you':

THE BALLAD OF SOMETHING EXTRA	*LA BALLADE AU RABIOT*
Night is slowly approaching From the top of the flimsy tent. Over a cheerful meal Everyone digs into their bowl, From the pot a little bit, Remains of an excellent stew. We hold out our bowl again, And someone says, 'There's extra!'	*La nuit s'approche lentement* *Du faîte de la tente frêle.* *Devant un repas pris gaîment* *Chacun puise dans sa gamelle.* *De la marmite une parcelle,* *Reste d'un excellent fricot.* *On tend à nouveau son écuelle,* *Et quelqu'un dit : 'Y a du rabiot !'*
The dawn of day, lightly, Comes and brushes against us with its wing. We awake suddenly And think of rising... without zeal! But in the street, a turret Rings out four strokes high in the air; Then, closing our eyes again, We say to each other, 'We have time… extra time!'	*L'aube du jour, légèrement,* *Vient nous effleurer de son aile.* *Nous nous éveillons brusquement* *Et songeons au lever... sans zèle !* *Mais dans la rue, une tourelle* *Égrène quatre coups bien haut ;* *Alors, refermant la prunelle,* *Nous nous disons : 'C'est du rabiot !'*

On his hard bench, when the pauper
Dreams of his eternal misery,
He tells himself he has no more money
To look for in his pouch,
And this feeling nags at him!
Suddenly, at the fold of his pullover,
A folded note is revealed:
'My God,' he says, 'I have some money…extra money!'

Sur son banc dur, quand l'indigent
Rêve à sa misère éternelle,
Il se dit qu'il n'a plus d'argent
À chercher dans son escarcelle,
Et ce sentiment le harcèle !
Soudain, au pli de son tricot,
Un billet plié se révèle :
'Mon Dieu, fait-il, j'ai du rabiot !'

Imprisoned by the German
For…criminal activity,
I was facing the fatal punishment
Destined by a formal law,
But was deported without a word.
I did not have this cruel end,
And I still had my life!
Heaven said to me, 'It's precious time…extra time!'

Emprisonné par l'Allemand
Pour activité… criminelle,
J'étais au fatal châtiment
Voué par une loi formelle,
Mais fus déporté sans un mot.
Je n'eus pas cette fin cruelle,
Et ma vie est demeurée, elle !
Le ciel m'a dit : 'C'est du rabiot !'

Envoi

Prince, life is still good,
To leave it already, so soon…
I'll have another bowl!
Yes, I agree: 'This is something extra!'

ENVOI

Prince, la vie est encore belle,
Pour la quitter déjà, si tôt…
J'en prends encore une gamelle !
Oui, j'en conviens : 'C'est du rabiot !…'

Appendix 1

The Report by Prof. R.V. Jones, Advisor to Sir Winston Churchill and King George VI, on the V-1 Plans Supplied by Michel Hollard

During the Second World War, Professor Reginald Victor Jones headed the RAF's Scientific Intelligence Unit, an organisation as yet unique in the world. In his book *Most Secret War*,[1] he tells how he was informed about the mysterious enemy installations.

> He [Michel Hollard] was 41 years old when the Second War broke out, and his feelings after the French capitulation were so strong that he finally crossed into Switzerland to make contact with our Embassy to offer his services in any capacity in which he could help. He was subsequently to make another 48 unofficial crossings of the border. He set up a small network which survived where others were caught, because he used no radio. One of his contacts was a young, freshly qualified, engineer called André Comps. Hollard himself had already heard of the ski-site activity; and when he discovered one at Bonnetot le Faubourg [*sic*] he made a personal reconnaissance, managing to penetrate the site by collecting a wheelbarrow that he spotted in the ditch outside it, and wheeling it in as though he were a workman. He noticed the intended line of something that was probably a launching catapult, and he was the kind of man who always carried a pocket compass. When he worked out the alignment of the catapult later that evening, it pointed in the direction of London. It had been his report that alerted us specifically about the ski sites, and now he was to resolve our question of the construction. He enlisted André Comps, and persuaded him to

volunteer for a job with the Germans as a draughtsman. Comps got the job, and succeeded in copying the plans of every building at the Bois Carré site, including the general outline of the base and rails of the launching catapult. This last plan he had to copy from the original that he had to remove temporarily from the coat of the German engineer supervising the construction [...] It was a brilliant piece of espionage, complementing what Hollard had already done us. It also contained a neat element of humour, for it described the site as 'B^2' as may be seen if 'B' is an abbreviation for 'Bois' and it is remembered that 'x^2' in French is called 'x carré'.

As for Hollard himself, he went on working until he was finally arrested by the Gestapo on 5 February 1944. He was atrociously tortured by the Gestapo, including the bath treatment where the victim was submerged in a bath of cold water and violently beaten every time he put his head above the surface, so that he nearly drowned, only to be revived and have the treatment started all over again. The Gestapo failed to break him even after five or more repetitions, and they finally sent him to a concentration camp. He was one of those both fortunate and strong enough to survive, and I was to have the pleasure of providing the detail for the citation for his D.S.O.

Appendix 2

Richard Anthony Young's Report on the V-1 Plans Supplied by Michel Hollard

The Flying Bomb[1] by Richard Anthony Young, a former RAF officer and a radar specialist, gives an account of the different phases of the discovery of the V-1, based on the archives of the War Cabinet 'Crossbow' Committee, chaired by Lord Duncan Sandys.

> Early in September, agents in northern France began sending reports to London about installations of a new kind being put up under German direction in the Somme and Seine-Inférieure. One report contained a rough plan of a concrete platform having a compass bearing noted along its main axis. It had come from Michel Hollard, a self-appointed agent and resistance organiser who had gained entry to the site at Bonnetôt le Faubourg [*sic*] disguised as a labourer, and noted down the bearing of the launching platform with a pocket compass before returning to Auffay, whence he had set out. Shortly afterwards he organised a contact in the site office at Bois Carré, a site near Abbeville.[2] From this young engineer Hollard obtained two traced sets of contractors plans showing the site and details of the principal buildings. These, and a list of eight sites nearby, were received by Intelligence on 28 October.
>
> Information contained in the drawings was confirmed by Sortie E/463 on 3 November which revealed that the site at Bois Carré and four others differed from any installations previously seen. The presence of elements common to all of them suggested a similarity of purpose; at each site the concrete platform was aligned on London.

Appendix 3

The Birth of the V-1

Before the First World War, thus at the dawn of aviation, a French officer, René Lorin, had already imagined the principle of an unmanned jet bomber. The power driving the machine came from a pulse jet developed by the engineer Georges Marconnet. At the time, these inventions were considered utopian.

A long time afterwards, under pressure from events, the German engineers Paul Schmidt and Robert Lusser worked on developing the same idea. Their flying bomb, having hinted at tremendous destructive power, was officially named V-1. They were given the task of carrying out the Kirschkern (cherry stone) programme, whose aim was nothing less than the destruction of London under a deluge of fire.

Description

The pilotless aircraft looked like a big cigar with wings, surmounted by its stovepipe propulsion (pulse jet) unit. Several models succeeded each other, differing slightly in size, capacity, weight and performance. The main data and capacities of these machines were similar to the following figures:

Length:	22ft 11½ in to 26ft 3in (7 to 8m)
Diameter:	2ft 7½ in to 2ft 9½ in (0.80 to 0.85m)
Length of pulse jet (nozzle):	10ft 6in (3.20m)
Wingspan:	17ft ½ in to 17ft 8½ in (5.20 to 5.40m)
Explosive charge:	1,764lbs (800kg)
Fuel:	110 to 132 UK gallons (500 to 600 litres) 132 to 158½ US gallons (500 to 600 litres)
Cruising speed:	404mph (650km/h)
Flight altitude:	2,625 to 3,937ft (800 to 1,200m) at the end of the flight
Possible range:	155 miles (250km)

Principle of Propulsion

The machine's forward movement forced a determined volume of air through the duct of the pulse jet and opened a series of valves, invading the combustion chamber. The injected fuel mixed with oxygen was set off by an electric spark. The explosion caused the valves to close and forced the air violently backwards. At the end of the combustion, the valves opened again under the forward pressure of air and the process started again. The cycle was repeated about forty-five times per second, with a terrifying roar.

We have many eyewitness accounts of the V-1's arrival. When the rumbling noise suddenly stopped, this announced the beginning of its plunge, indicating the area where it was going to crash and explode.

Appendix 4

How the V-1 was Launched

The V-1 couldn't take off under its own power. Its power plant – the pulse jet – needed a violent movement of air to start working. The machine therefore had to be catapulted at a high enough speed (155mph minimum) to give it enough range. The first 100 or so launch ramps would have largely accomplished their programme of devastation if the Allied air forces had not almost completely destroyed them.

The English named this first generation of catapults after 'Bois Carré', the nearby base at Yvrench (Somme), for which they received the plans from Michel Hollard and André Comps. This type of launch site was made up of a series of buildings spread out over a vast, roughly rectangular area measuring about 400 by 250 yards. A network of concrete paths served ten or so buildings used for storage, assembly, fuel supplies, settings, guiding and the machine's initial propulsion. A non-magnetic building (no iron components) was used for setting the automatic navigation system. The storage buildings could contain ten machines lined up in a row. These bunkers were about 87.5 yards long and comprised a curved end resembling the tip of a ski when seen from the sky. This peculiarity, designed for suppressing the blast effect during air raids, helped the Allied pilots identify them.

The Allied air raids forced the Germans to change their launching method. Within a few months, they'd set up a host of other ramps that were both simpler and better-camouflaged. The Allies called this new generation of launch ramp 'Belhamelin', after a hamlet near Cherbourg over which the RAF had been carrying out photographic reconnaissance.

The Luftwaffe technicians invented several V-1 launching systems using carrier aircraft. The Heinkel He 111 turned out to be the best suited for this function, but its use was rather sporadic.

Appendix 5

Between the Devil and the Deep Blue Sea

In October 1939, as the German columns started sweeping across Europe, Hitler only listened distractedly to the information reaching him about the new weapons being tested. The sight of his troops going from lightning success to lightning success exalted him and he considered their equipment was good enough for them to be able to carry out his ambitious expansionist projects in the near future.

The Treaty of Versailles (28 June 1919), which ended the First World War, severely limited and halted Germany's future armament. Strangely enough, there was nothing in it about restricting rocket development. Indeed, this field, which was soon to open up ever wider horizons, was considered at the time as being limited to popular fireworks and quite definitely unsuited for combat. As pictures of missiles are very familiar to us today, it's difficult for us to understand why those who drew up the treaty neglected the military application of pyrotechnics – an art already put into practice by strategists in Antiquity.

Some of the German scientists noticed this shortcoming and were quick to point it out discreetly. Their writings gave rise to fireworks enthusiasts, often amateurs, who were soon able to launch projectiles that were much more powerful than the usual party fireworks. The city of Berlin provided the sorcerer's apprentices with an area that quickly became known as *Raketenflugplatz* (rocket launch site). Meanwhile, the German Ministry of Defence created another establishment at Kummersdorf, Brandenburg, dedicated to testing the propulsion of machines into space.

These installations, the first of their kind, soon turned out to be too cramped for experiments in long-range firing. In 1936, Hitler agreed to create a huge research department and ballistics test centre on the Baltic coast at enormous cost. A real city reserved for this secret military industry sprung up at Peenemünde, on the island of Usedom. This rugged, wild land, which until then had been frequented above all by keen fishermen and hunters, suddenly lost its romantic cachet when it became an ultramodern fortress.

Several factories and large areas were specially set up to study, test and build different sorts of long-range missiles. The two main types of machines developed there differed radically. One was shaped like a large shell with tail fins. It pointed towards the sky almost vertically before being fired and was aimed at its target after describing a wide curve at a very high altitude. The other one was a small, pilotless jet plane. It was sometimes called an aerial torpedo.

The Reich's masters only took these revolutionary inventions fully into consideration after the crushing defeats their troops suffered at the end of 1941 onwards (retreats costing them catastrophic human and material losses on the Soviet, Libyan and Egyptian fronts). These reversals caused the myth of German invincibility to wane in some parts of the world. However, there were rumours flying around despite the inevitable secrecy. They announced the imminent arrival of invincible weapons.

Decisions concerning how to use these new machines of war were taken at several meetings held in the Wolfsschanze (Wolf's Lair)[1] during the winter and spring months of 1942–43. Hitler personally chaired the commissions, which were attended in turn by the following dignitaries:

- Albert Speer, Minister of Armaments and War Production
- Wilhelm Keitel, Chief of the General Staff
- Alfred Jodl, Chief of Operations
- Hermann Göring, Reichsmarschall, Head of the Luftwaffe
- Heinrich Himmler, Reichsführer-SS
- Hans Jeschonnek, Luftwaffe Chief of Staff
- Walter Dornberger, Lieutenant General (Engineers), in charge of the Peenemünde base
- Wernher von Braun, Chief Engineer

The critical situation the German troops were in on the various fronts didn't dispel any rivalry there was among those responsible for the new weapons. The Wehrmacht had set its sights on the rocket on which the engineers Wernher von Braun[2] and Walter Dornberger were working. But the delicate settings the missile needed, the numerous accidents occurring during the trials, its ruinous cost and the demands it made on fuel that were hard to satisfy led to an accumulation of delays.

At the head of the Luftwaffe, Reichsmarschall Hermann Göring was working to make it a priority to adopt the unmanned aircraft for which he was responsible. Provided its launch sites were completed, the machine was considered as being operational.

A combination of not only technical but also economic and relational factors made this weapon, now called the V-1, the first 'vengeance weapon'. Because the rocket was put into service later, it was given the name V-2.[3]

***

So, it was on the V-1 that the hopes of Hitler and his advisers were first pinned, while waiting for the arrival, if necessary, of the rival missile.

Appendix 6

Pilgrimage - The Tribute Paid to Michel Hollard by Sir Christopher Mallaby, Great Britain's Ambassador to France (1993-1996)

In 1943, as autumn approached, the inhabitants of the little Norman town of Auffay and its environs noticed that the occupying army was making a strange commotion on their land. They were to learn later that the flying bomb called the V-1 had been discovered in their area, before being visited by the Allied air forces.

In 1994, the Auffay municipality decided to name the square in front of the Auffay railway station after Michel Hollard. It is not far from where the hero made his crucial discoveries.

The inauguration ceremony for the Place Michel Hollard took place on Saturday, 12 November 1994 and was presided over by Sir Christopher Mallaby, the British Ambassador to France. In his speech, made in French, the diplomat said on behalf of Queen Elizabeth II:

> We are gathered here to remember a man, a man of principles, a hero. […] During the First World War, Michel Hollard showed his bravery and patriotism. During the Second, he was once again a true hero.
>
> This square will henceforth bear the name of this exceptional man. He devoted his life to the defence of liberty, in his country and in mine. He played a key role in saving London and ensuring the Allied victory.
>
> He risked his life to carry out his numerous missions for the British intelligence services in Switzerland, bringing them extremely important information. Right here in Auffay, the terrible threat that the V-1 weapon posed to London began to come to an end.

Thanks to the information supplied by Michel Hollard, more than 100 launch sites were obliterated by Allied aircraft. Today, we pay tribute to a man. But along with him, we also pay tribute to his friends, the agents in his Agir network – not forgetting those who did not return from the concentration camps – and to the railway workers at Auffay, thanks to whom he was able to discover and measure the first V-1 flying bomb.

Michel Hollard was a man of goodness, courage and principles. He will not be forgotten, either in his homeland or in mine.

I am now honoured to unveil this plaque and to name this square: *Place Michel Hollard.*

How can I express in a few words the reaction of my compatriots to the exploits of Michel Hollard? As well as the many French decorations he received and so richly deserved, for the courage he showed during both world wars, Michel Hollard was awarded the Distinguished Service Order for services rendered to my country during the last war. It is almost unprecedented for a non-British citizen to receive such a distinction.

Please allow me to read the citation that at the time accompanied the decoration awarded to Reserve Captain Michel Hollard, subsequently promoted to Lieutenant Colonel. It is remarkable for its brevity and the sense of understatement the English Language is so fond of:

DISTINGUISHED SERVICE ORDER (DSO) CITATION

'This officer in January 1942 organised and conducted, with the greatest skill and devotion for two years, a highly successful information service in favour of the Allied Cause in Northern France.

'He, at great personal risk, reconnoitred a number of heavily guarded V-1 sites and reported thereon with such clarity that models thereof were constructed in this country which enabled effective bombing to be carried out.

'His courage, devotion to duty and unsparing efforts were a constant inspiration to his team.

'Finally arrested in February 1944 by treachery, he was deported to Germany, from where, after severe privations and despite torture under which he revealed nothing, he succeeded recently in escaping.'

Without the exceptional information supplied by Michel Hollard, the V-1 attacks against London would have been at least six times more serious than they were and would have lasted six months longer. The damage would have been disastrous. And the victims, countless.

As General Eisenhower said:

'If the Germans had succeeded in perfecting and using these new weapons six months earlier than they did, our invasion of Europe would have proved exceedingly difficult, perhaps impossible.'

The Commanding Officer of the British XXX Corps, General Sir Brian Horrocks, said quite rightly that Michel Hollard was 'literally the man who saved London'.

I was 6 or 7 when Michel Hollard used to travel between France and Switzerland. I remember perfectly well the fear caused by the V-1s which hit Great Britain. I remember very well the whistling sound they made when they fell. Thousands of people like me owe their lives to this man and to the sacrifices of the French Resistance fighters. Thousands more, thanks to them, did not know grief or suffering. It is to renew the expression of my country's profound gratitude that I am here today.

Appendix 7

'Redemption' - A Poem by Michel Hollard Whilst Deported to Neuengamme, Dedicated to His Son Florian

REDEMPTION

To my son, Florian

Over there, in the land where the sun is shining,
Where people can talk without shouting
Where in every eye, sparkles a gaze,
Where joy and laughter remain;
In this Paradise that they wanted to take from us,
There is a cottage where you can hear
Pieces of music you have forgotten.

A handsome lad, whose heavenly eyes
Colour his pale face with azure,
Is the master of sound: every gesture
Awakens a note or recalls a melody,
And seeks to give a passionate life
To such a concerto whose voice haunts us,
And makes us dream even in hell.

Beloved musician from the gentle lands
Whose arrangements go to a heaven too far away,
Your notes of silver once lost
Could they not change their fate,
Visit those places where there is no heart,
Where only horror still dwells,
Where everything is cursed, even in the morning?

Could they not enlighten our souls
And remind us that there is a heaven...
A harmonious world that your art proclaims
And that the joy of living is real?
Make them ring out over our misery
So that we know it is ephemeral,
And that their power alone is eternal!

RÉDEMPTION[1]

À mon fils Florian

Là-bas, au pays où le soleil brille,
Où l'on sait parler sans pousser des cris
Où dans tous les yeux le regard scintille,
Où sont demeurés la joie et les ris ;
Dans ce Paradis qu'on voulait nous prendre,
Il est un chalet où l'on peut entendre
Chanter des morceaux qu'on a désappris.

Un beau jouvenceau, dont les yeux célestes
Colorent d'azur le visage clair,
Est prêtre des sons : chacun de ses gestes
Réveille une note ou rappelle un air,
Et cherche à donner une vie ardente
À tel concerto dont la voix nous hante,
Et nous fait rêver jusque dans l'enfer.

Cher musicien des douces contrées
Dont les accords vont au ciel trop lointain,
Tes notes d'argent un jour égarées
Ne pourraient-elles pas changer leur destin,
Visiter ces lieux où le cœur s'ignore,
Où seule l'horreur peut loger encore,
Où tout est maudit, même le matin ?

Ne pourraient-elles pas éclairer notre âme
Et nous rappeler qu'il existe un ciel...
Monde harmonieux que ton art proclame
Et que le bonheur de vivre est réel ?
Fais-les retentir sur notre misère
Pour que nous sachions qu'elle est éphémère,
Et que leur pouvoir seul est éternel !

Bibliography and Acknowledgements

Bibliography

AMOUROUX Henri, *La Grande Histoire des Français sous l'Occupation*, Paris, Robert Laffont, 1993.

BAILLEUL Laurent, *Les Sites V1 en Flandres et en Artois*, Hazebrouck, 2000.

BRUNET Pierre (Général), *Les Martyrs de Neuengamme*, Paris, Tallandier, 1975.

CUICH Myrone N., *Armes Secrètes et Ouvrages Mystérieux*, Tourcoing, 1996.

DEBUCHY Victor, *Les Armes Secrètes des Nazis*, Paris, Page Après Page, 2003.

DORNBERGER Walter (Général), *L'Arme Secrète de Peenemünde,* Paris, Arthaud, 1961.

DUCELLIER Jean-Pierre, *La Guerre Aérienne dans le Nord de la France*, Abbeville, Paillard, 2003, 2004, 2005.

DUFOUR Norbert and DORÉ Christian, *L'Enfer des V1 en Seine-Maritime*, Luneray, Bertout, 1993.

HASSEL Sven, *Liquidez Paris !,* Paris, Presses de la Cité, 1968.

JONES Reginald Victor, *Most Secret War: British Scientific Intelligence 1939–1945*, London, Hamish Hamilton, 1978.

JONES Reginald Victor, *The Wizard War: British Scientific Intelligence 1939–1945*, New York, Coward, McCann & Geoghegan, Inc., 1978.

LAPIERRE Dominique and COLLINS Larry, *Paris Brûle-t-il ?,* Paris, Robert Laffont, 1964.

MARTELLI George, *Agent Extraordinary*, London, Collins, 1960.

MARTELLI George, *The Man Who Saved London*, London, Collins (for The Companion Book Club), 1961.

MARTELLI George, *The Man Who Saved London*, New York, Doubleday, 1961.

MARTELLI George, *L'Homme Qui a Sauvé Londres*, Paris, Julliard, 1960.

MARTELLI George, *L'Homme Qui a Sauvé Londres*, Paris, Éditions des Arènes, 2016.

NOGUÈRES Henri, *Histoire de la Résistance*, Paris, Robert Laffont, 1967-1981.

NOGUÈRES Henri, *Le Suicide de la Flotte Française à Toulon*, Paris, Robert Laffont, 1961.

RÉMY, *Missions Secrètes. « Vergeltungswaffen »*, Geneva, Idégraf, 1977.

RICHARDOT Jean-Pierre, *Une Autre Suisse*, Paris, Le Félin; Geneva, Labor et Fides, 2002.

SAINT-CLAIR Simone and MONESTIER Marianne, *Cinquante-Huit Actions Héroïques de la Résistance*, Paris, Gründ, 1971.

YOUNG Richard Anthony, *The Flying Bomb*, London, Ian Allan Ltd, 1978.

Acknowledgements

Jeannine, my wife, became very interested in her father-in-law's historic mission. Page after page, this book has benefited from her ever-pertinent comments. I am deeply grateful to her.

I've naturally consulted, when needed, my sister Francine and my brother Vincent. I would like to thank them both as their brother.

I would like to thank the ASSVYA (Association Pour la Sauvegarde du Site de V-1 du Val-Ygot at Ardouval, Seine-Maritime) for its documentation, which they kindly allowed me to include. My thanks also to the following people who gave me their help and valuable statements.

Odette Allard in Paris
Réjane Barraud in Paris
Nicole Berrard-Poncet in Mijoux (Ain)
Jean Bonnet in Le Cerneux-Péquignot (Switzerland)
Robert de Bosmelet in Auffay (Seine-Maritime)
Roger Bramble in London
Michel Clément-Grandcourt in Dijon (Côte-d'Or)
Joseph Brocard in Gattières (Alpes-Maritimes)
Pierre Clément in Les Ventes (Eure)
Lady Duncan Sandys in London
François Delacroix in Bonnetot-le-Faubourg (Seine-Maritime)
The Cuenot Family in Besançon and Morteau (Doubs), La Chaux-de-Fonds (Switzerland)

Norbert Dufour in Lintot-les-Bois (Seine-Maritime)
Pamela Edwards in Borehamwood (England)
Patrick Frigère, Mayor of Mijoux (Ain)
Pierre Gaiffe in Le Vieux Châteleu (Doubs)
Jean-Pierre Grandy in Neuchâtel (Switzerland)
Doctor Michel Guisan in Yverdon-les-Bains (Switzerland)
Olivier Guisan in La Tour-de-Peilz (Switzerland)
Jean-Paul Gros, Honorary Mayor of Mijoux (Ain)
Marcel Gros in Mijoux (Ain)
Michèle Herzig-Rubenach in Paris
Charles Hirschy in La Brévine (Switzerland)
Phillip Jackson in Enghien-les-Bains (Val-d'Oise)
Alain and Florence Jaulmes in Massy (Essonne)
The Lionnet Family in Machilly (Haute-Savoie)
Sir Christopher Mallaby, former British Ambassador to France
Eleanor McClean in Belfast
Angus Martelli in Bridport (England)
Roger Merkelbach in Geneva
Josette Montgomery in London
The Neury Family in Machilly (Haute-Savoie)
The Paccot Family in Machilly (Haute-Savoie)
The Poncet Family in Mijoux and Échallon (Ain)
Rafaël Rabaey, former Mayor of Ardouval (Seine-Maritime)
André Rérat in Le Locle (Switzerland)
Donna Ross in Hackensack (USA)
Anne Roulet-Guisan in Lausanne (Switzerland)
Marielle Stamm in Neuilly-sur-Seine (Hauts-de-Seine)
Doctor Guy Troché in Albert (Somme)

Notes

Chapter 1 - Worrying Unrest

1. *Vert-de-gris* (grey-green colour called field grey or *Feldgrau*) was one of the French nicknames given to the soldiers of the Wehrmacht, referring to the colour of their uniforms.
2. In March 2004, I met the owner of the Bonnetot-le-Faubourg site, Mr François Delacroix, whose parents were already living near the site in 1943. Vestiges of the site Michel Hollard discovered could still be seen.
3. The Hôtel d'Annecy, 207 Rue de Bercy, Paris 12^{e}, no longer exists. In front of the building built in its stead, a stela perpetuates the memory of the twenty martyrs of the Agir network. Until the very end of his life, Michel Hollard came every year to place a wreath in tribute to his departed comrades. He never failed to organise this yearly commemoration, in the presence of the survivors of his gradually diminishing team. From 1990 onwards, the memorial's neighbours would see him still coming, often alone despite his great age, to lay flowers on the memorial.

Chapter 2 - Cradle of a Vocation

1. A German peasant trickster of the fourteenth century, whose merry pranks were the source of numerous folk and literary tales.
2. Like the Greek philosopher, Michel Hollard preferred the sun's rays to all the gold in the world.
3. With old age perhaps as an excuse, Michel Hollard was no doubt excessively magnanimous. At 91, he and his wife were violently attacked by a burglar. When the police arrested the culprit, whose speciality was aggressing old folk, he refused to press charges because he thought the thief was 'pitiful and irresponsible'.
4. There was German blood in his veins on his paternal grandmother's side.
5. Near a mighty oak uprooted by a storm, the fabulist has a humble reed say to the contrary: 'I bend, and do not break!' in 'The Oak and the Reed' ('*Le Chêne et le Roseau*').
6. Killed in action.

Chapter 3 - A Hero at 19

1. Henri Gounelle, killed in action on 21 June 1915 at the age of 20, was already a recognised writer and poet with promising talent. In Paris, a tribute paid by the nation has perpetuated his name in the Panthéon, at the Sorbonne and in the Lycée Louis-le-Grand. Michel Hollard went on to marry his sister, Yvonne Gounelle.

Chapter 4 - Refusing Defeat

1. The verses of the French translation of 'If—' by André Maurois are not in the same order as the original in English. The version in French ends with the above stanzas.

Chapter 5 - Survival and Challenge

1. What was even more distressing was to see businessmen making money shamelessly by trading with the occupiers.
2. A wealthy acquaintance, who didn't hide his sympathy for the Vichy government, publicly reproached the engineer who'd given up his job. At the same time, he ostensibly offered the unemployed man a handout, which was naturally refused.

Chapter 6 - A Daring Undertaking

1. A cheval-de-frise is a portable obstacle, consisting of a wooden frame covered with spikes or barbed wire, used by the military to close off a passage or block enemy advancement.
2. While the war was raging, nobody thought of giving the Resistance movement created by Michel Hollard any particular name. It was only when he came back from deportation that he chose to call his network 'Agir'. The present account, however, uses this name even if it is an anachronism. During the war, the British intelligence services had given its leader the secret military code Z 165.
3. The commune of Montlebon, which he often went through on his way to the border, now has a street named *Michel Hollard*.

Chapter 7 - Enchantment

1. This was Mr Raymond Rérat, the head of the customs office at La Brévine-Chobert. The office no longer exists, but the building has survived, almost unchanged.

2. Michel Hollard only found out the soldier's full identity, André Gagnaux, the following year.

Chapter 9 - The Second Attempt

1. In the summer of 2002, the writer of this book managed to bring together the surviving Cuenot children: Marcelle, Marie-Louise, Victor, Maurice, Gilberte and Guy. The group, just as fervent as it had been, honoured the memory of their family in the barn on Mont Châteleu. This memorable building has become an inn, fitted out by Pierre Gaiffe, the grandson of the pit-sawyer in Derrière-le-Mont.

Chapter 10 - *Bienvenue*

1. During the Second World War, the Swiss Army wasn't always fully mobilised. During periods of less tension, a rotation system enabled part of the army's strength to go back to civilian life, whilst regular forces were retained for military service.
2. Later, Michel Hollard was informed there was a risk of complicity between certain people and the Nazis. He was warned that the German secret services had access to the Swiss hotel registers. With the agreement of the Federal Authorities, he used other names.
3. The British Ministry of War.

Chapter 11 - Amateur Secret Agent

1. This was most likely the military pool at Satory, outside Versailles, where the Germans had set up a big armour base.

Chapter 12 - Reinforcements

1. The air force of Nazi Germany.
2. When peace returned, Gaston Ségur was promoted to the post of *receveur des finances* (tax collector) in Le Havre. The town and its port having been devastated by the war, the civil servant and his friend Michel Hollard founded an association linked to the former Agir network, with the aim of contributing to rebuild the martyred city.

Chapter 13 - The Olivier Giran Tragedy

1. This is how the Hollard family jokingly abbreviated their new address, located in Place Paul-Painlevé, Paris 5e.

2. Uncovered by true Dutch patriots, the traitor didn't escape for long the punishment meted out to traitors in wartime.
3. In their mousey grey uniforms, female personnel of the German Army were given this nickname in France not without humour.
4. Geheime Staatspolizei: the German secret state police.
5. After accusing the son, being responsible for the father's arrest and that of other patriots, the traitor went looking for his victims on Swiss soil. There he ran into Resistance workers getting ready to go back into France. He followed them and had them arrested. The Swiss Intelligence Service found out what he was up to and arrested him when he returned to Switzerland. He was sentenced to death but in the meantime, Germany had capitulated just at the moment he was to be executed. Under Swiss law, there is no death penalty in peacetime, so his sentence was therefore commuted to life imprisonment.

Chapter 14 - Hide and Seek

1. Madame Madeleine Boulanger became an active member of the Agir network, in which she played a centralising role.

Chapter 15 - Kaleidoscope

1. At the time, even the most modest clockwork mechanism was valuable. When peace returned, Joseph Brocard, who carefully hung on to the watch, confided to his former boss that never had a lesson been more humiliating.
2. Nevertheless, an underground newspaper published from 1940 onwards was called *Résistance*, a term at the time still rarely used in the sense of 'revolt against the occupier'.

Chapter 16 - A British Entreaty

1. The southern part of France administered by the Vichy government which was not occupied by German troops until 11 November 1942.

Chapter 17 - Extending the Network

1. Vergeltungswaffe 1: Vengeance Weapon 1.
2. *Fritz, Frisé, Fridolin*: all nicknames the French gave to the German occupiers.
3. French railways were still mostly steam-powered. The trains covering the greatest distances were drawn by the famous Pacific 231 locomotives.

4. Michel Hollard himself refused to consider this type of initiative as a real exploit. He only attached importance to actions he carried out in the field.
5. Later renamed the Hôtel Bristol.
6. Michel Hollard brought back a few packets from Switzerland where they were freely available.
7. When Hollard returned from deportation and learned of the tragic mistake, he set about rehabilitating his comrade's memory, cursed by misinformed members of the Resistance.
8. At 207 Rue de Bercy, Paris, 12^{e}.

Chapter 18 - Record Number of Illegal Crossings

1. My brother went to a secondary school where a Resistance group developed. After the German police raided the school, the headmaster, several teachers and pupils were condemned to death or deported. Vincent had to change his identity, and then flee. He was admitted to the École du Montcel in Jouy-en-Josas, run by Charles Jeanrenaud, a Swiss who was also a member of the Agir network.
2. In August 2002, as I was going through Machilly, I met up with several of the participants and witnesses of this adventure: Claude Neury, François Lionnet, Jean-Claude and Josette Piccot-Lionnet. They showed me the routes my father had taken.
3. On the fiftieth anniversary of the Liberation of Mijoux, on 21 August 1994, this commune of the Ain department, on the edge of the Jura Mountains, celebrated the inauguration of the newly restored Charlemagne Bridge. As a tribute to the memory of Michel Hollard and his brave local protectors, Denis and Alice Poncet, the epic story in which they were involved is now remembered at the entrance of the bridge on a stela bearing their effigies.
4. This affectionate nickname, chosen by the grandchildren for their grandmother, had been adopted by the whole family.
5. No doubt nobody would think of doing this with twenty-first century rolling stock, but during the Second World War these acrobatics were fairly common. Because there was no room inside the carriages, a lot of resourceful passengers often travelled hanging on outside, at their own risks and perils.
6. The telephone infrastructure at the time was still restricted to a limited number of individuals, especially in rural areas, and the post office was most often used as a relay.

Chapter 19 - Harbour Graveyard

1. During the 1950s, a famous commentator of French-speaking Swiss radio stated, before retiring, that the broadcasting of that news had perhaps affected him more than any other during his career as a journalist.
2. The navy of Nazi Germany.
3. How the German police got wind of the meeting so quickly is unknown. Alexandre Roman was deported to Dachau, Jean Maiffret to Sandbostel and Louis Maiffret to Neuengamme. None of them survived the hell of the concentration camps.

Chapter 20 - The Joseph Brocard Odyssey

1. The Institut National de l'Audiovisuel (INA) has several accounts of these events, given by the people who had experienced them.
2. Colonels du Pasquier and de Montmollin went personally to the French patient's bedside.
3. Joseph Brocard was born in 1920. At the beginning of the twenty-first century, he was still a keen witness of the period, despite the after-effects of his ordeal which happened so long ago.

Chapter 21 - Eureka!

1. The rumour came from accurate information, but the weapon (the future V-2) was not ready.
2. Heeresversuchsanstalt Peenemünde (Peenemünde Army Research Centre), a secret establishment for testing missiles and long-range rockets, was an organisation located on the island of Usedom, off the Baltic coast. Towards the end of August 1943, an Allied night-time air raid partly destroyed it.

Chapter 22 - Infiltration

1. General Fritz Todt was known for having directed the building of the German motorways as well as the famous Siegfried Line, designed to protect the Reich from its western neighbours intending anything aggressive. He founded a vast industrial state enterprise which he managed until his death in an aircraft accident in February 1942.

Chapter 23 - The Monster in its Lair

1. There were several launching ramps in the Auffay area.

2. The Germans were unable to prevent their structures from being seen by the people of Normandy and Picardy. As they were short of labour, the Germans had to enrol forcibly a lot of Frenchmen by force to work on the new construction sites. Resistance movements were organised among the unwilling recruits. There was a lot of sabotage, followed by executions, sometimes including hostages.
3. Flak (*Fliegerabwehrkanone*): anti-aircraft guns.
4. The French, English and German archives, although sometimes contradictory, enable researchers to estimate that no fewer than 400 V-1 launch sites in all were under construction. More than three quarters of these sites remained as rough land or disappeared under the bombs.
5. Fearing that too many elements of this large infrastructure would be discovered, the Luftwaffe found other ways of launching the missiles using aircraft. There were even several models designed to be used by suicide pilots. It was claimed that the poor men could still hope to escape death. These volunteers had to bail out of the aircraft when it was on its last dive at 500 mph! Hitler rejected this extreme measure.
6. The Germans continued installing their 'light ramps' in the spring of 1944, after Michel Hollard had been arrested. Pierre Carteron and other members of the Agir network managed to track down almost half of them. Jean-Henri Morin and Joseph Legendre, who successively replaced their leader after he'd been caught, managed to get to Lausanne to warn O.P., the English contact. The new V-1 bases which escaped being bombed didn't work very well. There were a lot of botched launchings, often deadly for the technicians and the neighbourhood.

Chapter 24 - Betrayal and Arrest

1. The former schoolhouse soon collapsed under the bombs. A group of officers and technicians were holding a meeting there. Its main members were killed.
2. Victor Guerreau, an engineer and test pilot with the aircraft manufacturing company Morane-Saulnier, had joined the Agir network. Having access to the aerodrome at Villacoublay, he was able to inform the Allies regularly about the intense enemy air traffic.
3. At the beginning of the twenty-first century, the little bar became an Indian restaurant. Twice a year, on 11 November and 8 May, the City of Paris decorates a marble plaque with flowers, thus perpetuating the memory of the four arrests made there on 5 February 1944.

4. Simone Boirel, arrested at Pierrelatte, was probably denounced by the same woman who said she was her friend. After several weeks in prison, she managed to get out of all the accusations and was released.
5. Located at 3 and 5 Rue Mallet-Stevens, Paris 16e.

Chapter 25 - The Abyss

1. Henri Lauth, chorus master of the Paris Opera and cousin of Michel Hollard, and his wife took them in at the beginning of this critical period. Charles Jeanrenaud, a Swiss citizen and member of the Agir network, ran the École du Montcel at Jouy-en-Josas, near Versailles. He had no hesitation taking in the family of his Resistance boss, hiding them in the institution that already sheltered several other people on the run.
2. One might ask why the Germans didn't try to check the identity of all the passengers getting off the train. In fact, they didn't like checking in public since this required a lot of personnel and created crowd movements which were difficult to control.
3. 'Thank heavens for helping me put up with their savagery. Those pitiful men got tired more quickly than I did!' he later concluded, magnanimously.

Chapter 26 - 'In Defeat: Defiance'!

1. In 1997, Mr Toulouze, director of Fresnes Prison, allowed me to visit the places where my father had stayed fifty-three years earlier. They had hardly changed.
2. The first two verses of the poem *'Sommeil'* ('Sleep') by Michel Hollard (probably written in 1937).
3. That is to say without demanding the usual food ration tickets.
4. In reality, Michel Hollard only saw Francine accompanied by a friend. Our mother was prevented from coming because she was urgently reorganising the network.
5. 207 Rue de Bercy, Paris 12[e] (in front of the Gare de Lyon).
6. In a poem entitled, not without humour, *'La Ballade au Rabiot'* ('The Ballad of Something Extra'), Michel Hollard later expressed the astonishment that this reprieve had inspired in him (see the poem in the Epilogue).

Chapter 27 - Down into Hell

1. Michel Hollard, however, had only had a very vague foreboding. He had no idea of how barbarous the concentration camps really were.

2. Both men then suffered the same fate. Jean-Henri Daudemard, deported to Neuengamme, also survived. He was repatriated on 5 June 1945.
3. SS: Schutzstaffel (Protection Squad), the Nazi military police.
4. Exploiting these unfortunate people went even further sometimes. Those responsible for Nazi medical research naturally chose their guinea pigs from among the concentration camp population. Gold teeth were systematically wrenched from the jaws of the dead. In certain cases, before ending up in the crematoria, corpses supplied raw materials for industrial use.

Chapter 28 - Neuengamme Concentration Camp

1. *Kapo*: *Kameraden Polizist,* a Nazi concentration camp prisoner charged with overseeing other prisoners.
2. To keep costs down, the SS administration got rid of its stock of colourful cast-offs first before starting to use its reserve of new, blue and white striped uniforms made for the convicts. Michel Hollard never wore one of those uniforms.
3. *Vorarbeiter*: foreman, a detainee selected by the SS working under the supervision of military and sometimes civilian engineers.
4. *Blockführer*: the barrack leader chosen by the SS from among the detained. In this case, he was a common law German prisoner.
5. One can easily imagine that if these two dates had been inverted, the undertaking to free Europe would have become even more hazardous.
6. After being sent home, Michel Hollard polished up and completed the poems he'd created in his mind at Neuengamme.
7. *Lagerältester*: the camp leader (or camp elder). A detainee designated by the SS to maintain discipline, especially at night. This person under the enemy's orders was generally even crueller than his new masters.

Chapter 29 - Floating Tomb

1. People were dying all the time. When the corpses were lifted up, they were strung up by a rope tied to a limb, the neck or the waist. Before disappearing through the hatch, they twirled around sometimes for a long time above the living.
2. Another prisoner, the young Phillip Jackson, also climbed up onto the deck. He did this just before the tragedy took place, thus saving his life.
3. Michel Hollard never knew that the *Thielbek*'s engines had broken down.
4. A verse from the Gospel According to Saint Matthew, engraved on Michel Hollard's tomb in Gorniès cemetery (Hérault department).
5. When they were repatriated, most of the survivors of the group claimed that a contagious feeling of peacefulness had touched them at that moment.

6. The number reported by General Brunet in *Les Martyrs de Neuengamme.*
7. Francine was now the holder of a Red Cross first aid certificate.

Chapter 30 - Renewal

1. For the sake of clarity, the present book uses the name Agir right from the beginning, even though it was chosen afterwards.
2. The poet Robert Desnos had managed to steal confidential communications from the staff of General von Stülpnagel, head of the occupying troops throughout France. As the writer's reports had been discovered, he was deported to Auschwitz, then transferred successively to Buchenwald, Flossenburg and finally Theresienstadt in Czechoslovakia. He died there of typhus on 8 June 1945, after being freed. Michel Hollard and Robert Desnos never had the opportunity to talk about their common literary passion.
3. Michel Hollard was in captivity when a daughter was born in Robert Rubenach's home. While fate threatened him with the worst, the little girl was named Michèle. Joseph Brocard and his wife were also thinking of their leader and friend when they chose Michel as the name for their son. Naturally, the founder of Agir agreed to be the children's godfather.
4. In 1961, the city of Paris placed a marble plaque on the facade of the building paying tribute to the fallen. Later, when the Hôtel d'Annecy was demolished, a stela was edified in its place to perpetuate their memory.
5. The number indicated by General de Gaulle in his *Mémoires de Guerre.*
6. BCRA: Bureau Central de Renseignements et d'Action, an organisation created in London in 1940–1941, attached to General de Gaulle's headquarters and given the task of uniting the various Resistance movements spread throughout France.
7. This letter is reproduced in the second plate section.
8. DSO: Distinguished Service Order, the highest distinction that Great Britain has exceptionally awarded to a few foreigners. Michel Hollard received his at the same time as Maréchal Leclerc.
9. Michel Hollard's main French decorations: Croix de Commandeur de la Légion d'Honneur, Croix de Guerre 1914–1918, Croix de Guerre 1939–1945 and Rosette de la Résistance...

Chapter 31 - *Agent Extraordinary*

1. When my father was more than 80, I asked him once again why he still hadn't made up his mind to publish his memoirs. 'I've written down a few

bits,' he answered, 'but several times now I've been bothered by physical as well as psychological problems which have forced me to give up. Now I'll most likely no longer take it up again.'

'And if somebody in the family wants to tell your story so it doesn't fade into oblivion?'

'You can, if you like!'

'But will I find the right words? And how long will it take? With my artistic work at the moment, I wouldn't have the time to write such a story.'

'Nobody is better qualified than you are to do it, when you can. There's no hurry!'

2. Collins, London, 1960.
3. Éditions Julliard, Paris, 1960.
4. The film *L'Homme Qui a Sauvé Londres*, by the film-maker Jean L'Hôte, is in the archives of the Institut National de l'Audiovisuel (INA). The acting couple Yves Montand and Simone Signoret was fascinated by the Michel and Yvonne Hollard epic and had agreed to play the hero and his wife in a scenario which had a feminine role tailor-made for the actress. Material difficulties made the negotiations break down.
5. Military and civilian figures regularly attended the Agir reunions. Among the most faithful and enthusiastic were General Brunet, General Bouchardon and the philosopher Vladimir Jankélévitch.
6. The flags which took part in the ceremony: Royal Air Forces Association; Résistance Belge; Société Nationale des Chemins de Fer Français (SNCF); Fédération des Amicales de Réseaux de la France Combattante (FARFC); Amicale des Déportés de Neuengamme; Amicale du Réseau Agir.
7. The British authorities, responsible for the Neuengamme camp since 5 May 1945, had withdrawn in July 1948. The Hamburg prison administration, once more in charge of the place, decided to turn it into a big modern detention centre. The families of the victims, the surviving deportees and the associations for safeguarding its memory protested energetically. In turn, German public opinion, alerted by the media, admitted that using such a site where 55,000 people had died was a form of profanation. Lengthy negotiations took place with the aim of reconstituting the jail in its original form. These led to the creation of a memorial site, inaugurated on 4 May 2005, on the sixtieth anniversary of the camp's liberation.
8. Beethoven's only opera tells of the struggle of the just against the tyrannical. It exalts selflessness, bravery and love, overcoming oppression in the end. Before the Ninth Symphony, it was already a hymn not only to joy, but to freedom.

Chapter 32 - The Providential German Cousin

1. As a tribute to the memory of this Franco-German relative, Michel Hollard's parents named their first daughter Jenny Juliette (birth certificate in Leysin, Switzerland, 25 August 1899), grandmother of Philip Sandt, co-translator of the present book.
2. Paul de Rapin de Thoyras came from a prestigious lineage going back to Charlemagne.
3. General von Choltitz, the Governor of Gross Paris (Greater Paris) in August 1944, is generally acknowledged as the benefactor who knowingly spared the city of Paris, which he had been ordered to destroy. Other historians think that the capital owed its escape to the collapse of the German Army, harassed by French insurgents at the approach of the Allied troops. In any case, Lieutenant von Bressensdorf's initiative is plausible and has to be taken into consideration.

Chapter 33 - Final Act

1. The final movement of the choral symphony contains the words, adapted by Beethoven, of the ode 'An die Freude' by Friedrich von Schiller.
2. Pastor Alain Hutter, the deceased's nephew, conducted the service. The more official ceremony had to be put off until the autumn. It took place in the Oratoire du Louvre church in Paris on Thursday, 21 October 1993.

Chapter 34 - Tributes

1. Albert Grandy, the officer's father, was a leading figure in a components factory in the French commune of Verrières-de-Joux, on the Franco-Swiss border. This factory was soon used as a hub for the members of the Agir team on the move. Willy Grandy, the soldier's younger brother, carried on with his studies in Paris. It wasn't long before he met Michel Hollard and joined his underground organisation.
2. Ernst von Bressensdorf, who died on 19 August 1994, only survived Michel Hollard by thirteen months.

Appendix 1: The Report by Prof. R.V. Jones, Advisor to Sir Winston Churchill and King George VI, on the V-1 Plans Supplied by Michel Hollard

1. The American edition is entitled *The Wizard War: British Scientific Intelligence 1939–1945* (Coward, McCann & Geoghegan, Inc., New York, 1978).

Appendix 2: Richard Anthony Young's Report on the V-1 Plans Supplied by Michel Hollard

1. Ian Allan Ltd, London, 1978.
2. This name (Bois Carré) was at first used to denote the type of site but later gave way to the more convenient and descriptive term: 'ski site'.

Appendix 5: Between the Devil and the Deep Blue Sea

1. This name given to Hitler's general headquarters near Rastenburg, in East Prussia (near Ketrzyn in present-day Poland), referred perhaps to the 'Wolf's Glen' scene in Carl Maria von Weber's romantic opera *Der Freischütz* (*The Freeshooter*). In this famous work, the hero concludes a pact with the devil in which all the bullets in his gun, save one, would never miss their mark.
2. After Germany capitulated, the rocket's main designer, Wernher von Braun, seemingly had no qualms about exercising his talents serving those he'd just been fighting.
3. The term *Vergeltungswaffe* seems to have been chosen for its initial letter, in response to the 'V for Victory' sign, used so many times by Winston Churchill. At the same time, the Peenemünde design office was also working on a rocket capable of reaching New York and Washington.

Appendix 7: 'Redemption' - A Poem by Michel Hollard Whilst Deported to Neuengamme, Dedicated to His Son Florian

1. Verses 1, 2, 4 and 6 comprise the English translation.

Index